Northside

a time and place

Warren Kirk

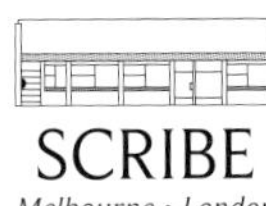

SCRIBE
Melbourne • London

Warren Kirk has been a documentary photographer for over 30 years. His previous books are the acclaimed *Westography* (2016) and *Suburbia* (2018). He lives and works in Melbourne's west.

Christos Tsiolkas is a multi-award-winning novelist, essayist, screenwriter, and playwright, whose most recent novel, *Damascus*, won the 2020 Victorian Premier's Literary Award for fiction. He lives and works in Melbourne.

Scribe Publications
18–20 Edward St, Brunswick, Victoria 3056, Australia
2 John St, Clerkenwell, London, WC1N 2ES, United Kingdom
3754 Pleasant Ave, Suite 100, Minneapolis, Minnesota 55409 USA

Published by Scribe 2020

Design by Allison Colpoys © Scribe Publications
Printed and bound in China by 1010 Printing Co Ltd

Scribe is committed to the sustainable use of natural resources and
the use of paper products made responsibly from those resources.

9781925849929 (hardback edition)

A catalogue record for this book is available from the National
Library of Australia.

scribepublications.com.au
scribepublications.com
scribepublications.co.uk

Introduction

Christos Tsiolkas

Some time ago, one evening in the early 1990s, a friend and I were walking down the southern end of High Street, Northcote, when we suddenly realised we were both hungry. We started looking for a place to eat. But gentrification had not yet crept across Westgarth Street, and, as it was mid-winter, there weren't any open restaurants or cafes in the vicinity. I knew we could trudge up to the pub on the roundabout on St Georges Road. My friend suggested we walk further up the hill, to the Croxton Park Hotel in Thornbury. Just as we were resigned to that walk, I glanced into the window of what initially seemed a dark and empty fish and chip shop. Far in the back I could make out a few men seated around a table, playing cards.

'Hey, Sol,' I called out to my friend. 'Let's try in here.'

As soon as we walked in, I felt guilty. The ovens and the grill were off, and the spotlessly shining bain-marie was empty. The men looked up, startled. A middle-aged woman, with a strong and beautiful face, a face harshly lined by experience, was sitting, smoking, at the nearest table.

'What do you want?' she asked.

'Sorry,' I answered in Greek. 'We thought we could get something to eat.' I nodded towards the gamblers. 'I realise we were mistaken.'

We had turned to leave when she stubbed out her cigarette, rose up from her chair, and said, 'I'll cook you something.'

Quickly, firing up the grill, she prepared us a small but tasty meal of grilled lamb, fried potatoes, and a green salad. We were so ravenous that we gulped the food down, and she and the men laughed at the enormity of our hunger.

'Dear Lord,' I heard one of the old men exclaim. 'Those poor children were starving!'

We weren't starving. Far from it. It was just that the food was delicious, and the kindness and generosity were humbling. She wouldn't take more than five dollars, and even that we had to force on her; and as we walked out the door, I glanced through the window again, to see her switching off the grill, and grabbing her gloves to wash down the surfaces.

Many years have passed since that quiet evening in Northcote. It was a time before smart phones, and so the place, the faces of the woman and the old Greek men — they only exist in memory. And now that this part of the north *has* become gentrified, memory, too, seems unreliable. I walk past the same strip, and I can't be sure of the location of that fish and chip shop. It seems more a dream now than a memory.

And this is why I am so grateful for Warren Kirk's photographs. His work gives that old north back to me. But unlike memory and unlike a dream, his photographs are bold, and the compositions and the framing are evidence of an artistic sensibility that is both exact and generous. His work is sharper than memory. The easy thing to assume is that my response to Kirk's art is an indulgence in nostalgia; that what I am gazing at when I look at his

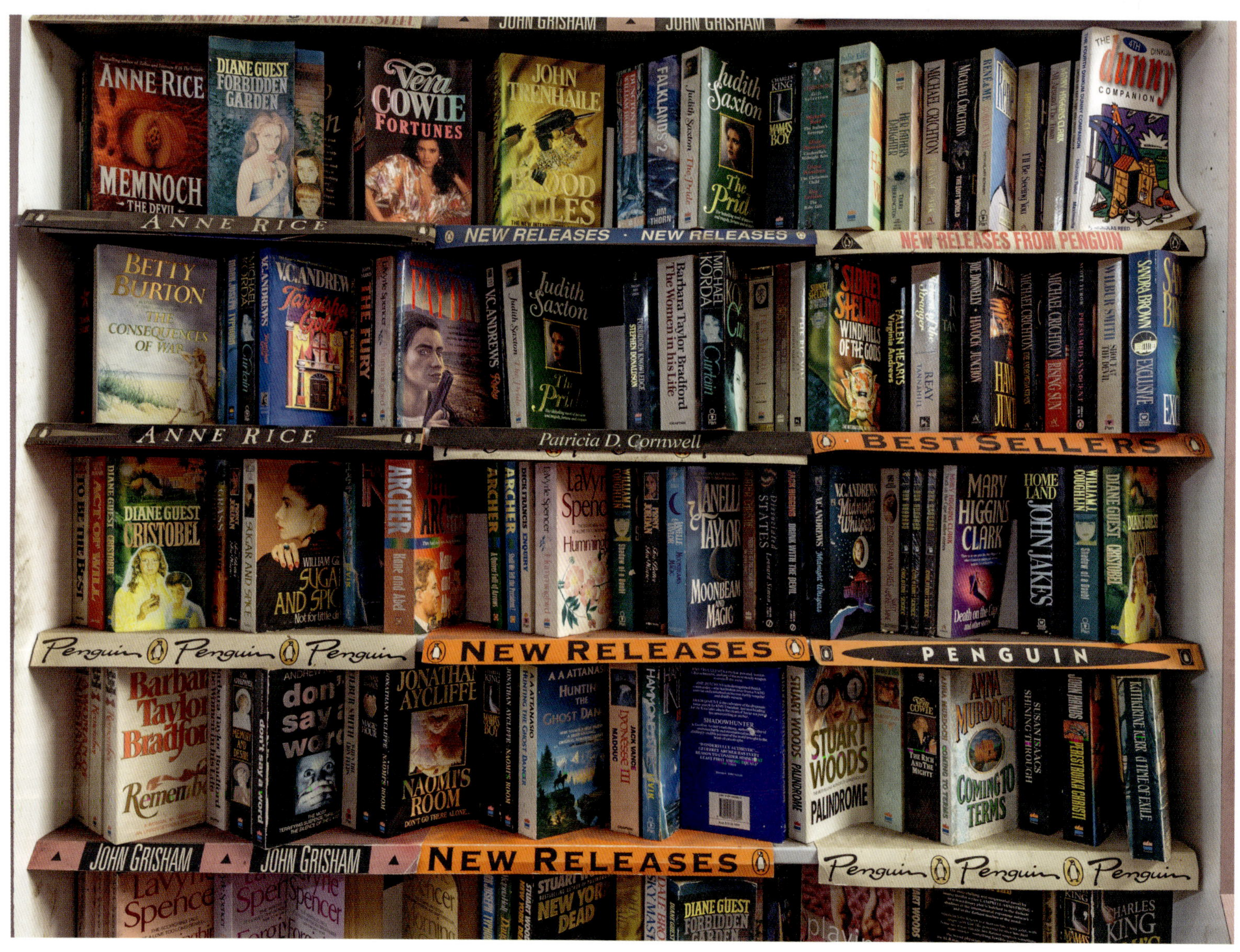

Princes Hill

photographs is the past. But that is to make a fundamental mistake about the integrity of his work. It isn't homage to the past. What his work does is ask us to recognise the beauty in what exists in the here and now in our northern streets. Yes, the milk bars have gone, replaced by expensive organic grocery stores, and hipsters sip coffee while tapping on their phones and laptops. But the barbershops are still there, where old migrants congregate on Saturday mornings to get their hair cut. And walking up High Street or Sydney Road or the Boulevard in Reservoir on a Sunday, I pass elderly Greek and Italian and Macedonian women, dressed simply and elegantly, walking in groups of three or four to catch the tram that will take them to the Catholic or to the Orthodox Church. Apartment blocks are rising everywhere in the north, but if you really look, if you really take heed of what is around you, you find that nestled between the high-rises are small stores and offices. Cobblers. Auto-electricians. Picture framers. Travel agents behind smoky, dusty windows: this one offers deals for those who want to return and visit family in the Mediterranean. This one advertises flights to East Africa and the Middle East. Globalisation and the gig economy haven't yet triumphed completely. Kirk's photographs are also quietly about resistance.

Like all great artists, Warren Kirk is *sui generis*. His photography is unlike any other photographer's work that I know. He captures a distinctly Australian urban landscape and face, but every image is imbued with a deep humanism and longing that I think can speak to everyone. The only other photographer's work that I can compare his to is that of Helen Levitt, the mid-twentieth-century documentarian of New York City. They both understand that it is in capturing the quotidian nature of a city that one finds its soul. As with Levitt, every photograph by Kirk also speaks to the discipline and maturity of craft. It takes a lot of precision and labour and time to make the universal seem accidental. Do Levitt's photographs now only speak to the past? Yes, for no artist is outside time. Gentrification and money have erased much of Levitt's New York City. But if you, like me, have had the good luck to visit New York, then you might have experienced the same burst of joy I have felt when I have turned onto an avenue or passed a group of children playing on a Brooklyn or Harlem street, and the moment has brought one of Levitt's photographs to life. The past isn't completely vanquished. It seeps into the present and is viscerally, tangibly alive. Warren Kirk's photographs, like Levitt's, are wonderfully alive.

Melbourne's north has been part of my life for five decades now. I grew up as a child of the inner city, and, even when I moved as a teenager, our family always returned to the north to visit cousins and friends in Northcote, Thornbury, and Reservoir. My early twenties and early thirties were spent in the inner north, and for the last twenty years, my partner and I have lived in Preston. It's impossible to walk down the streets and alleys and high streets of the north without memory and the present being in constant dialogue with each other. But it is also very easy to lose oneself in a podcast or in music blaring through head-phones; or there is the rush and stress of getting to the next appointment, and you stop looking at the world around you. You think you know it. But Warren Kirk's photographs give me pause. I remember my past lives, the past lives of the north, but I am also reminded to stop and look — really look — at the world around me. History, economics, migration, class, family, loneliness, and communion are what I discover in these images. In a word: humanity. It can be the diffident stare of a woman standing in front of an ornate garden that she is proud of. It is there in a handwritten note on the wall of a cluttered den of an auto-shop.

The familiar is made new when I look at these photographs. And I am reminded not to take my world or my city for granted. That's a great gift that Warren Kirk offers, and it is with great pleasure that I receive it.

Now when I want to remember that magical winter's evening in a Northcote that has long disappeared, I know that I can go to Kirk's photographs and I'll find a physical trace of that memory. It may not be the exact same face of that woman who kindly cooked us a meal, and it won't be the exact same gambling joint — but it will be what I am searching for. The past doesn't disappear. It leaves its traces everywhere.

—Christos Tsiolkas, February 2020

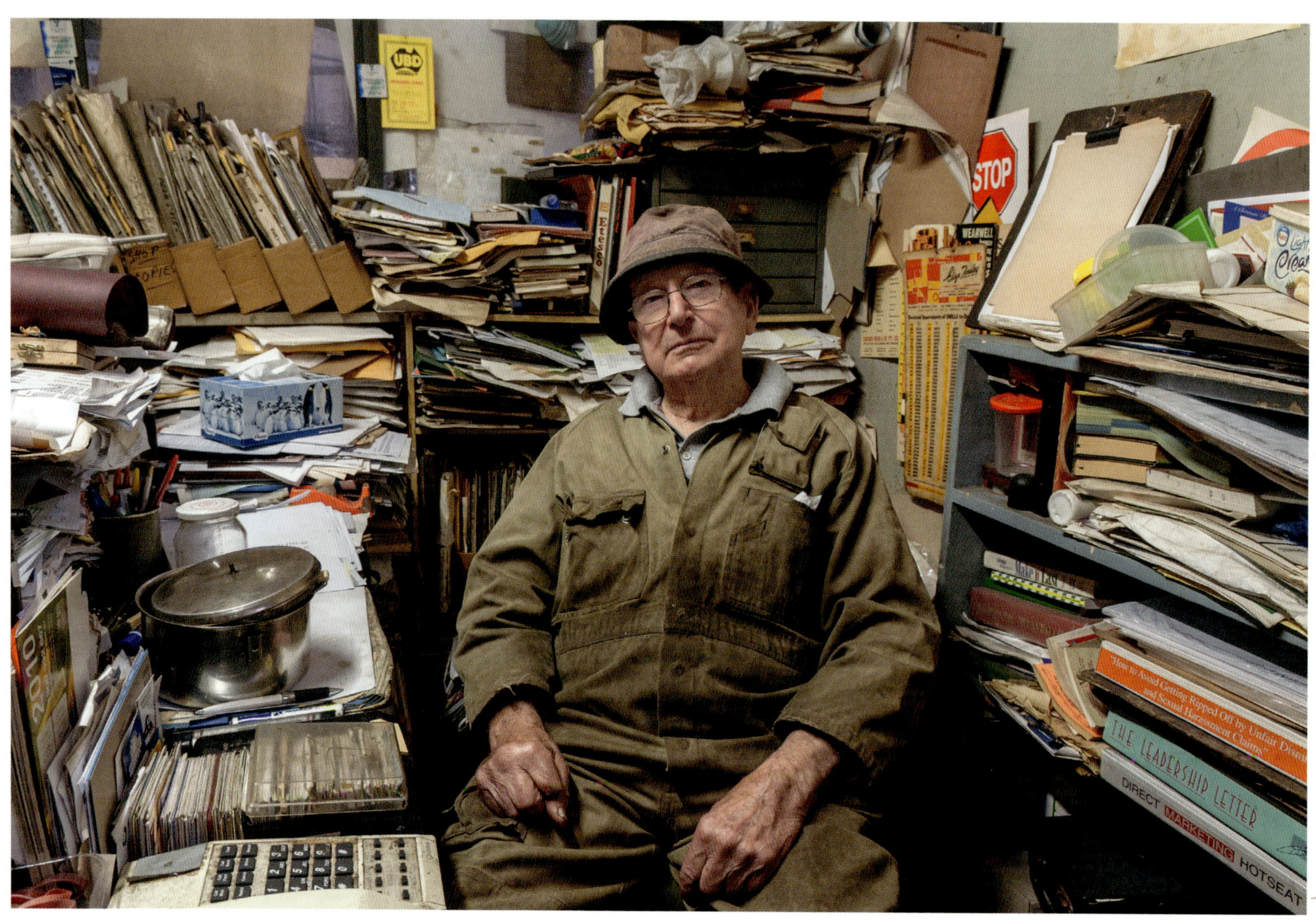

Coburg North

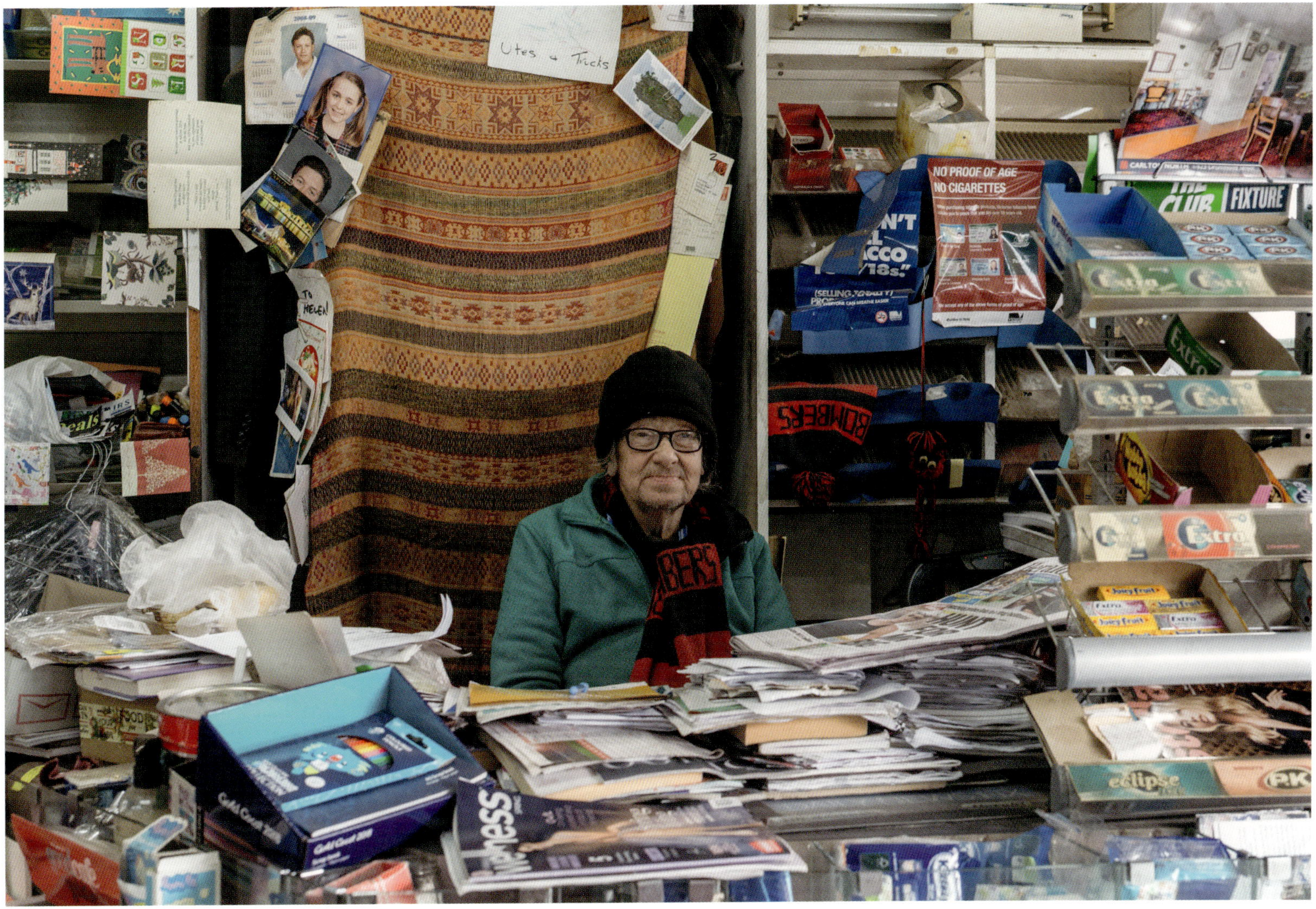

Princes Hill

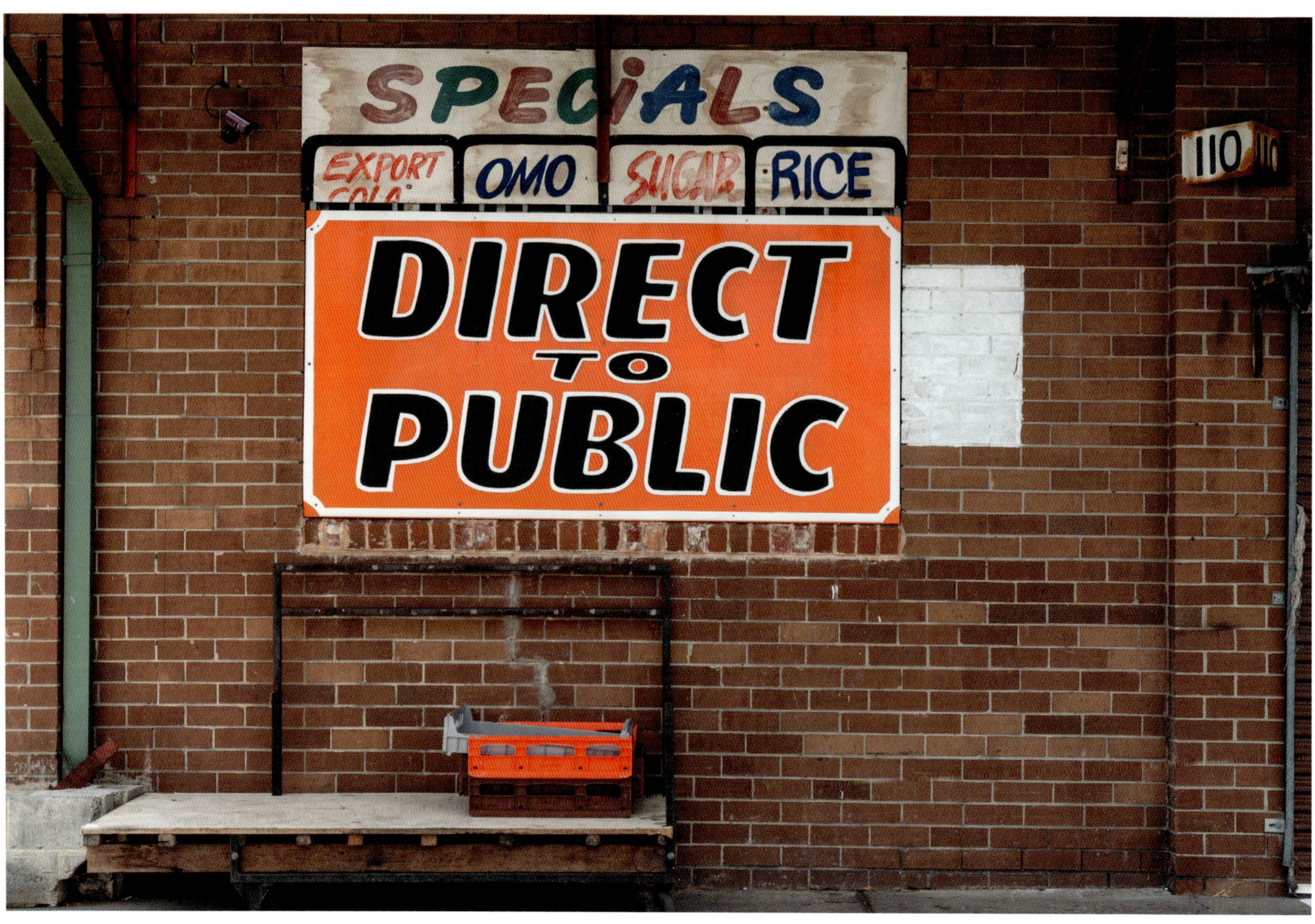

Reservoir

WARNING
COWLEY
SECURITY
(03) 9455 3366
HADDENS
GARDEN AND BUILDING
SUPPLIES
SAND SOIL SCREENINGS Ph 497 2740

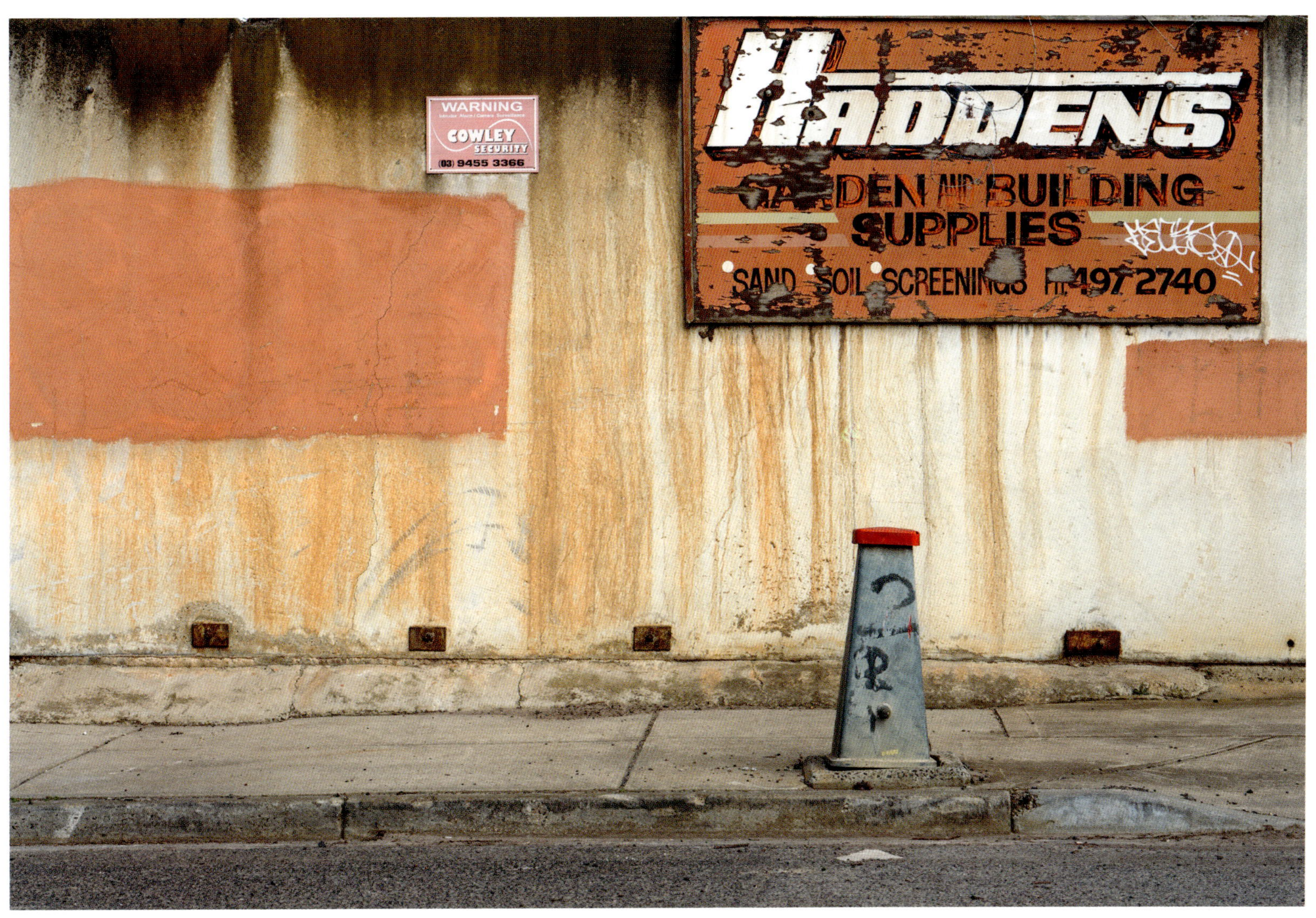

Thornbury

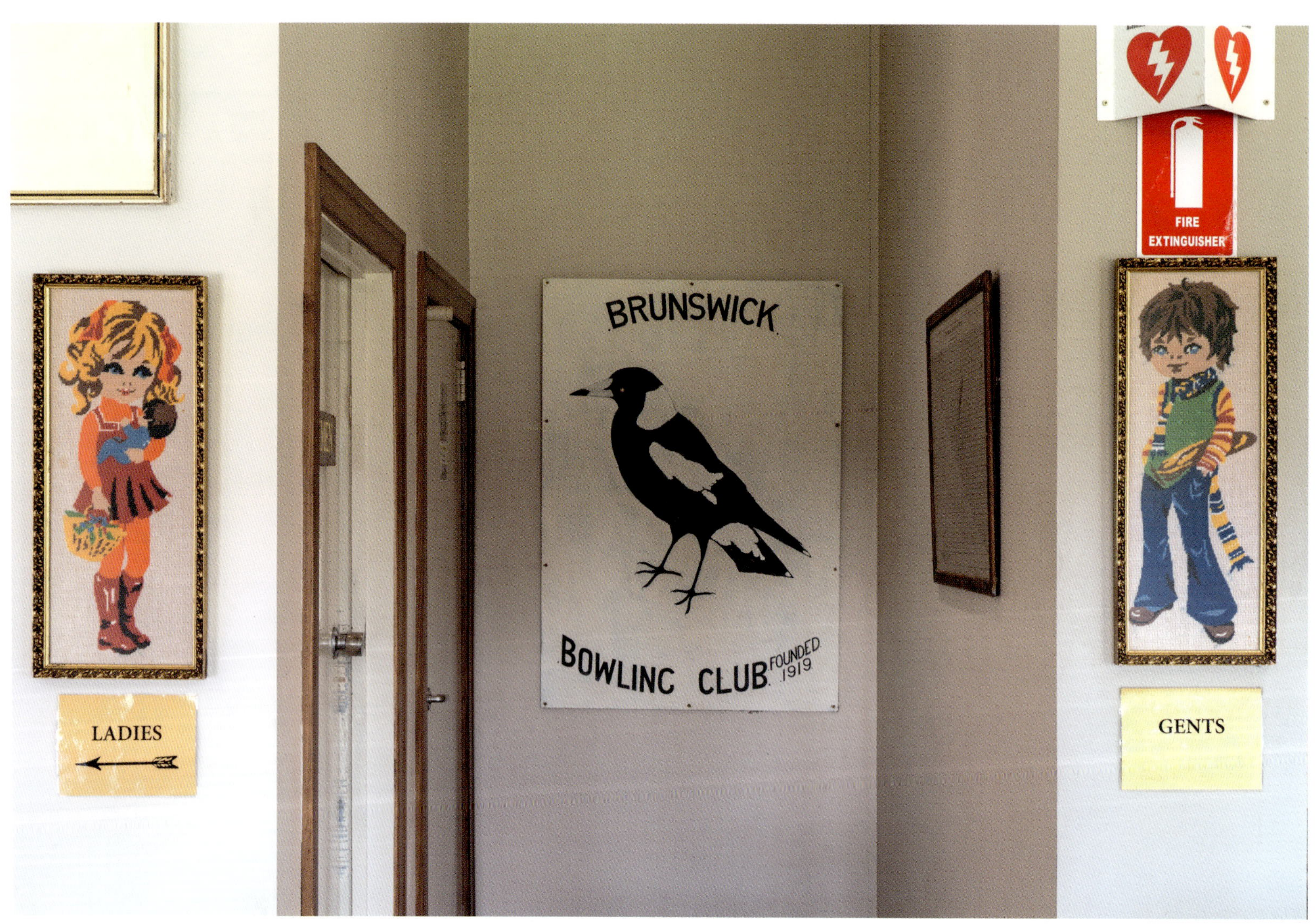

LADIES
BRUNSWICK
BOWLING CLUB FOUNDED 1919
FIRE EXTINGUISHER
GENTS

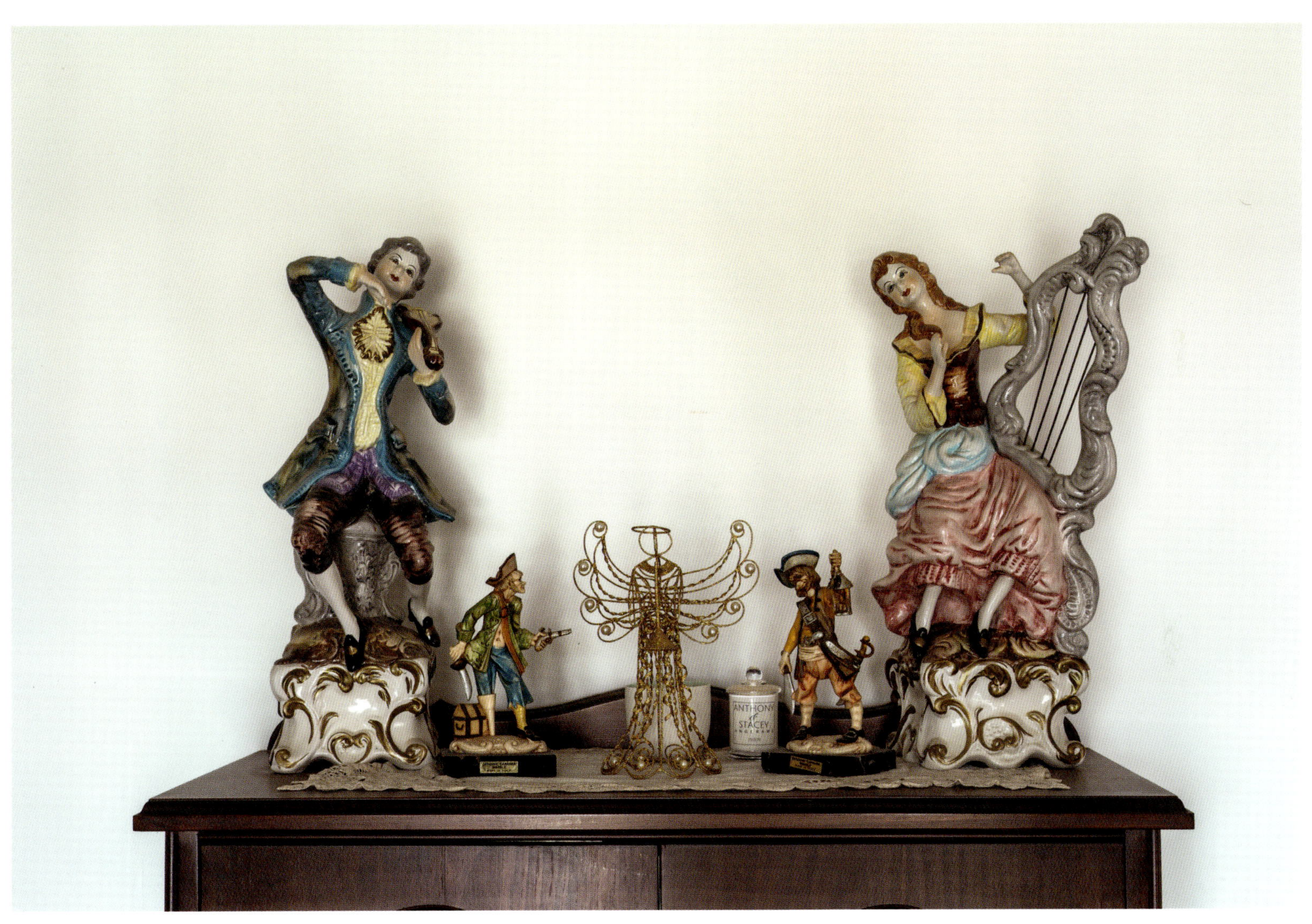

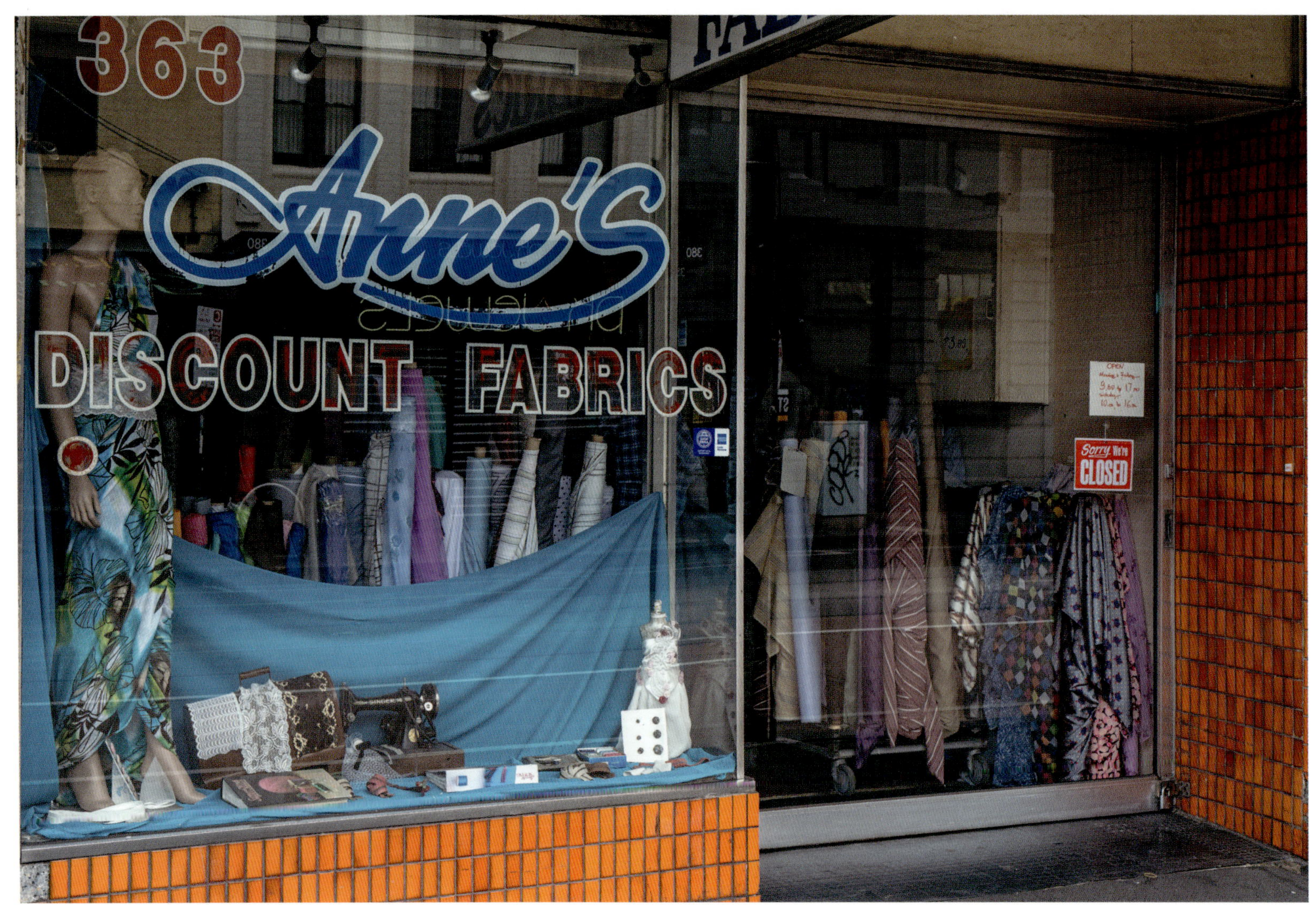
363
Anne's
DISCOUNT FABRICS
OPEN
Sorry We're
CLOSED

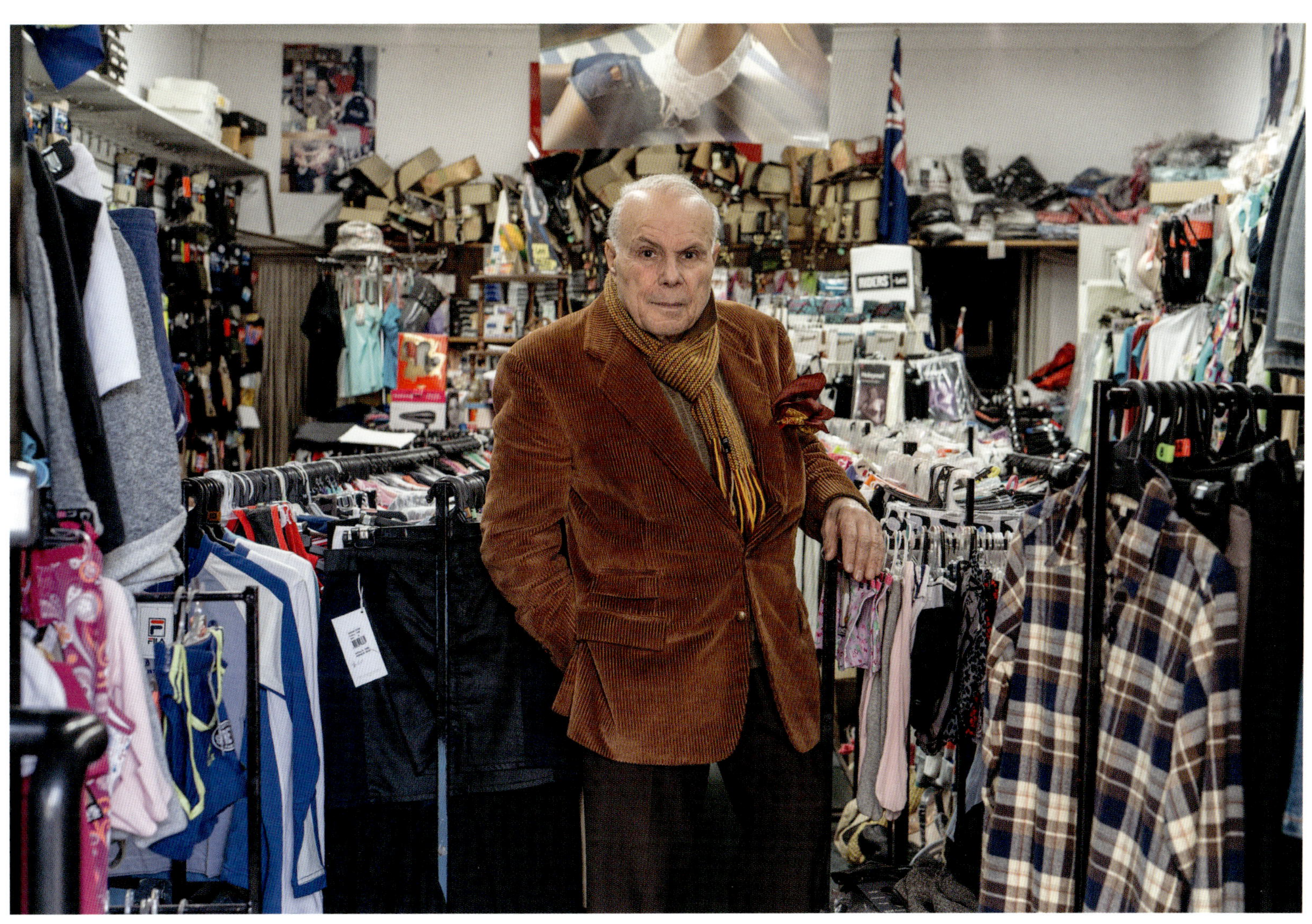

Brunswick East

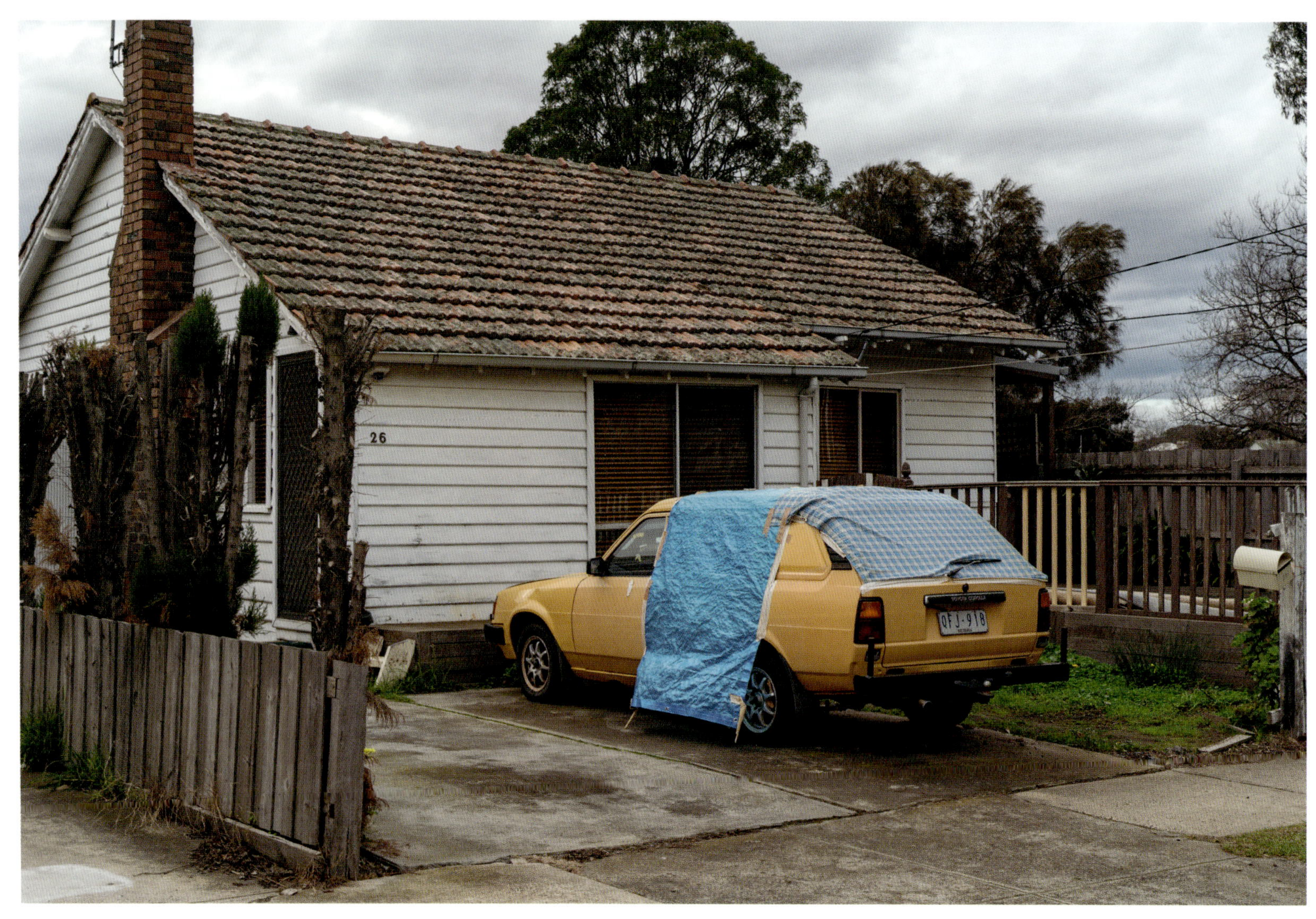

Brunswick West

12

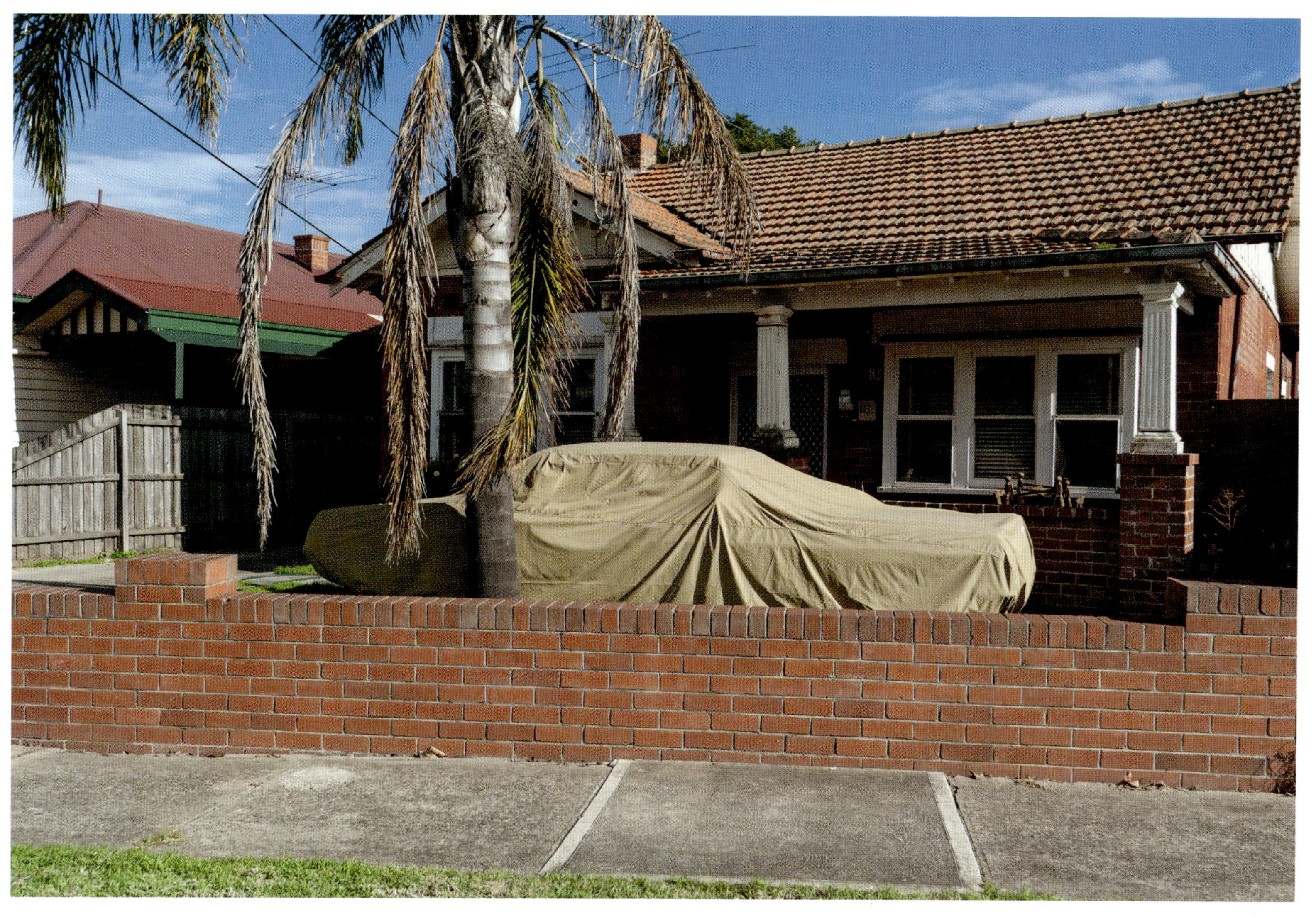

Coburg

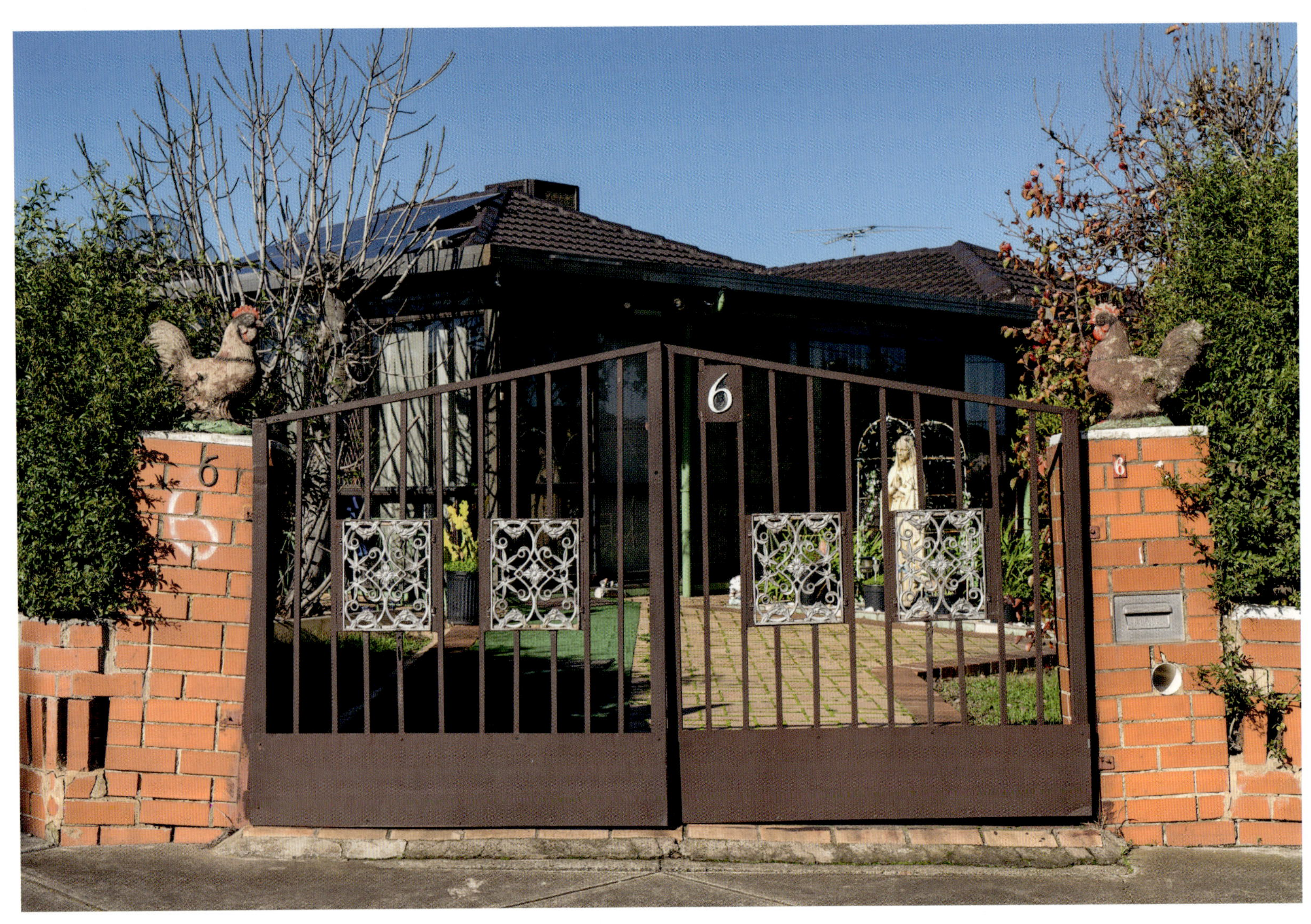

Campbellfield

14

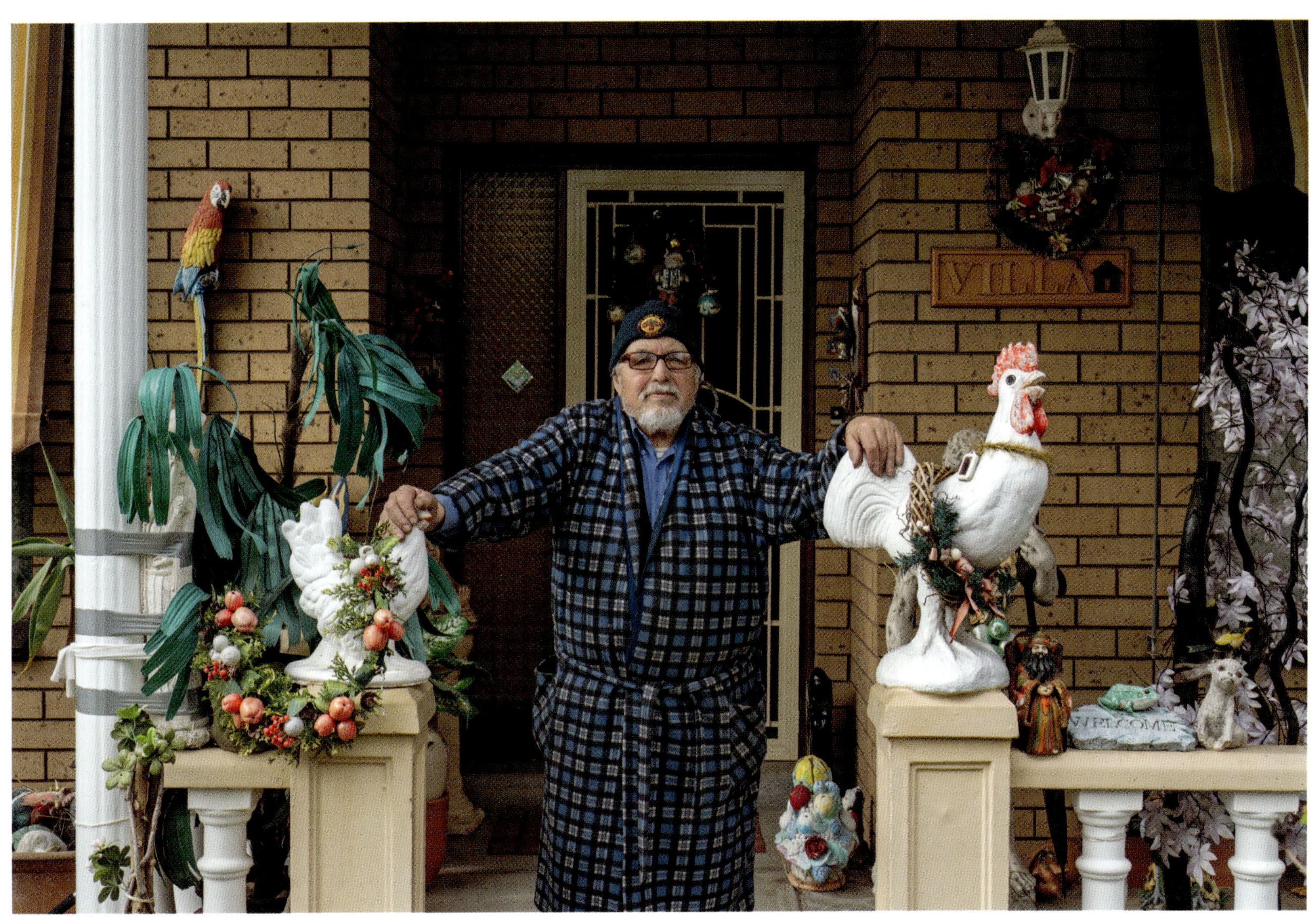

Coburg

SAM MIHELAKOS
FOR REAL SERVICE IN REAL ESTATE
ESTATE AGENTS
SM
Phone 387·3333
477 SYDNEY RD
CORNER BALLARAT ST
SAM MIHELAKOS ESTATE AGENTS
AUCTIONEERS
HOUSES WANTED
387 3333
INSURANCE AGENTS
SAM MIHELAKOS & CO. P/L
ESTATE AGENTS· R.E.I.V.

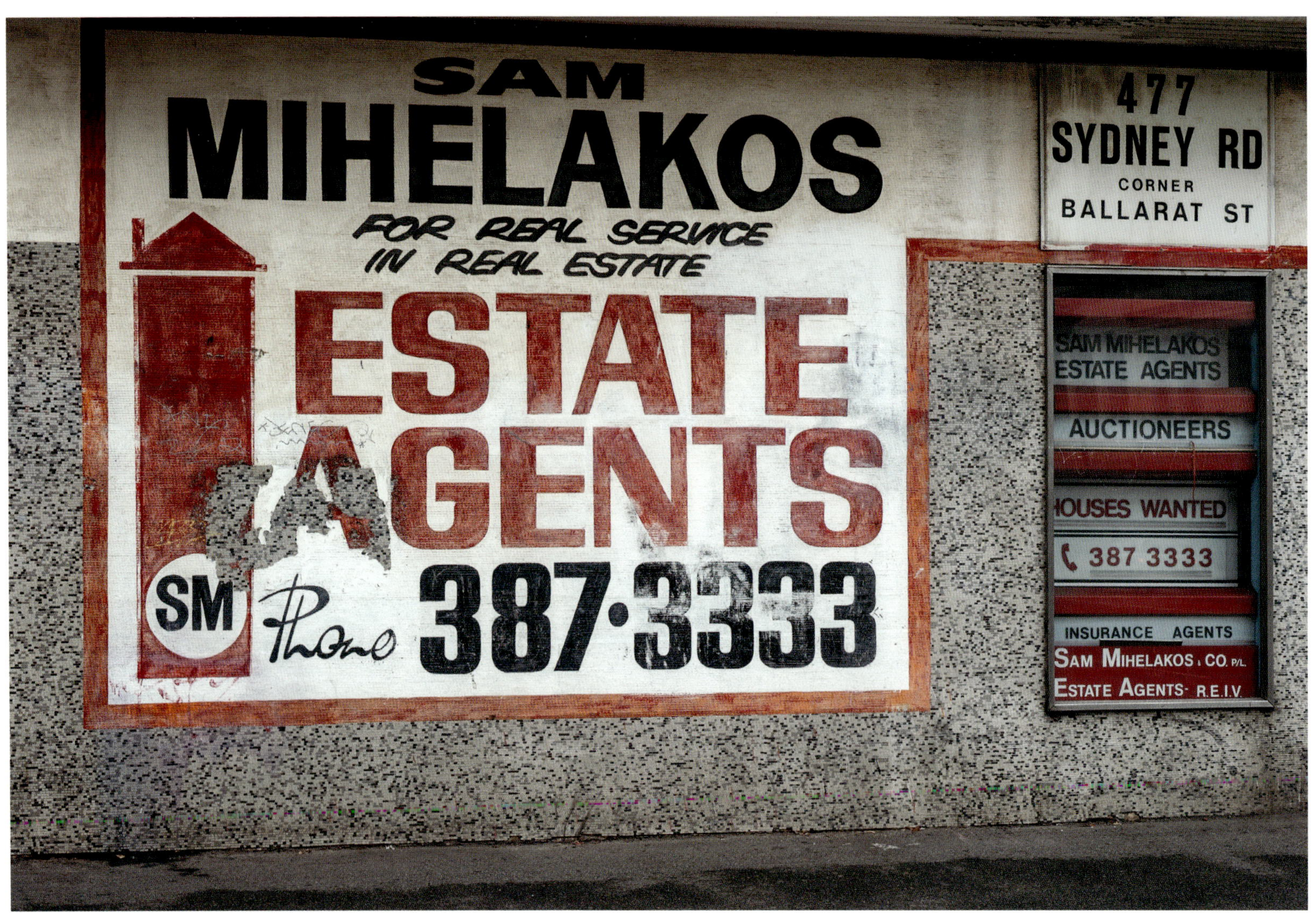

Brunswick

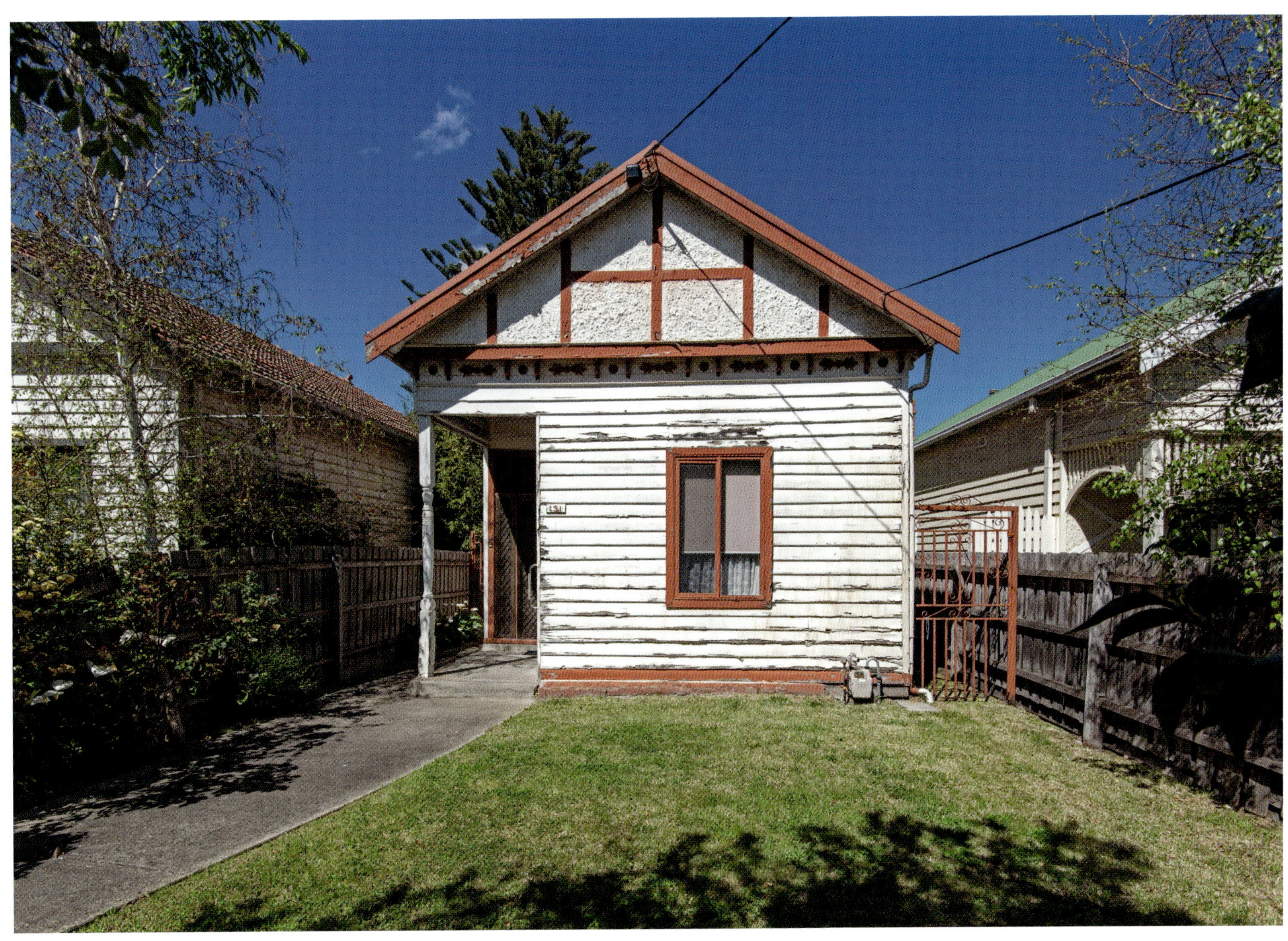

Thornbury

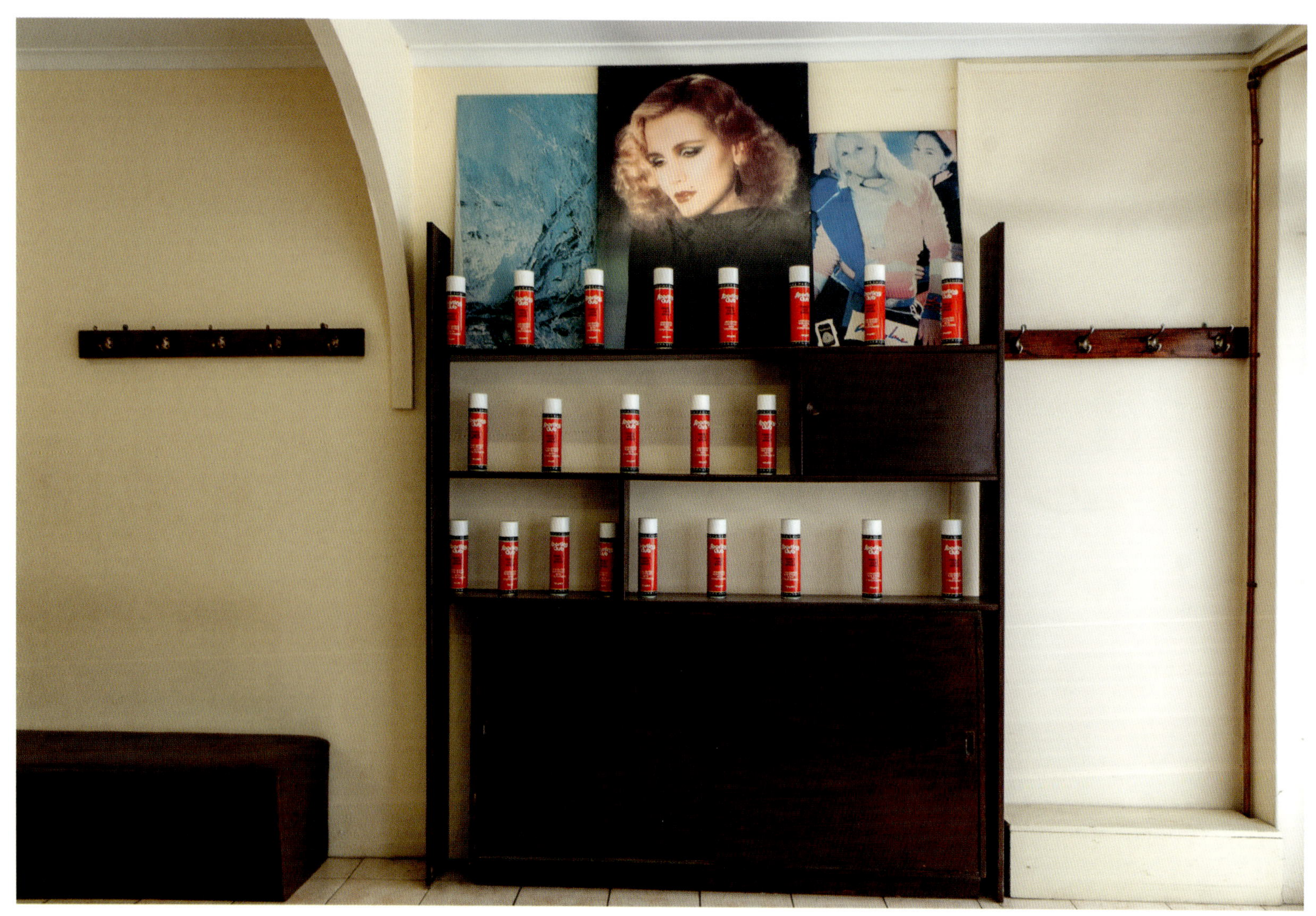

Hadfield

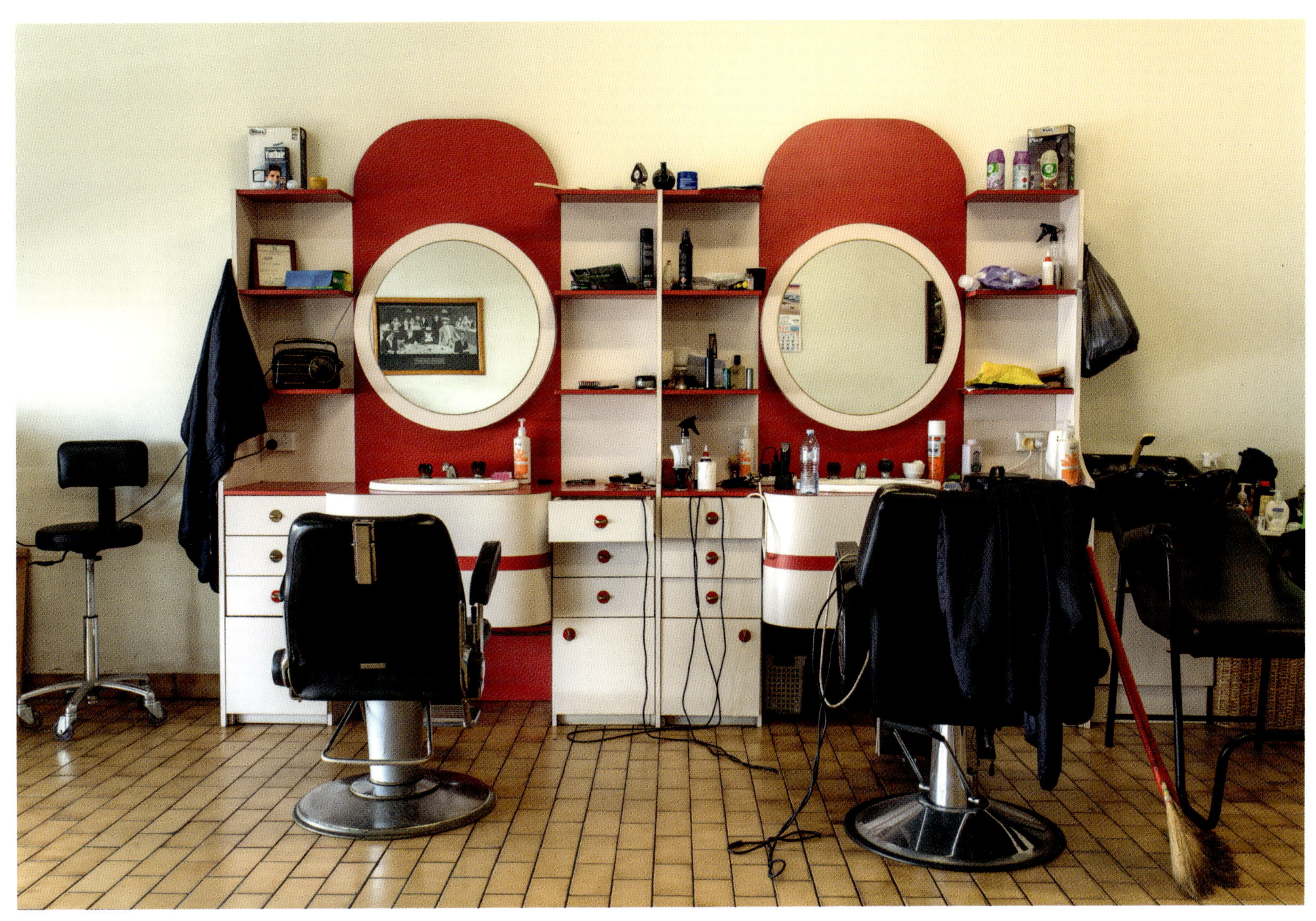

Reservoir

NOW LEANER THAN EVER
NEW FASHIONED PORK
WHOLE CHICKENS (No 13 + 14)
MARYLANDS
FILLETS
G & A LATINA CONTINENTAL BUTCHERS
2018
2017
SARAKOS

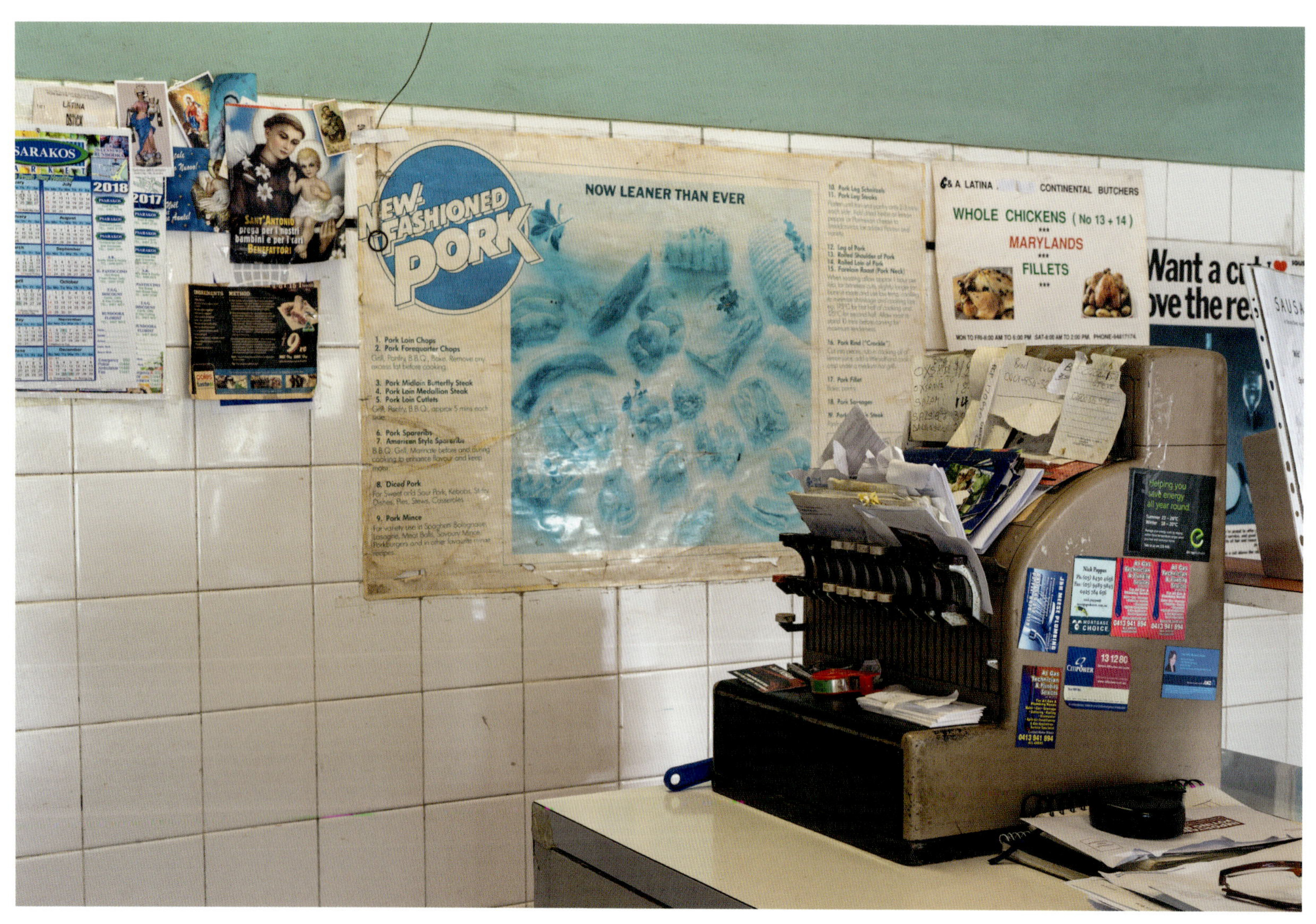

Northcote

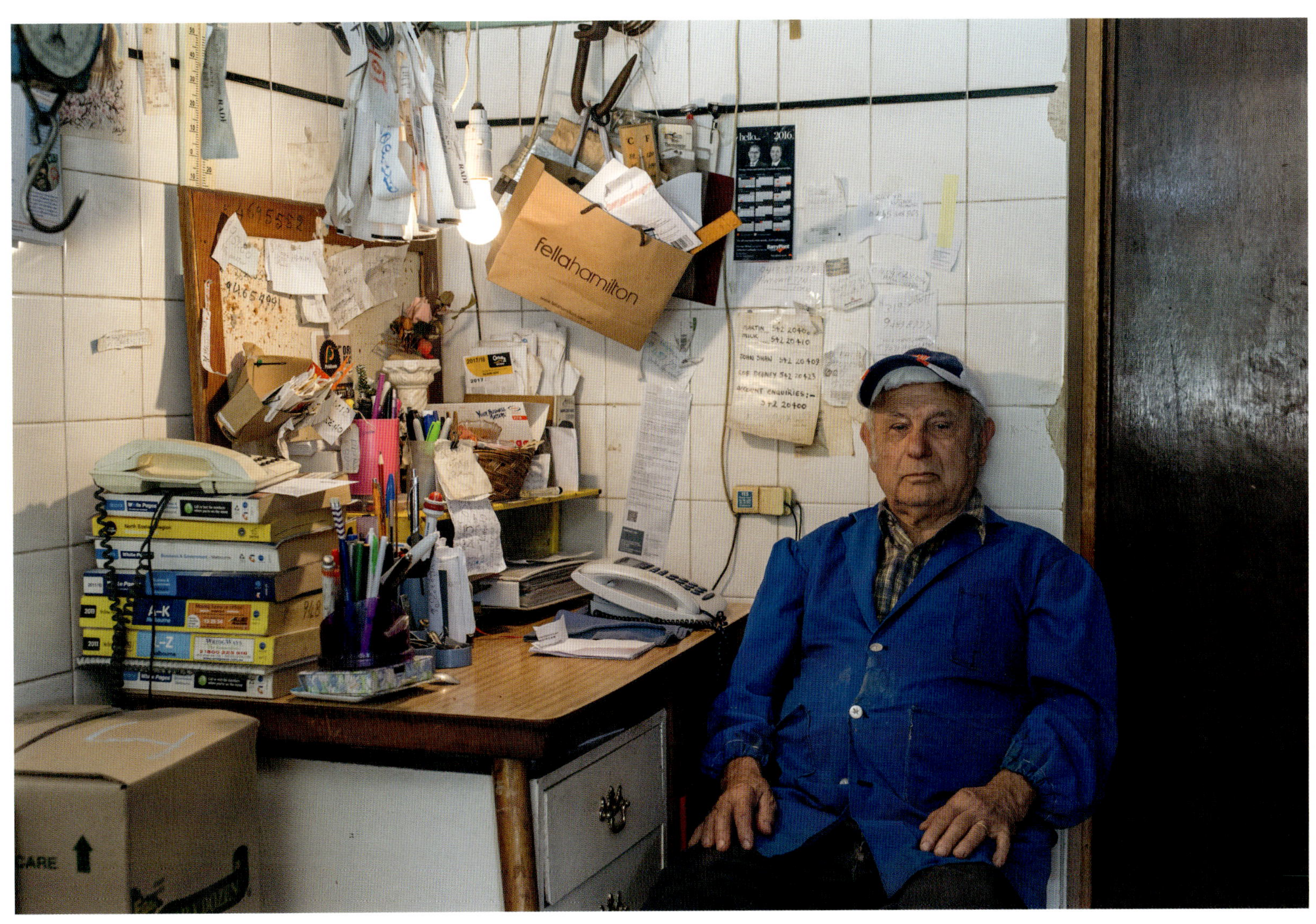

Northcote

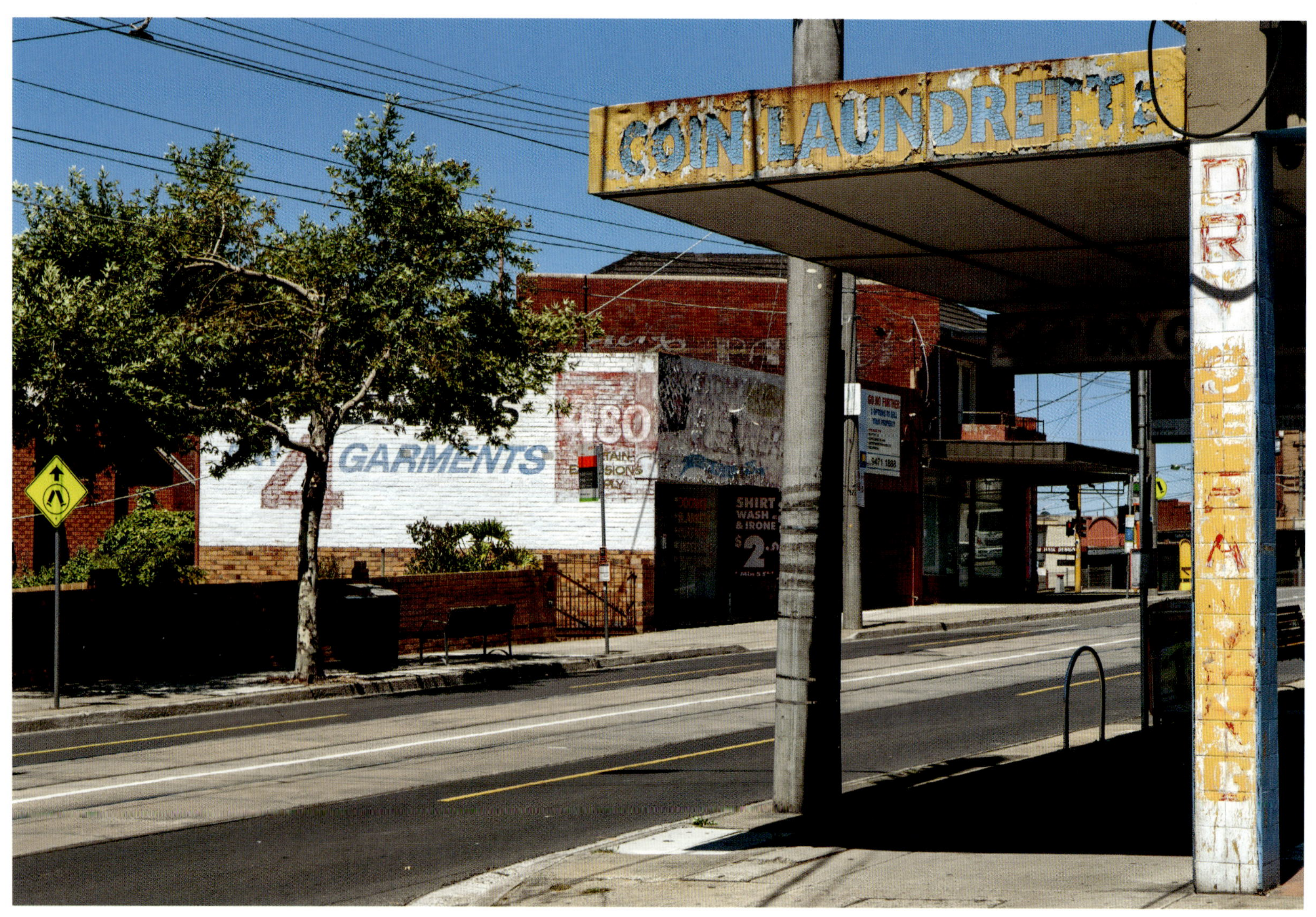

Reservoir

545
CHEMIST
ΕΛΛΗΝΙΚΟΝ ΦΑΡΜΑΚΕΙΟΝ
CHEMIST
ΕΛΛΗΝΙΚΟΝ
ΦΑΡΜΑΚΕΙΟΝ
ΣΙΑΜΙΔΗΣ
CHEMIST
CHEMIST
PROCESSING BY... QFL PROCESSING STEVE SIAMIDIS.
CHEMIST
FARMAC
ΦΑΡΜΑΚΕΙΟΝ
NESTLE'S CHOCOLATE
HAIRDRESSER
CHRIS
ΕΛΛΗΝΙΚΟΝ ΚΟΥΡΕΙΟΝ
SALE

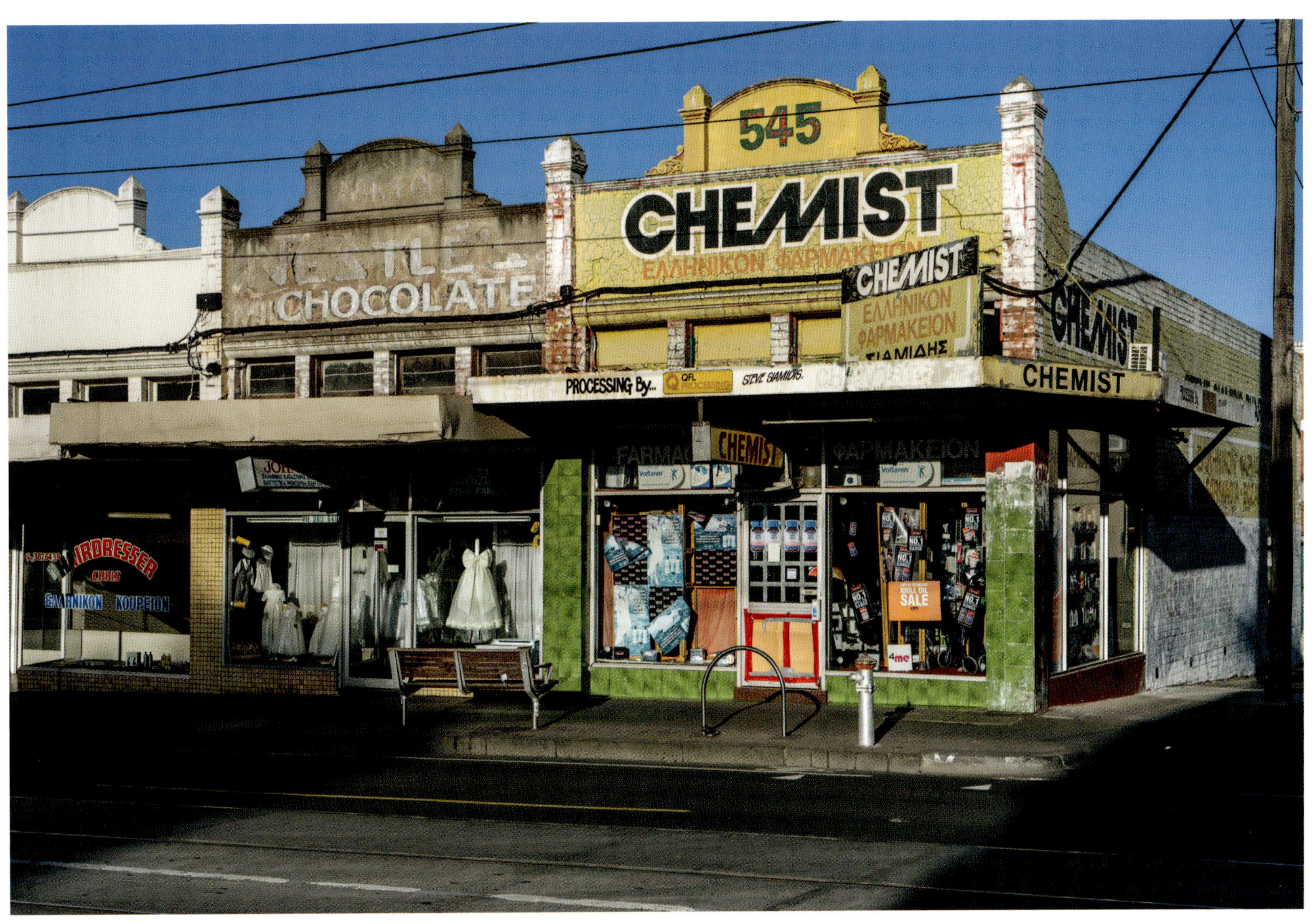

Brunswick

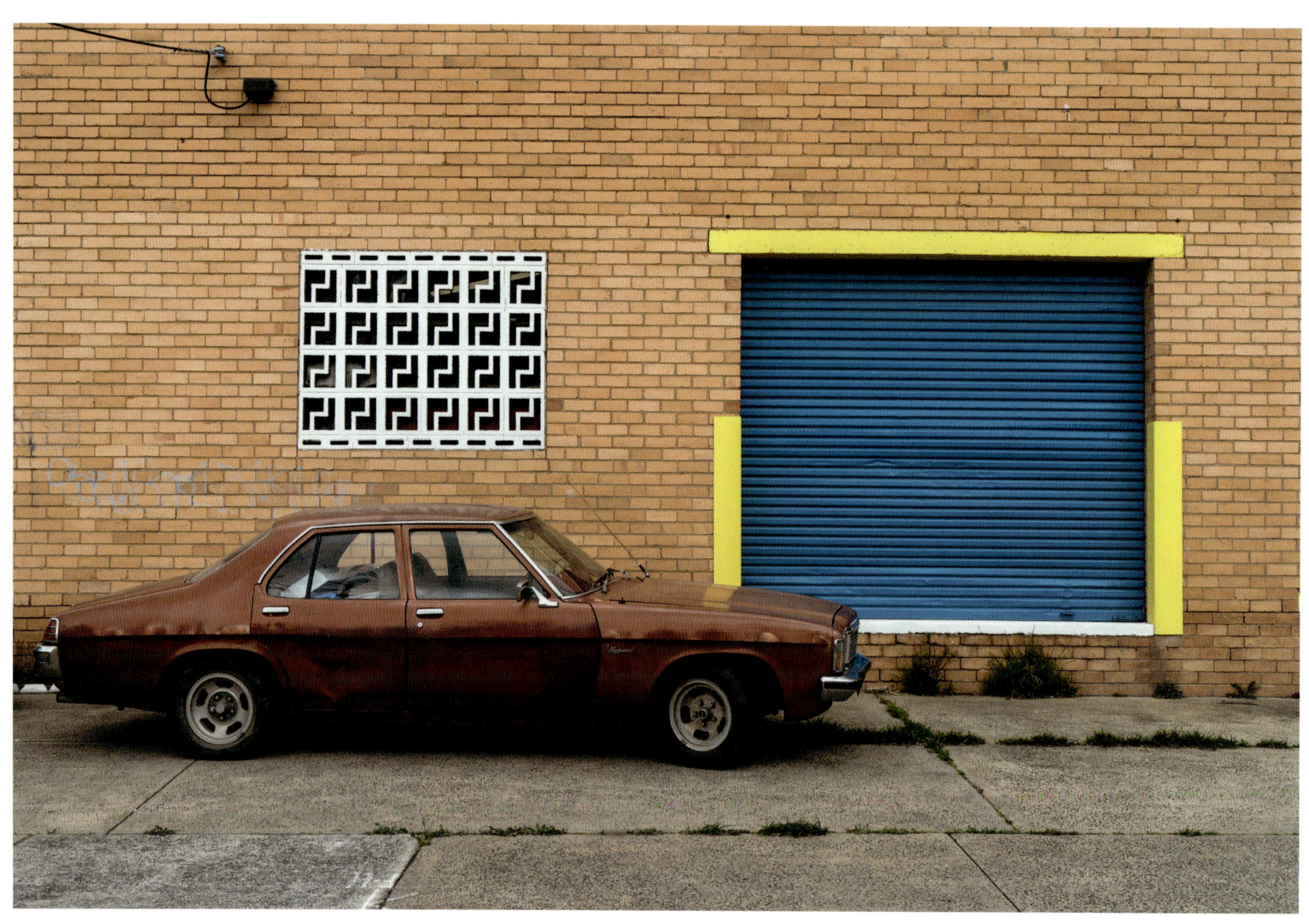

Coburg North

24

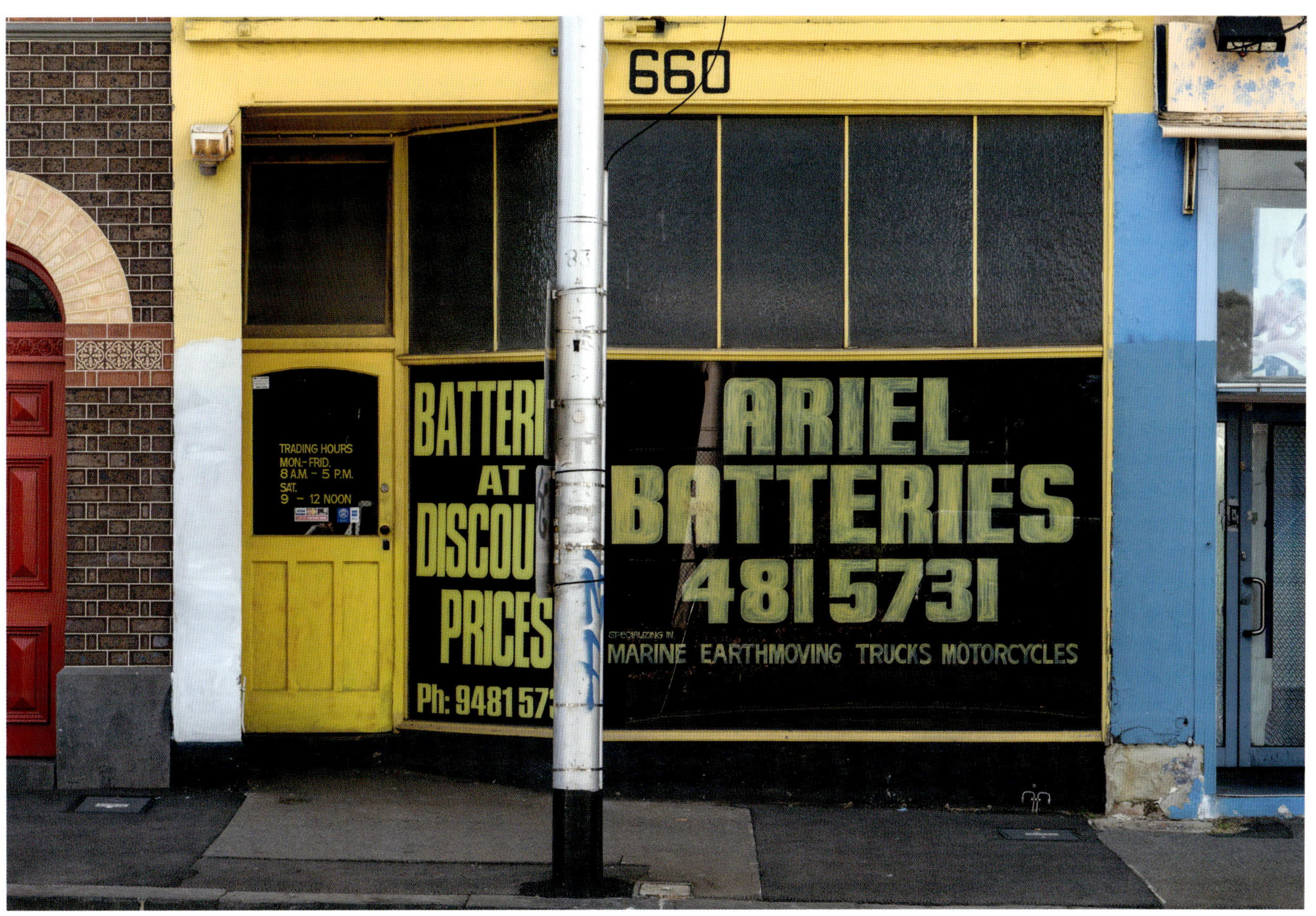

Clifton Hill

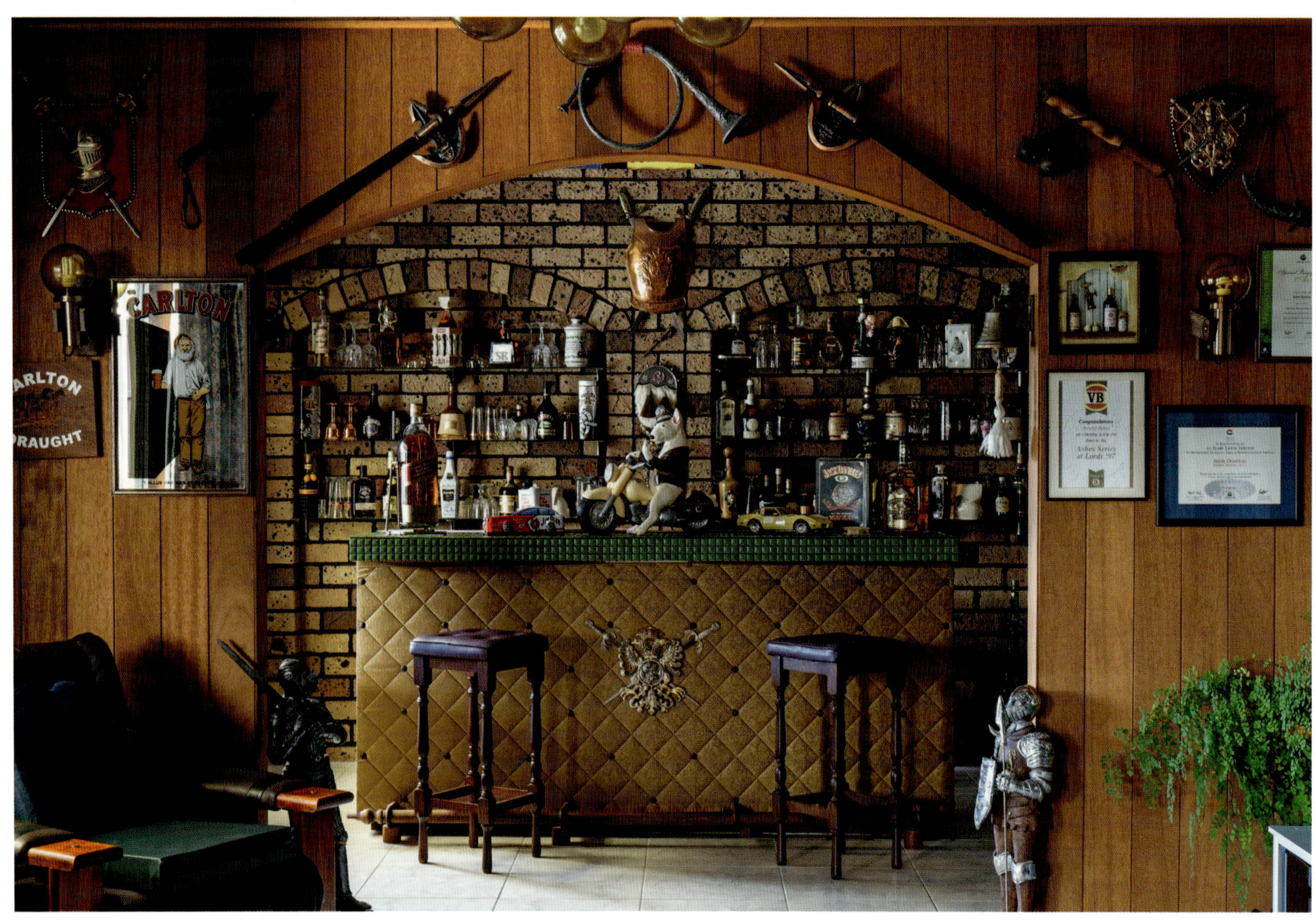

Hadfield

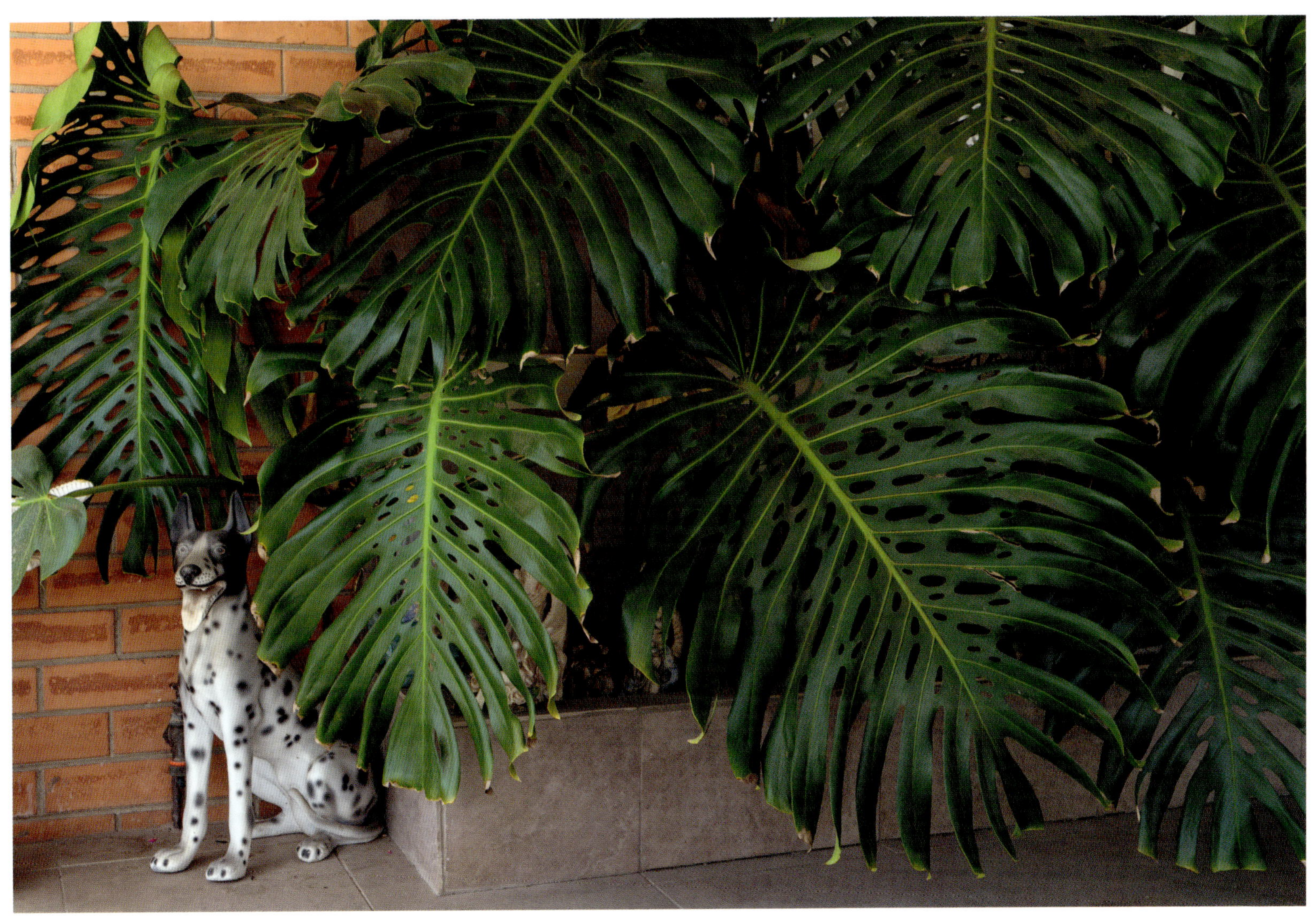

Reservoir

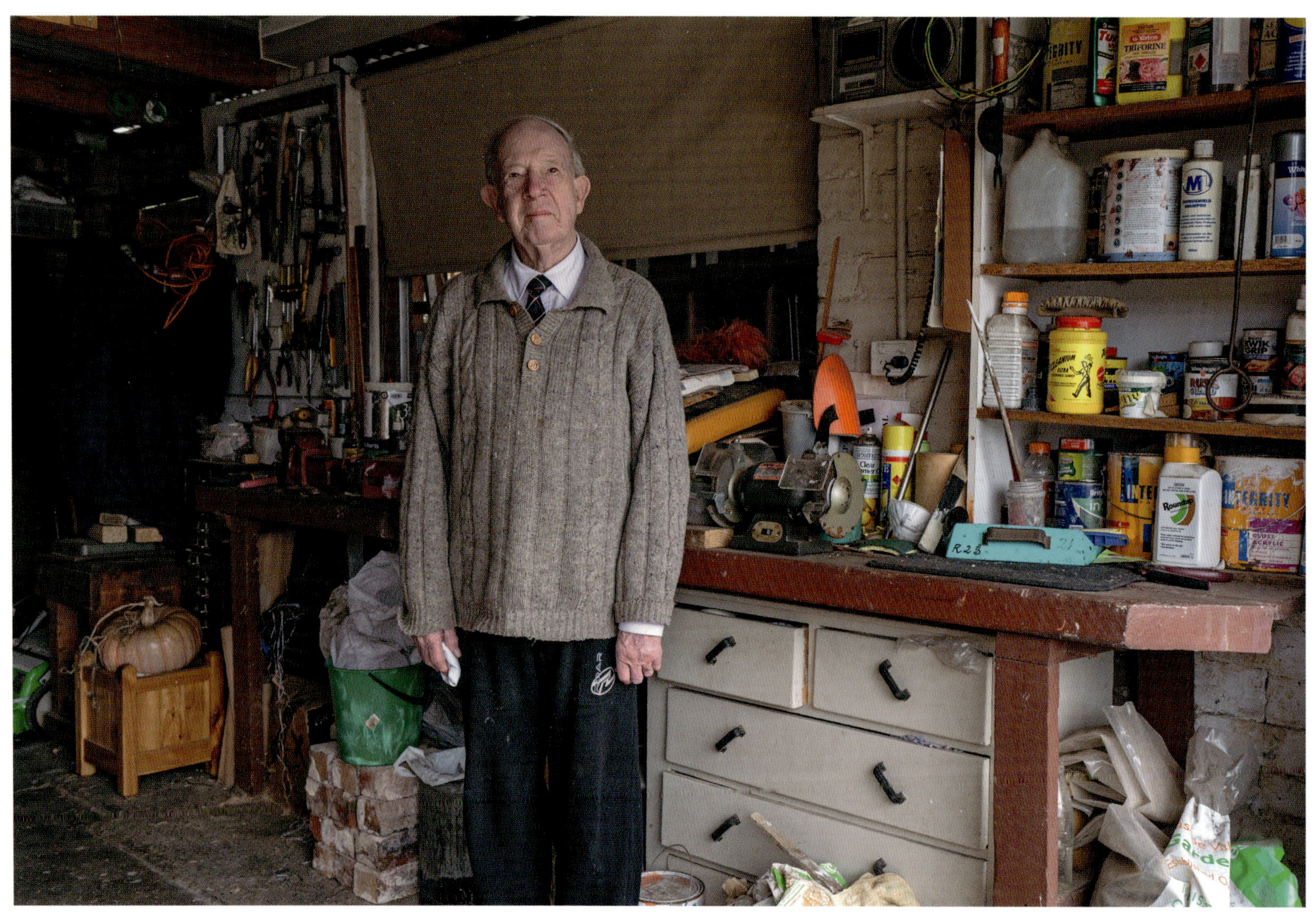

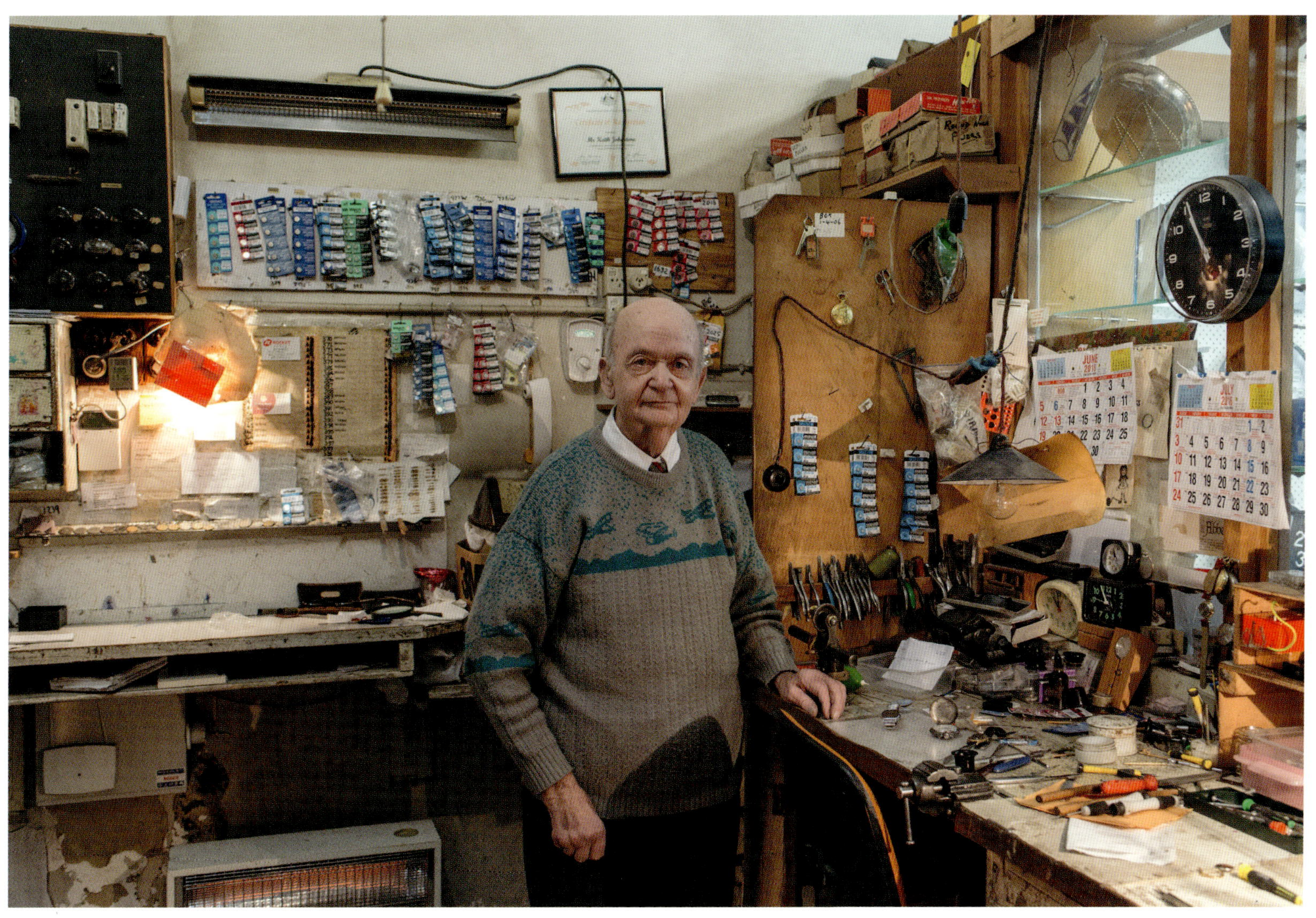

Coburg

VINCE MARTINO... THE BETTER
FRUIT SUPPLIERS
THE HOUSEWIVES FRIEND...
Quality-
153

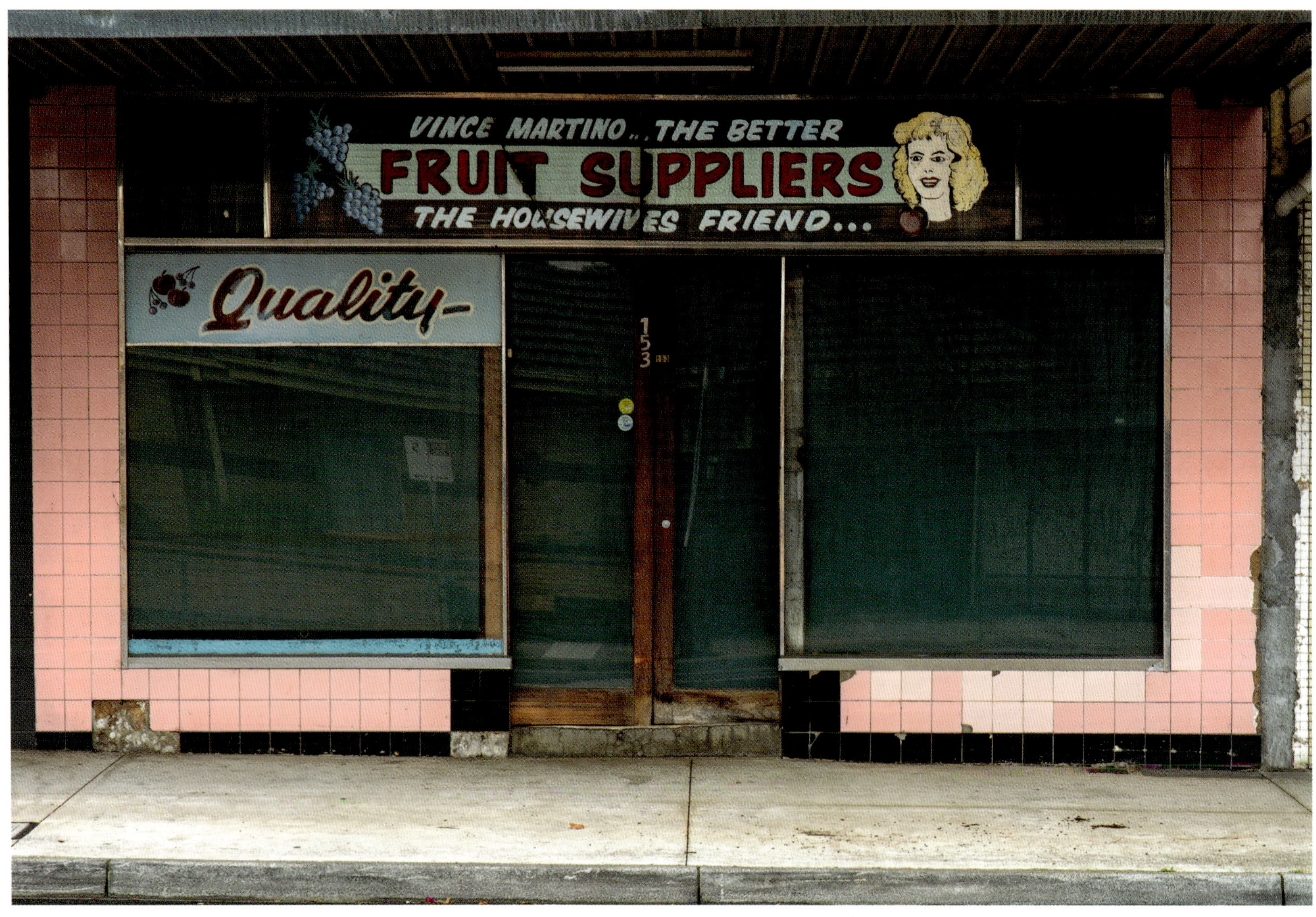

Thornbury

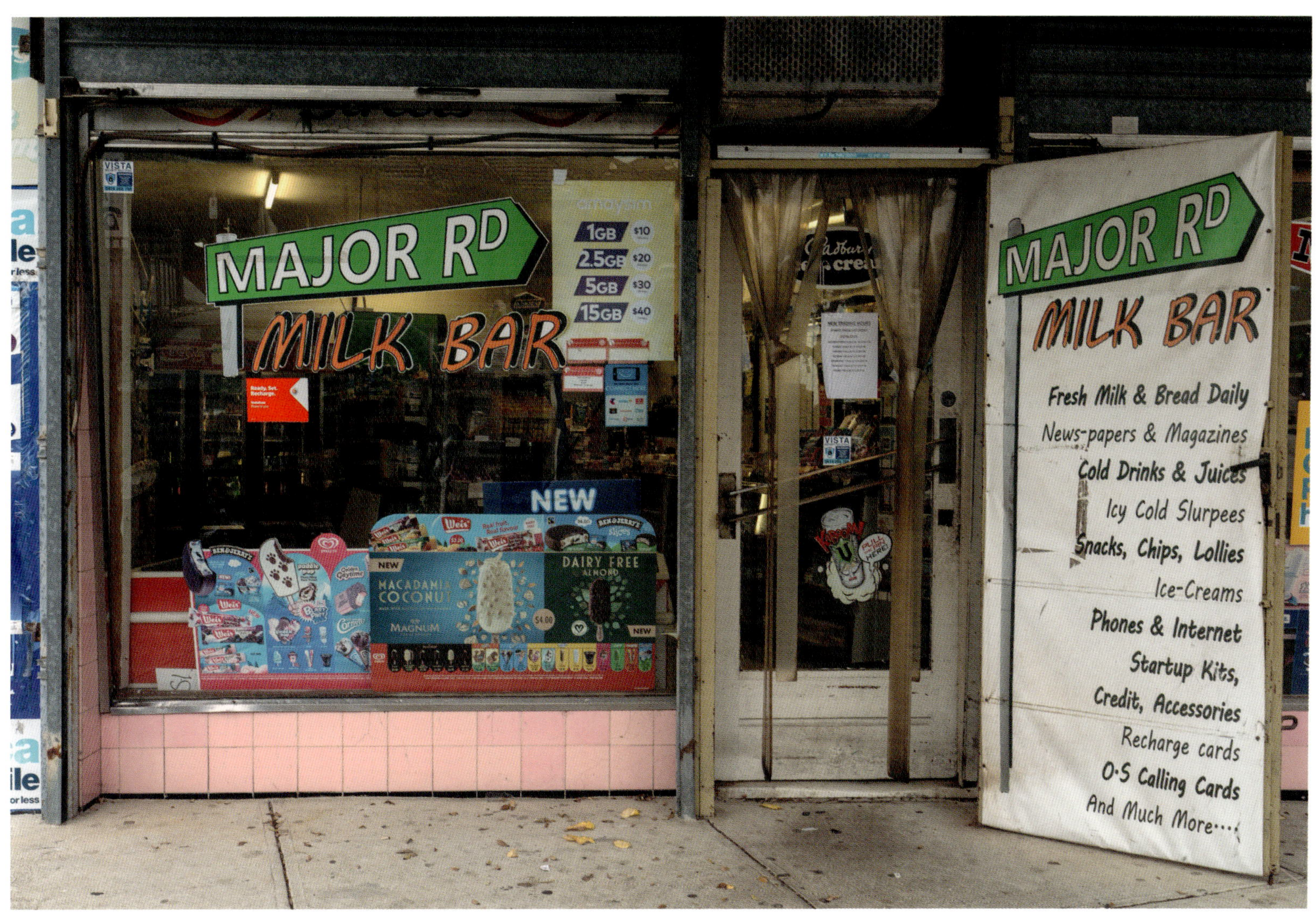

MAJOR RD
MILK BAR

MAJOR RD
MILK BAR

Fresh Milk & Bread Daily
News-papers & Magazines
Cold Drinks & Juices
Icy Cold Slurpees
Snacks, Chips, Lollies
Ice-Creams
Phones & Internet
Startup Kits,
Credit, Accessories
Recharge cards
O·S Calling Cards
And Much More....

1GB $10
2.5GB $20
5GB $30
15GB $40

NEW

DAIRY FREE
ALMOND

MACADAMIA
COCONUT

MAGNUM

$4.00

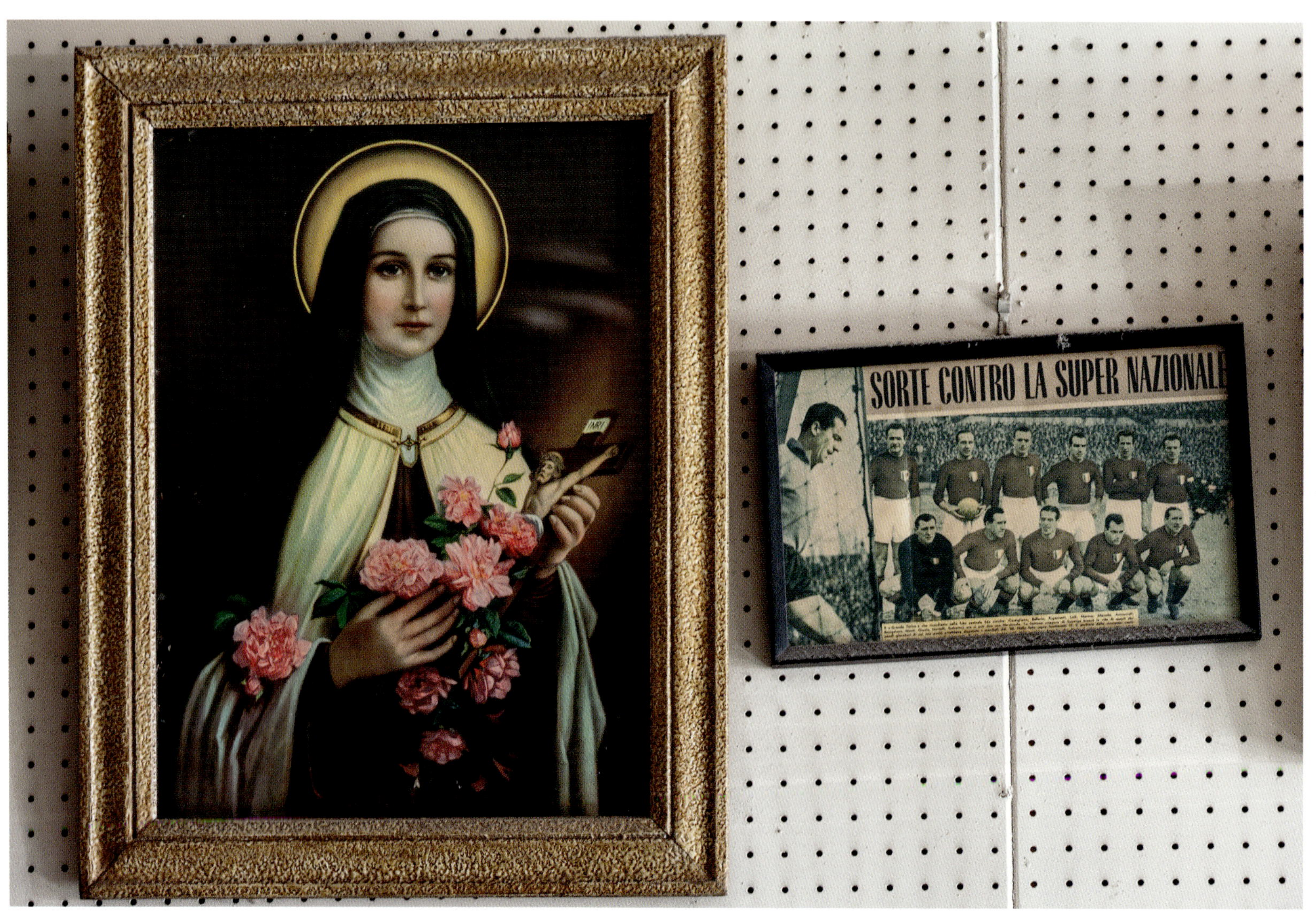

Collingwood

Tim Tam
Cadbury
Freddo
m&m's
PEPSI
Coca-Cola
MAGPIES
Reese's
Time Out

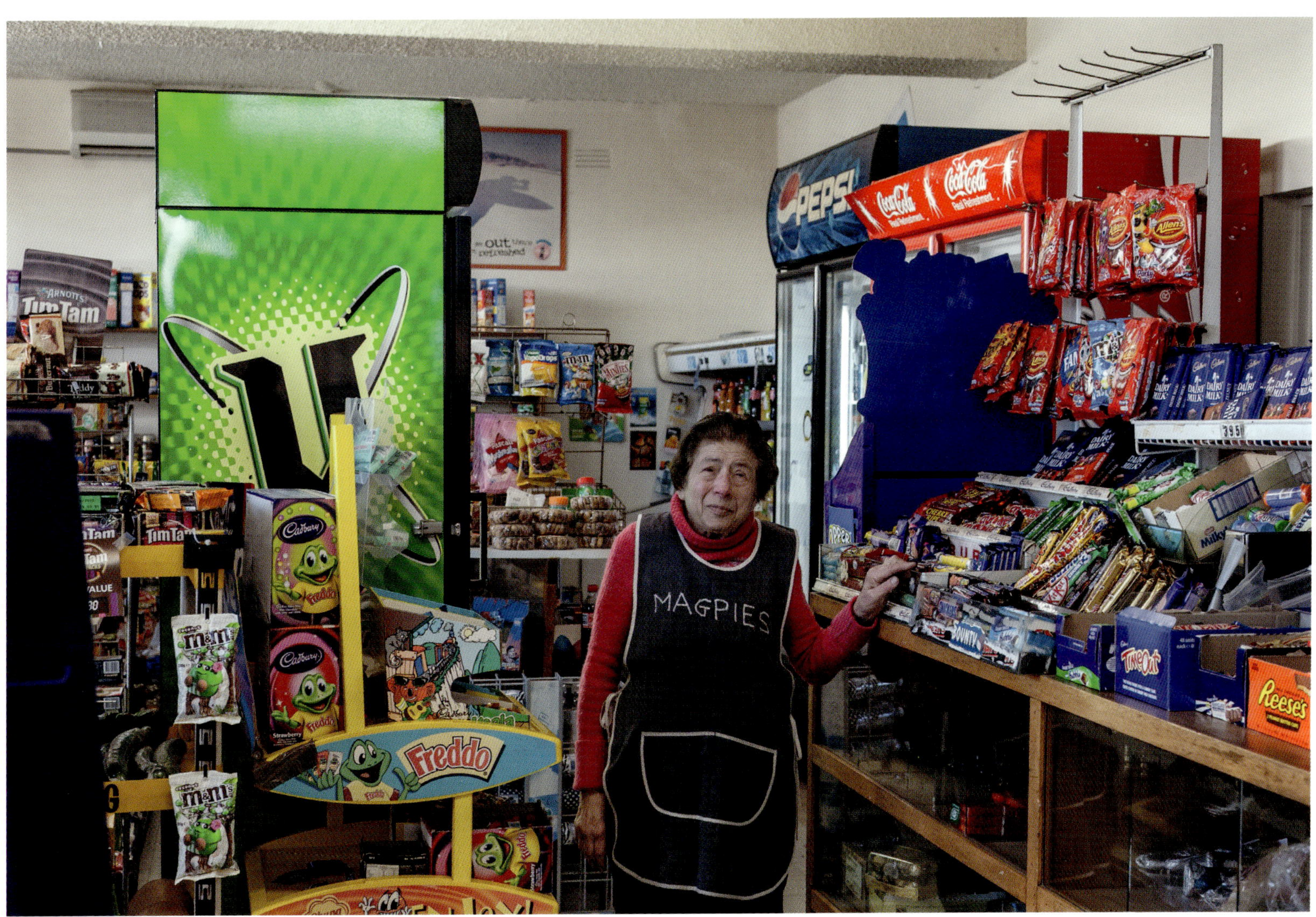

Abbotsford

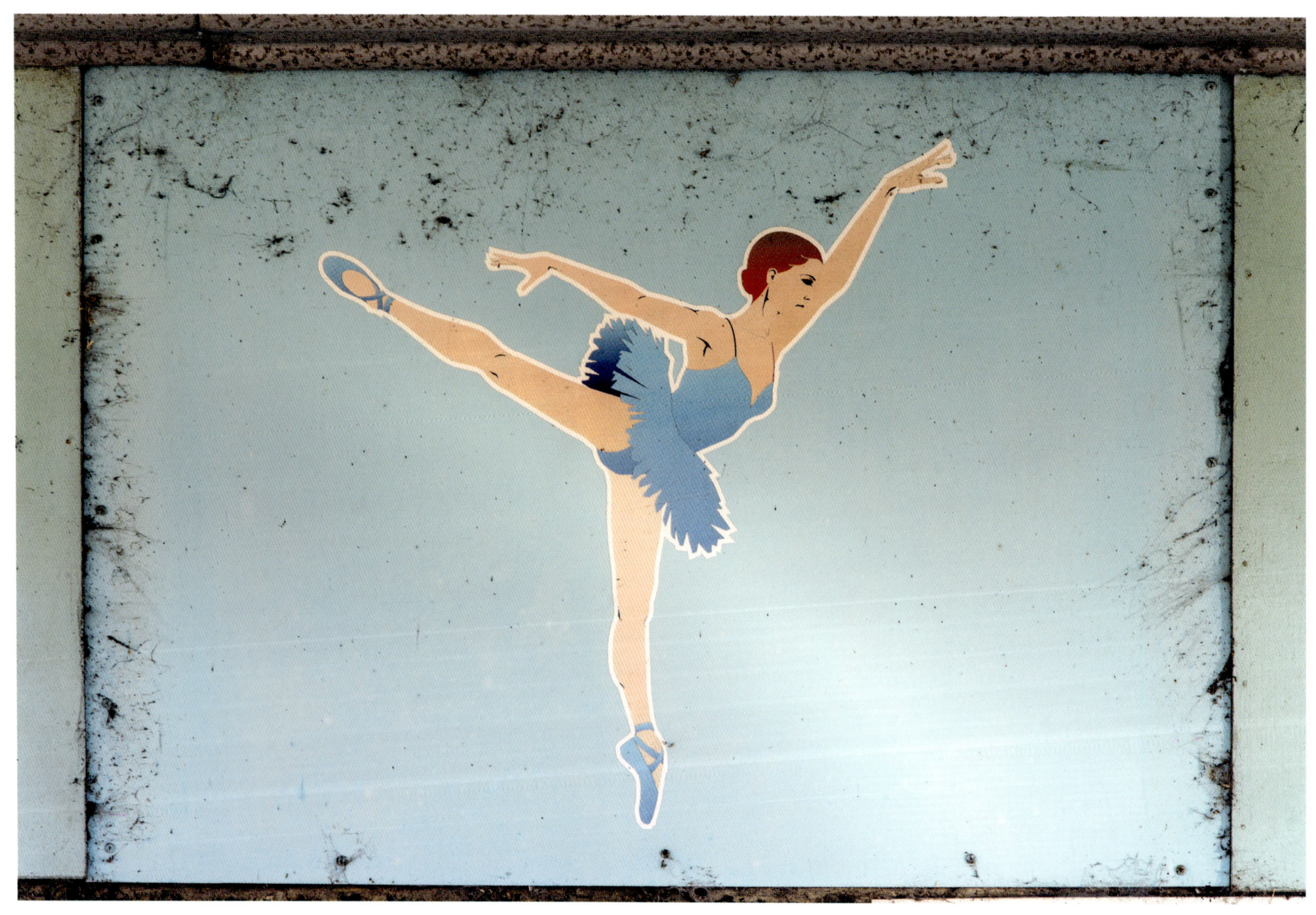

Pascoe Vale South

34

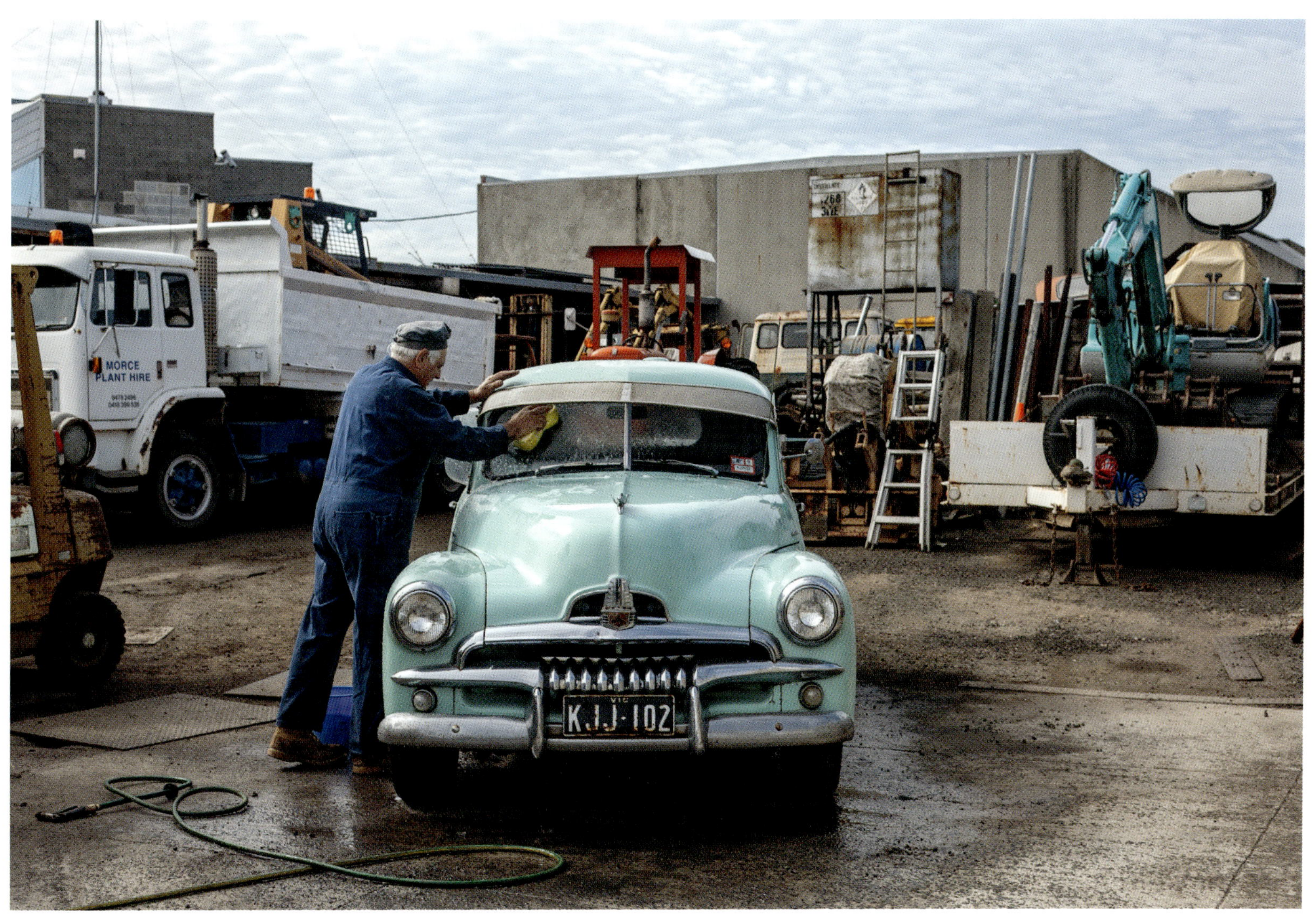

Preston

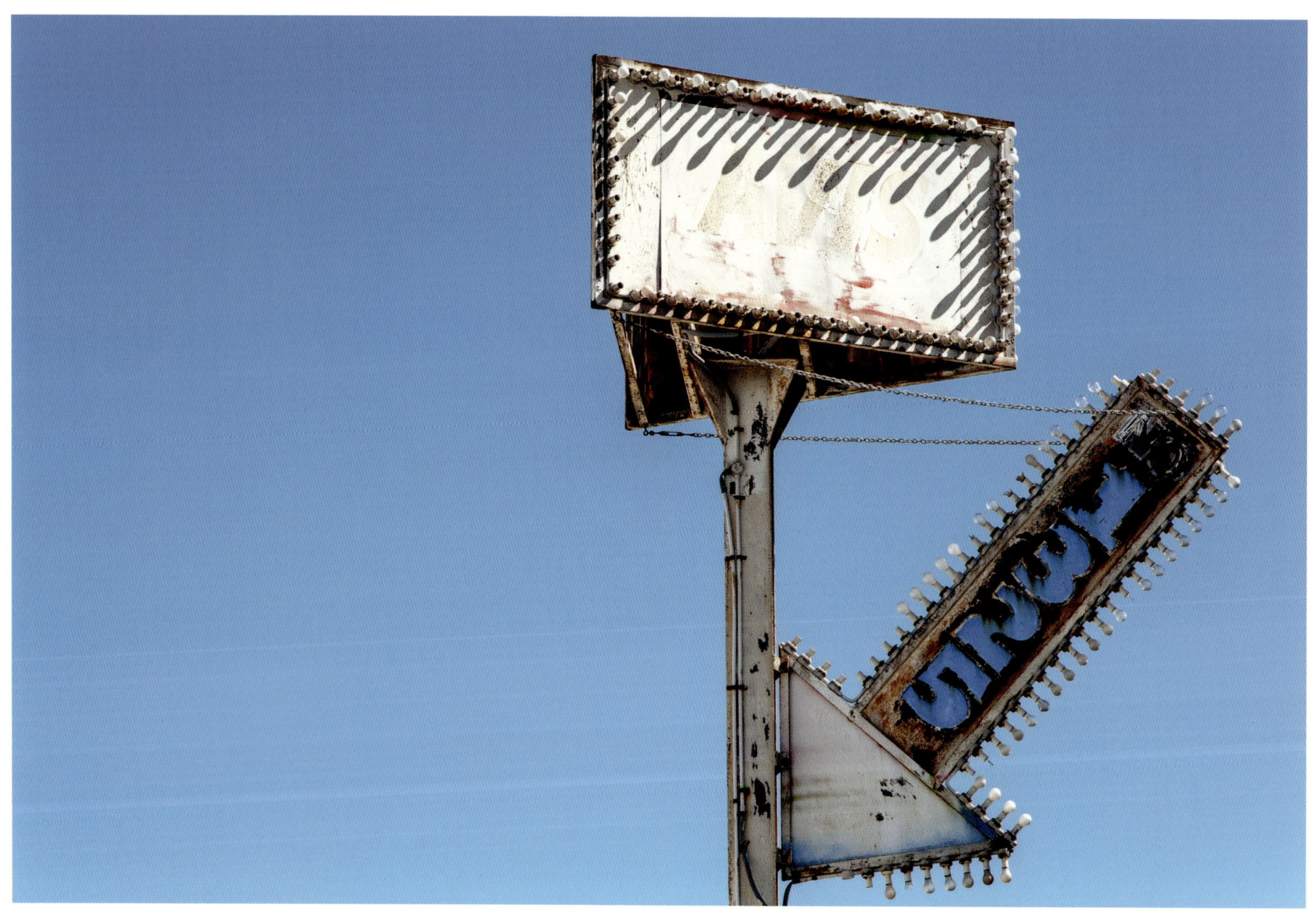

Fawkner

Video Library
TITALIAN DVD CENTRE
OPEN 7 DAYS
Largest Variety Of
ITALIAN MOVIES
PH. 9354 1379
TEMPO
Jellis Craig

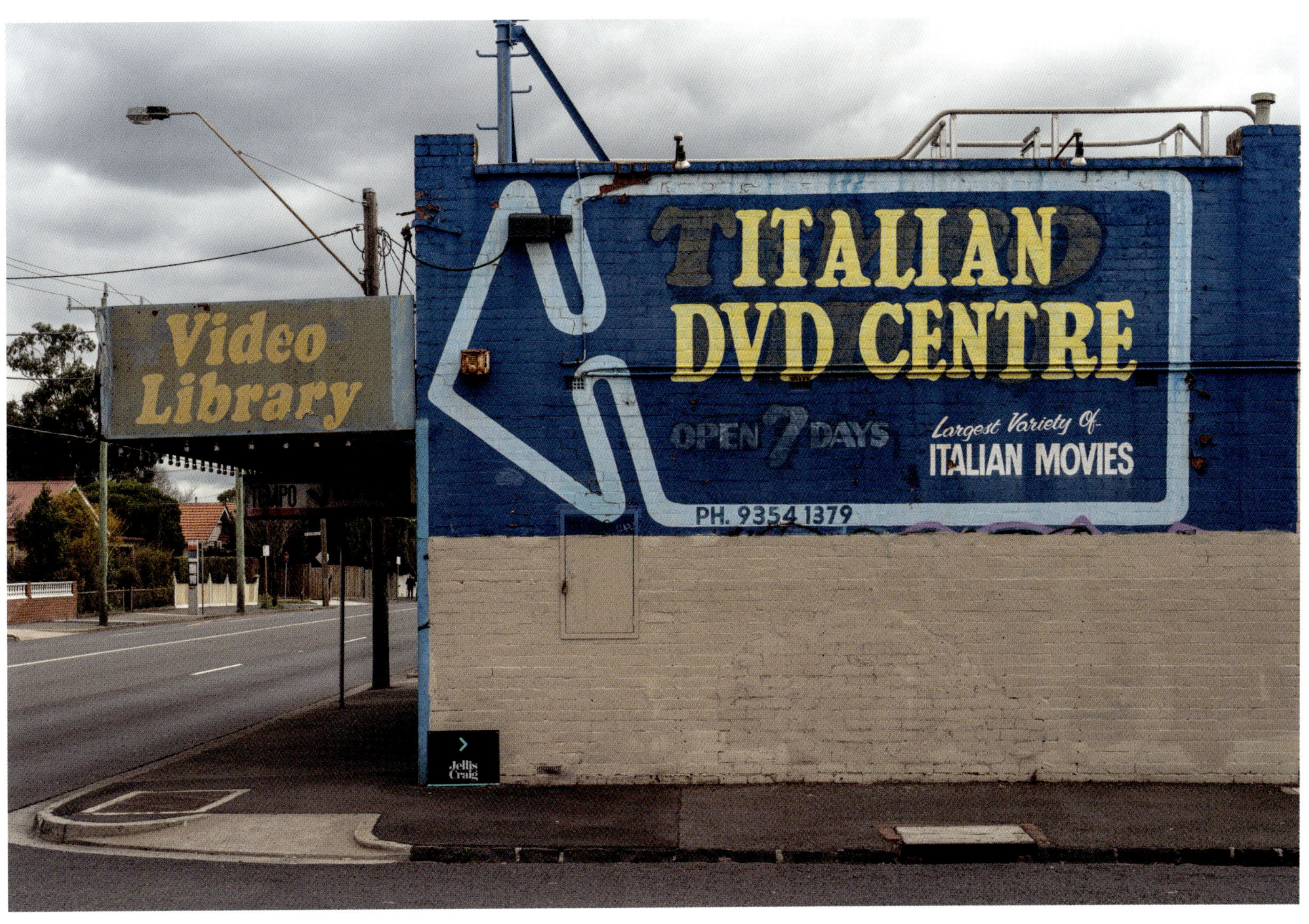

Coburg

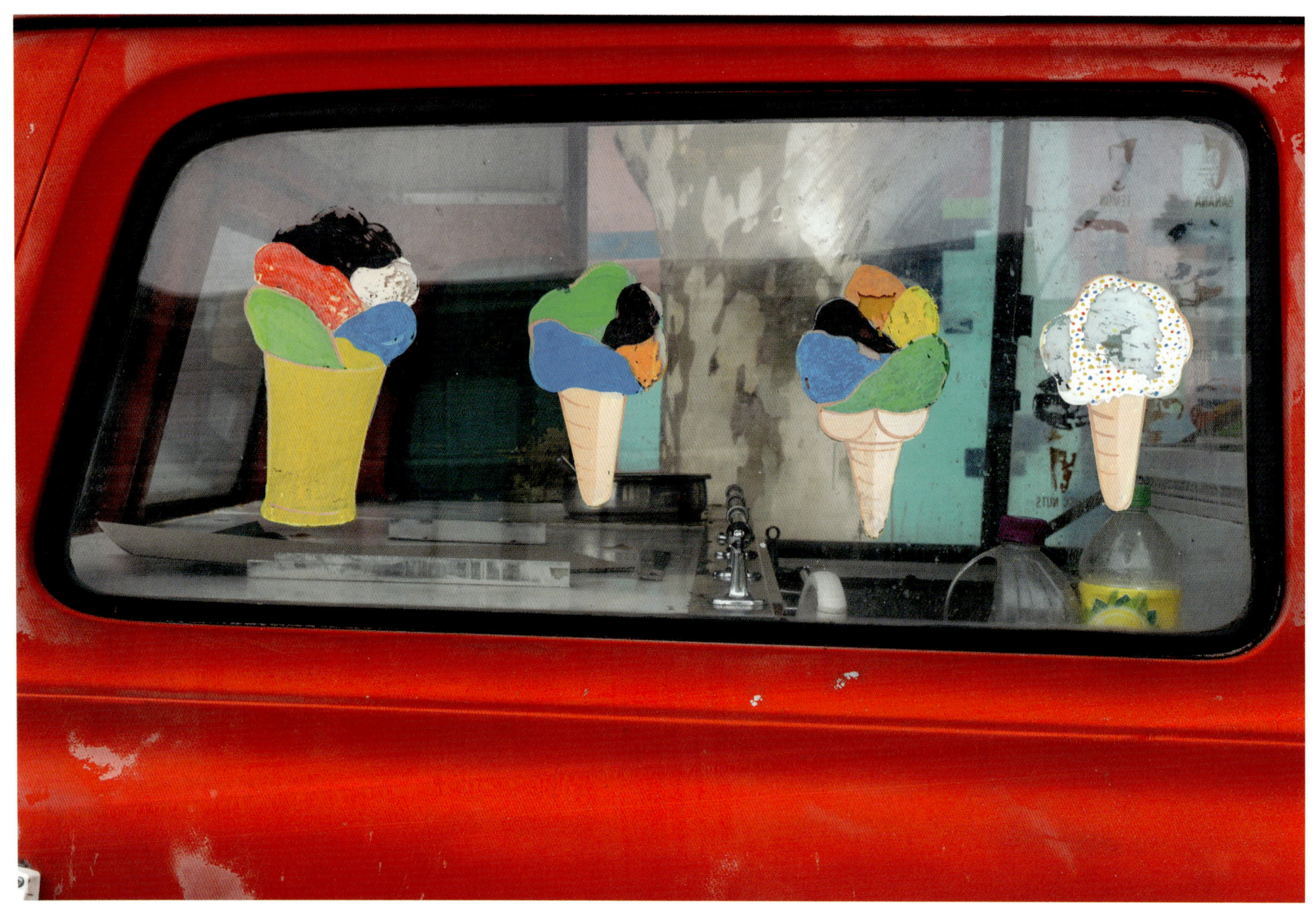

North Melbourne

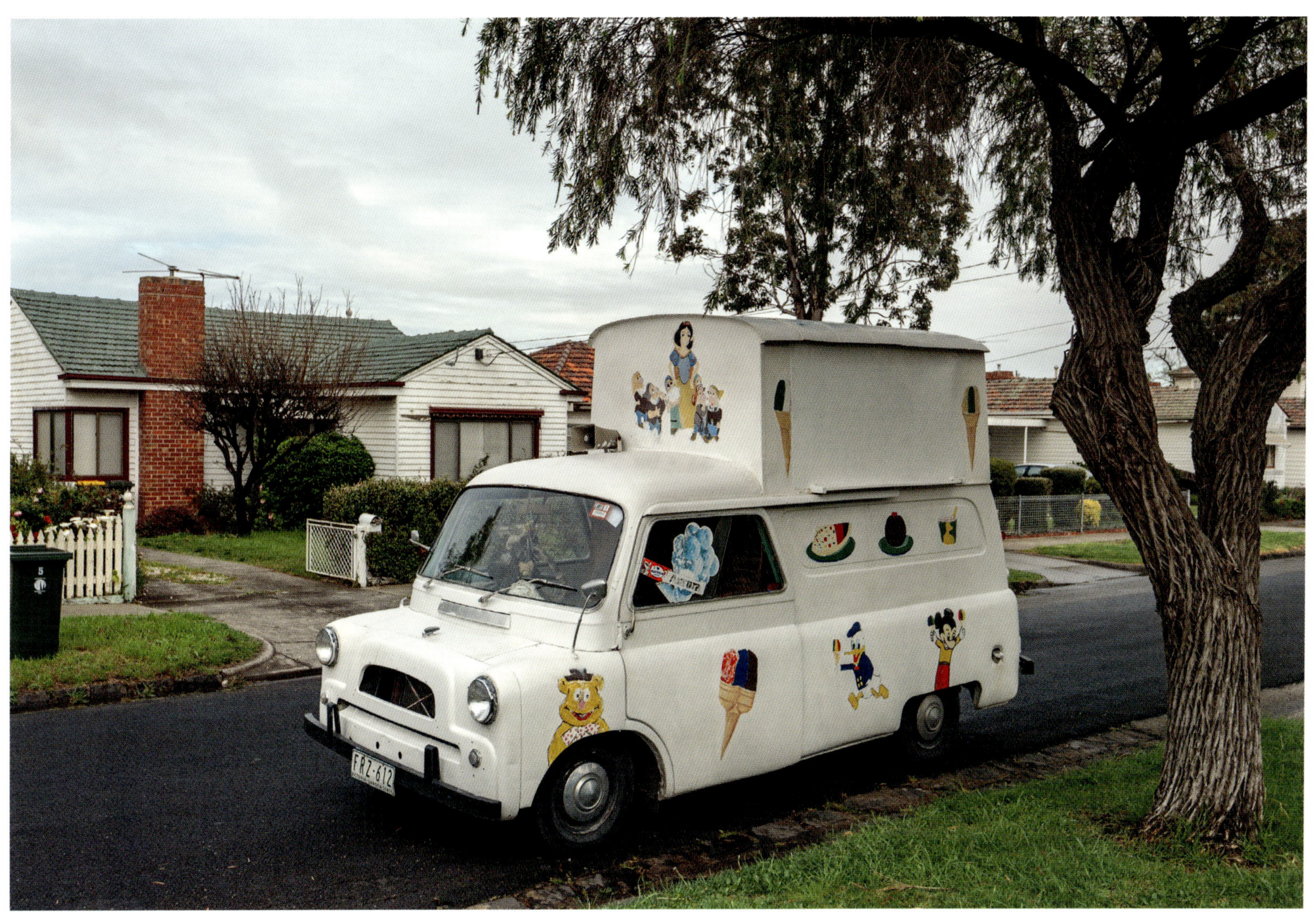

Pascoe Vale

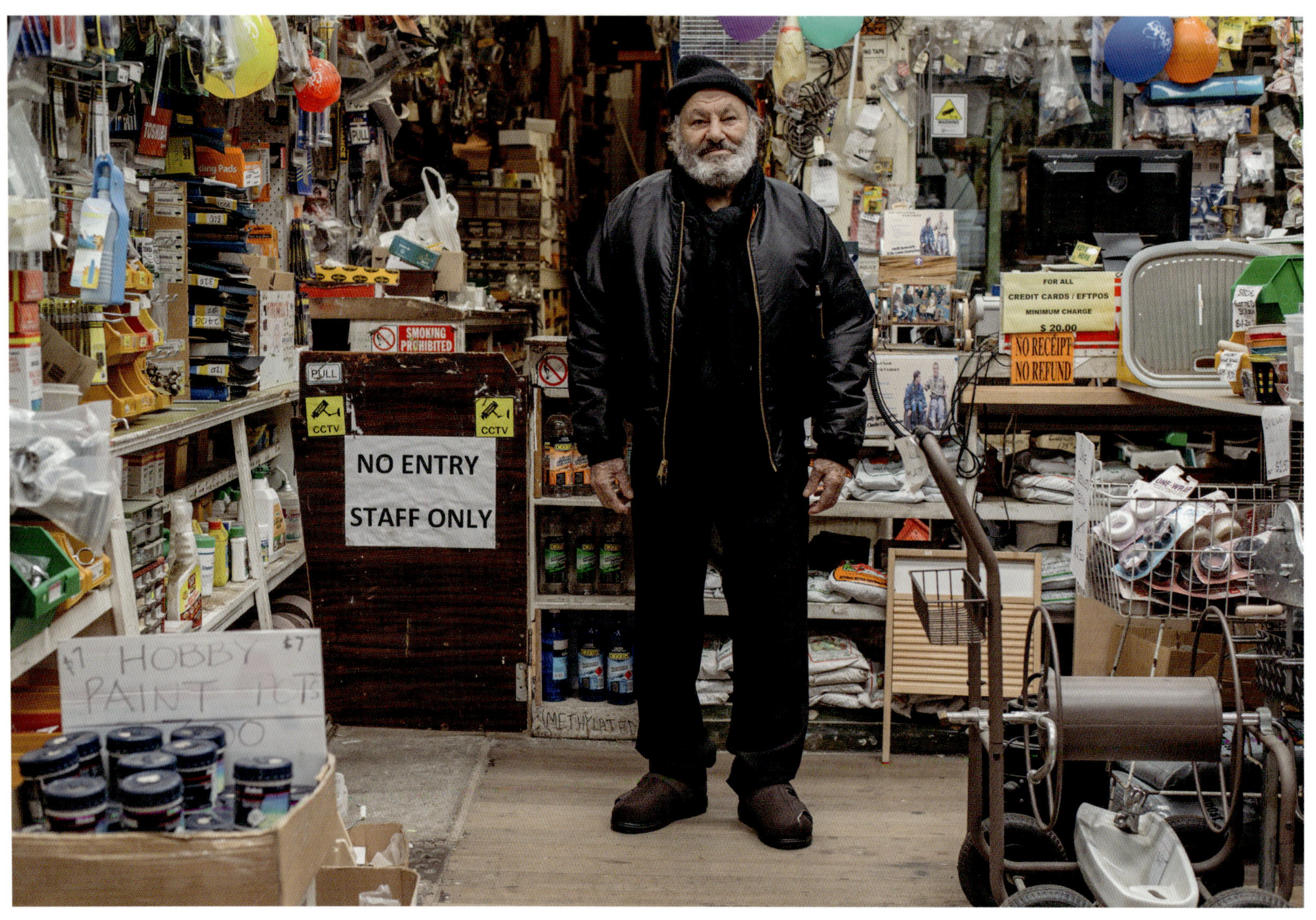

NO ENTRY
STAFF ONLY
SMOKING PROHIBITED
PULL
CCTV
CCTV
FOR ALL
CREDIT CARDS / EFTPOS
MINIMUM CHARGE
$ 20.00
NO RECEIPT
NO REFUND
HOBBY
PAINT POTS

$5
$4
#10
EACH
$10
$20
$20
$3
SMALL
CANDLE
AUGUST
2019
celebrate sp
fresh flowers
ENTINES
FEBRUA

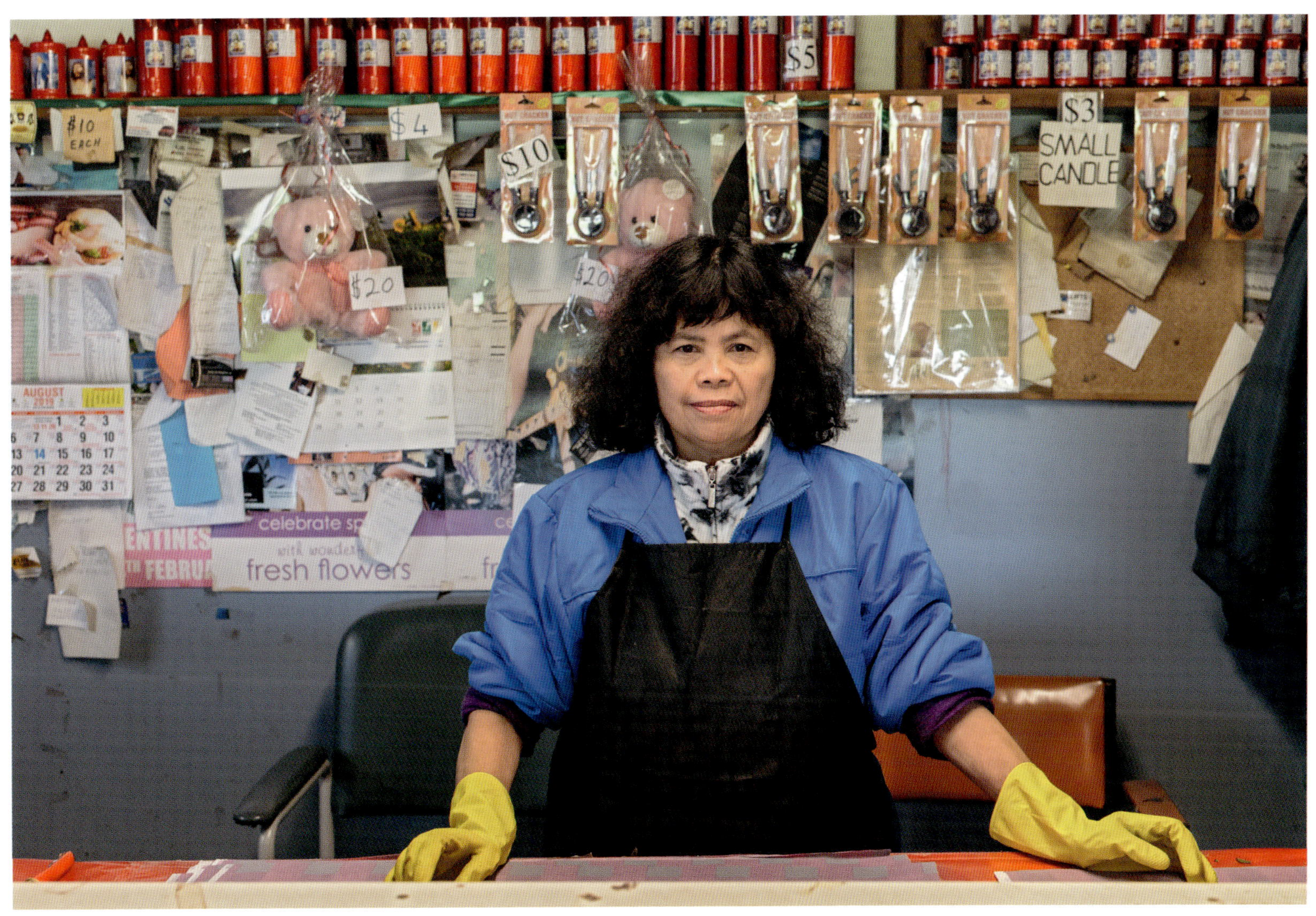

Reservoir

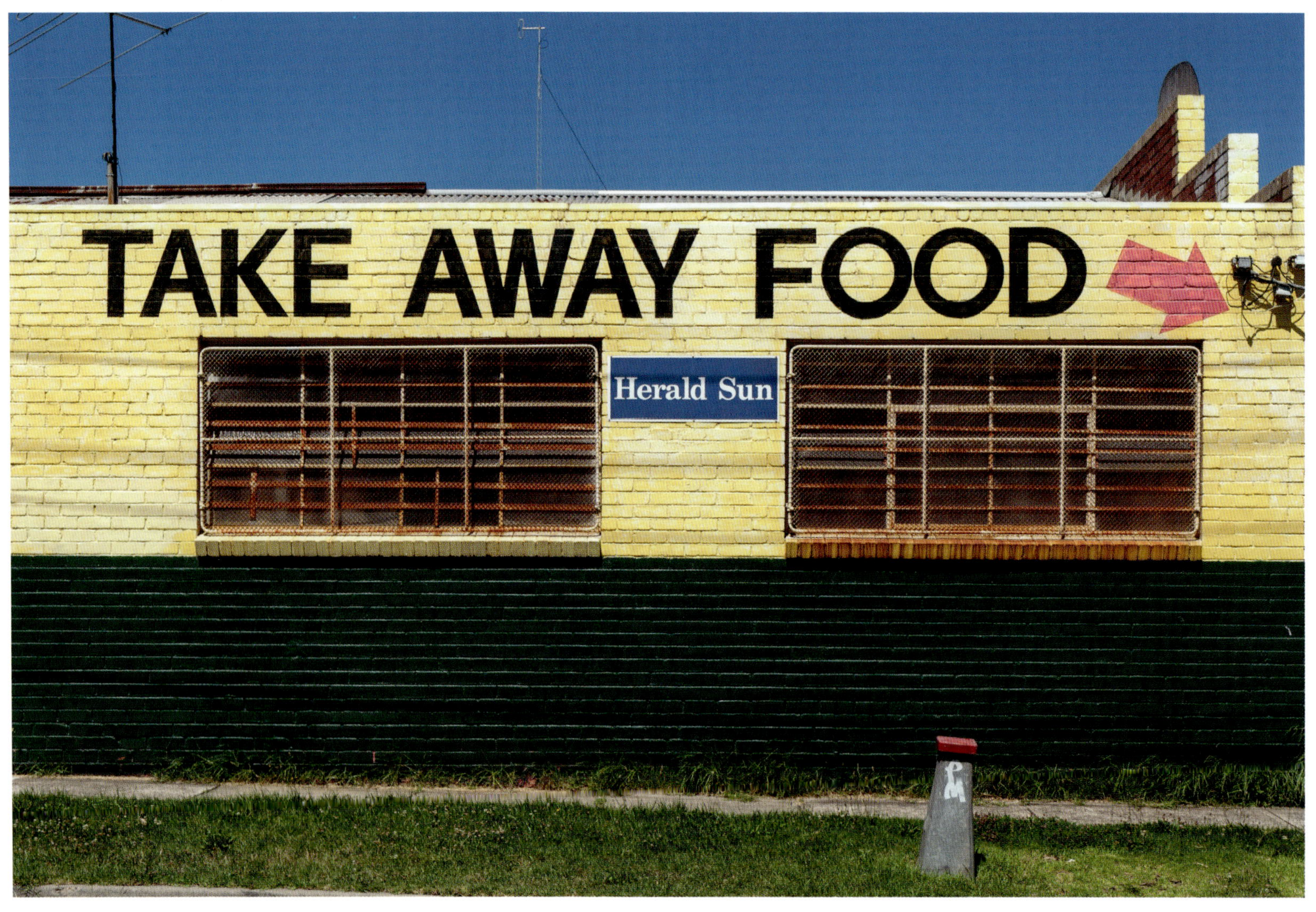

Heidelberg West

VICTORIA
IMPORT EXPORT Pty Ltd
Tel 3870230
TOOL'S
BMX BIKES,
KITCHEN
WARE
VICTORIA IMPORT
296
300

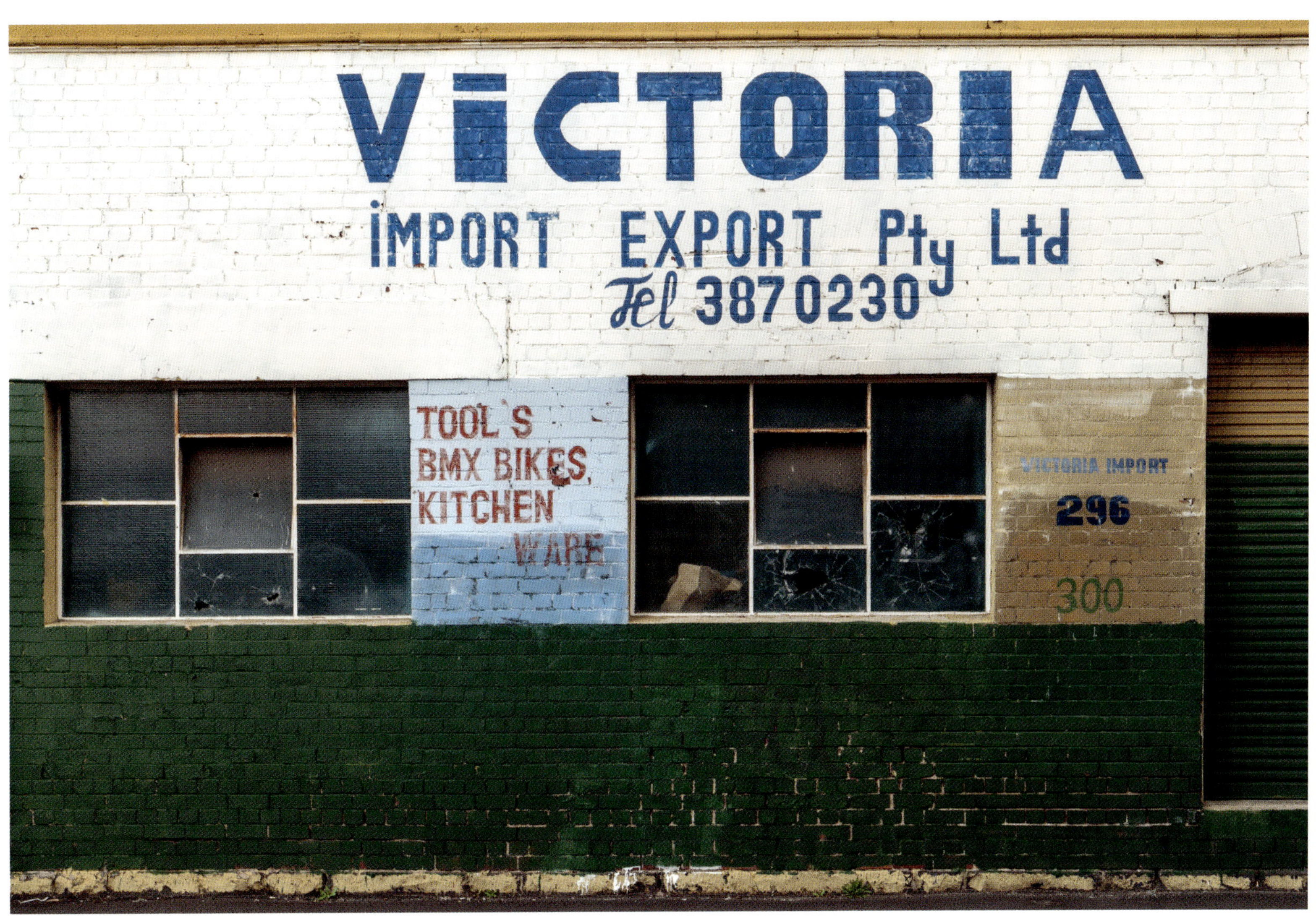

Brunswick

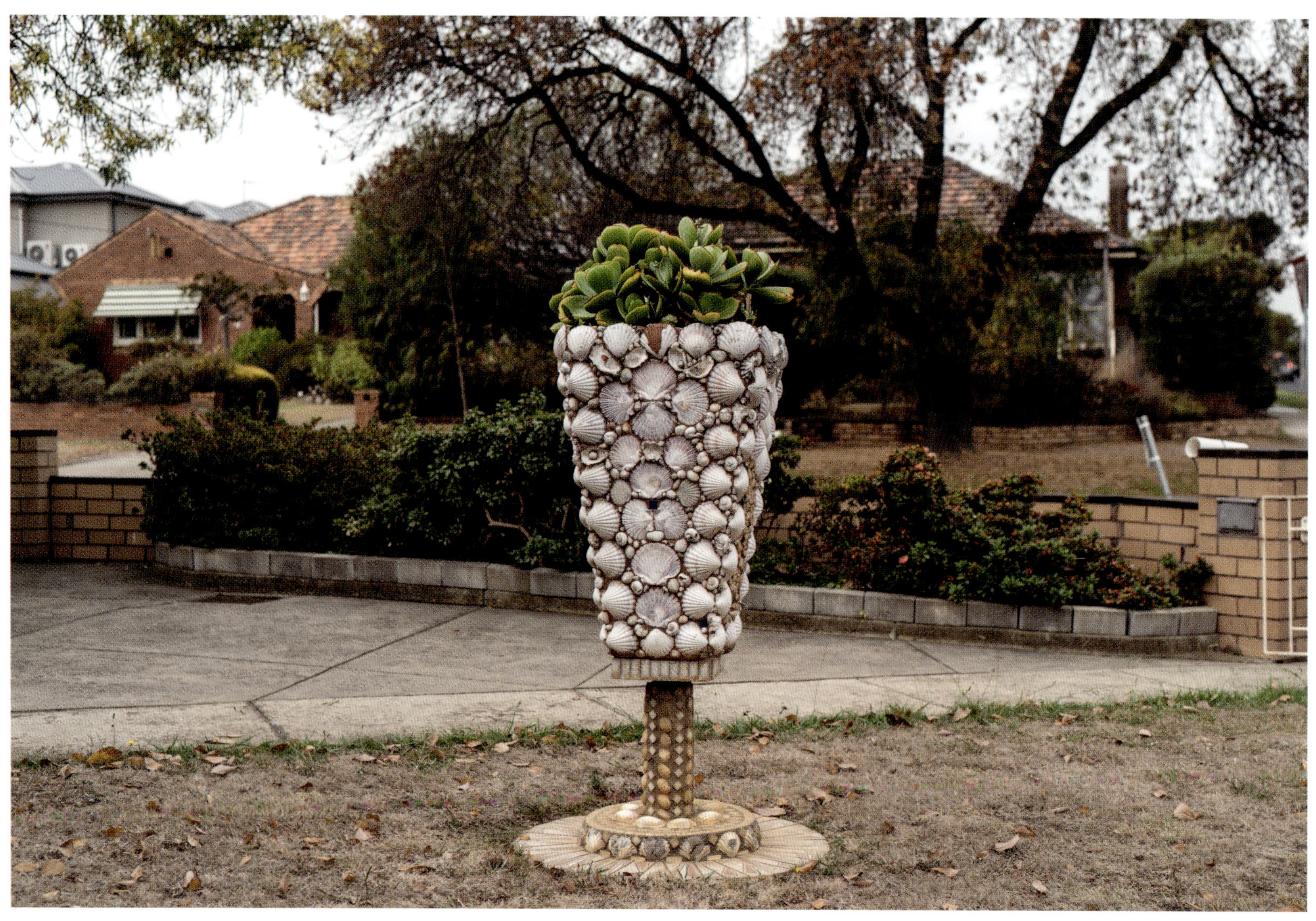

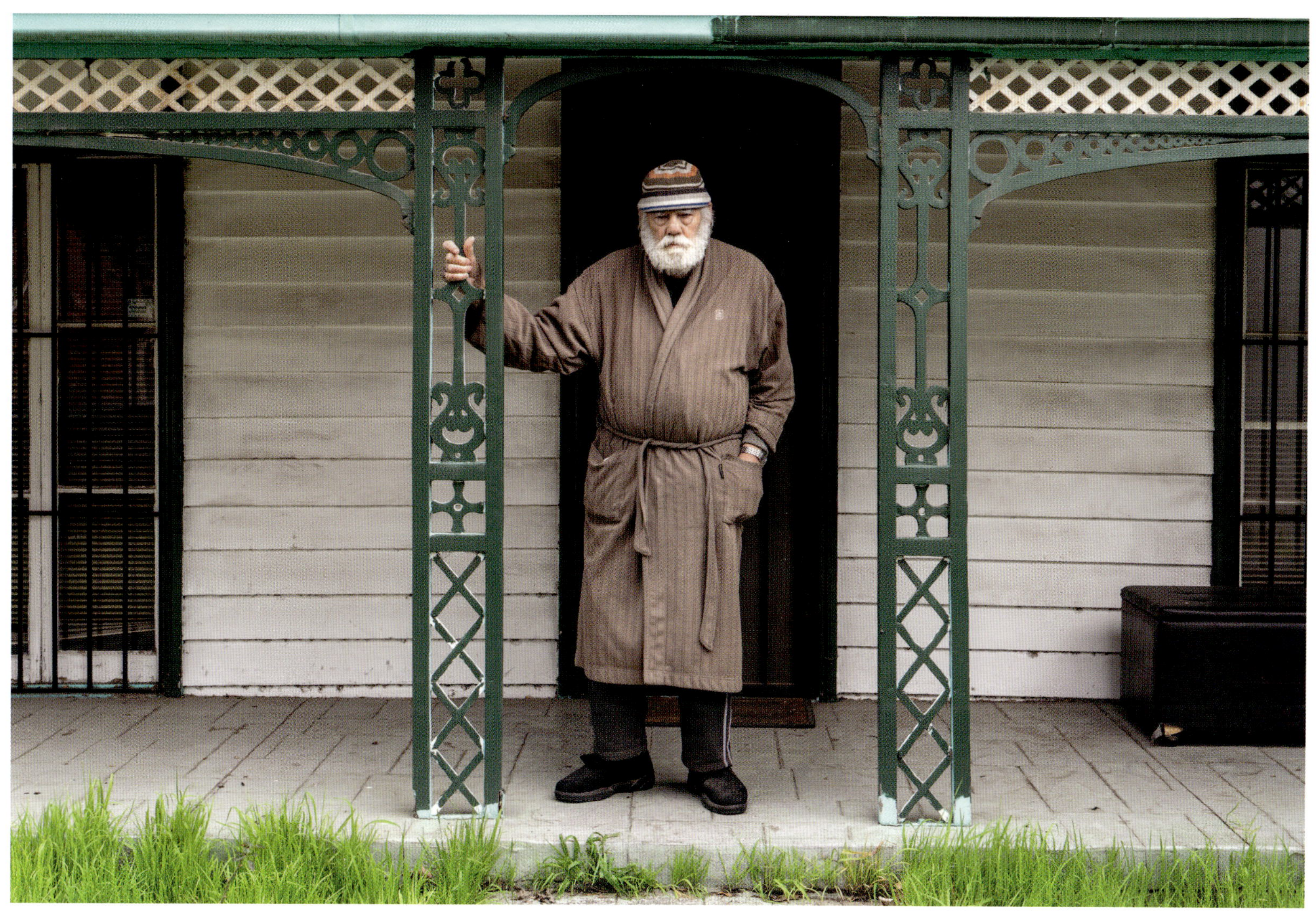

45

Carlton

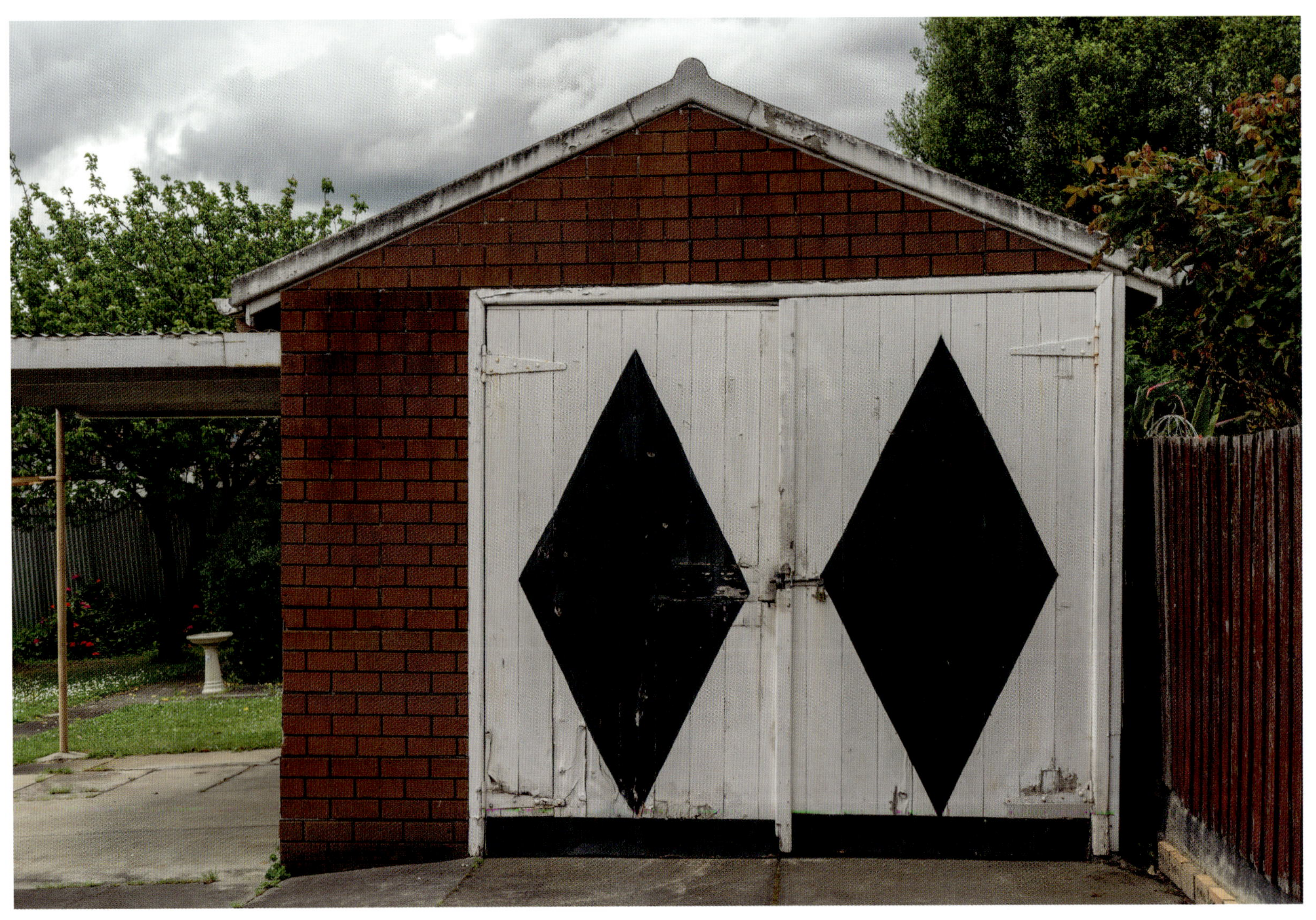

Reservoir

46

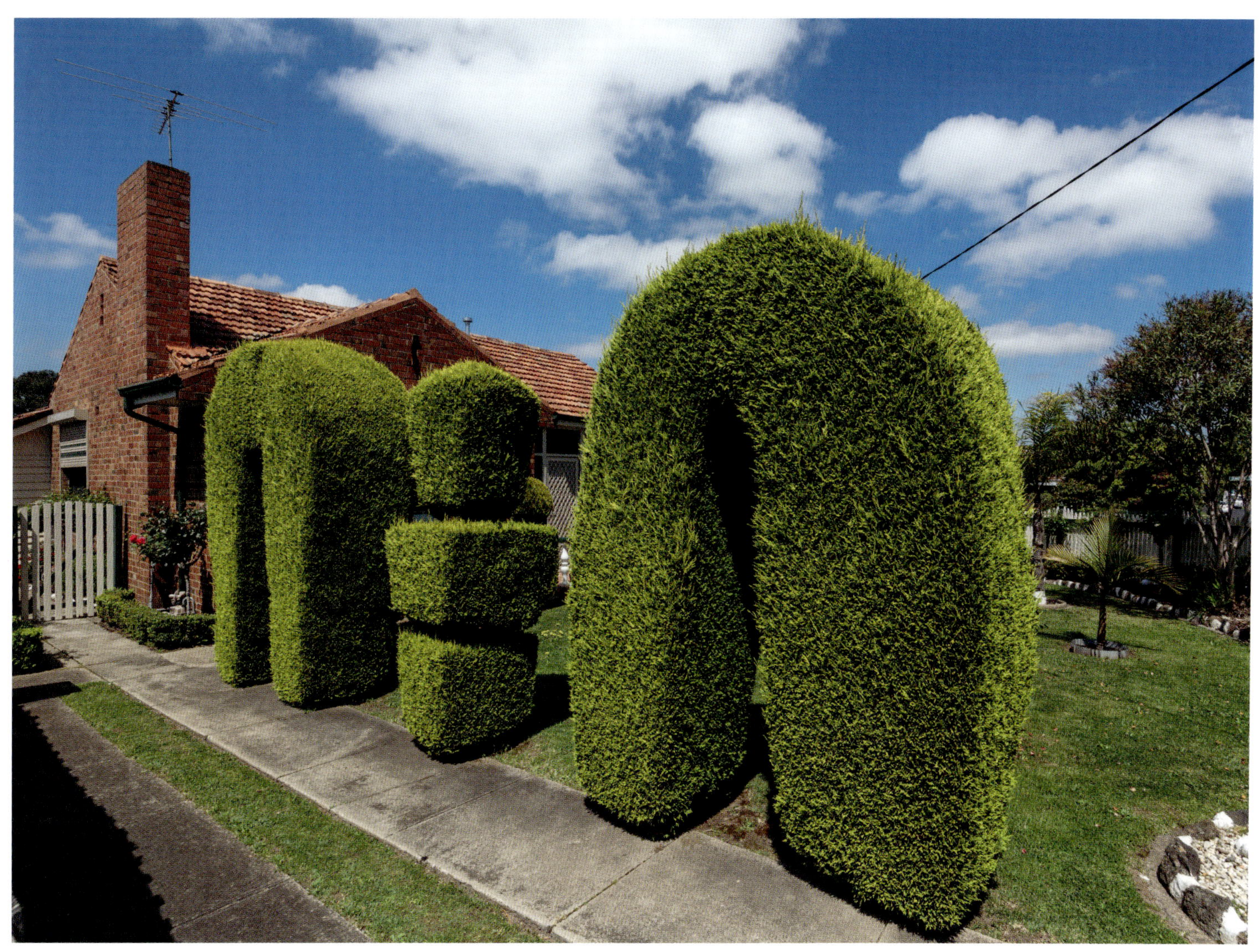

Coburg North

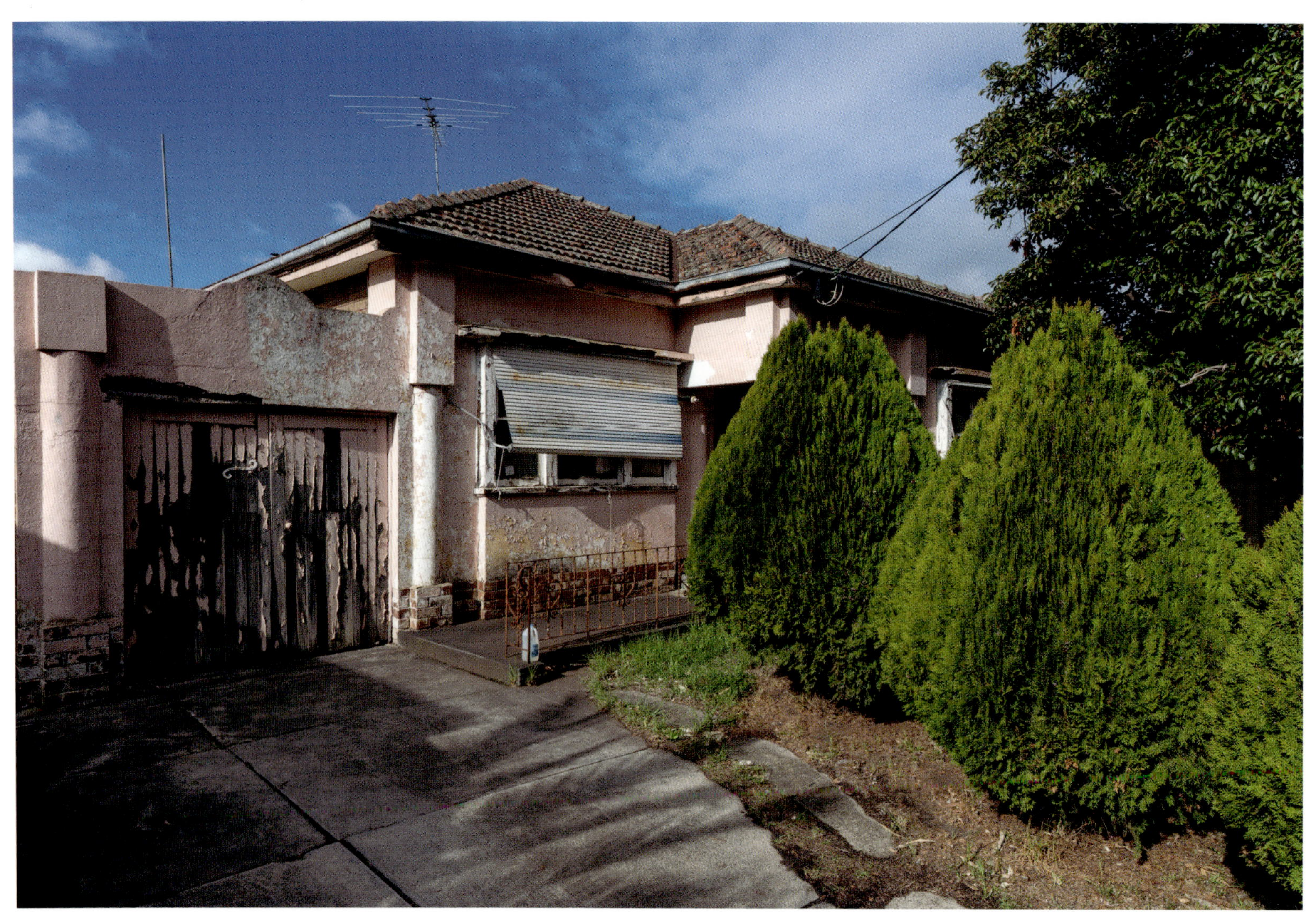

Reservoir

48

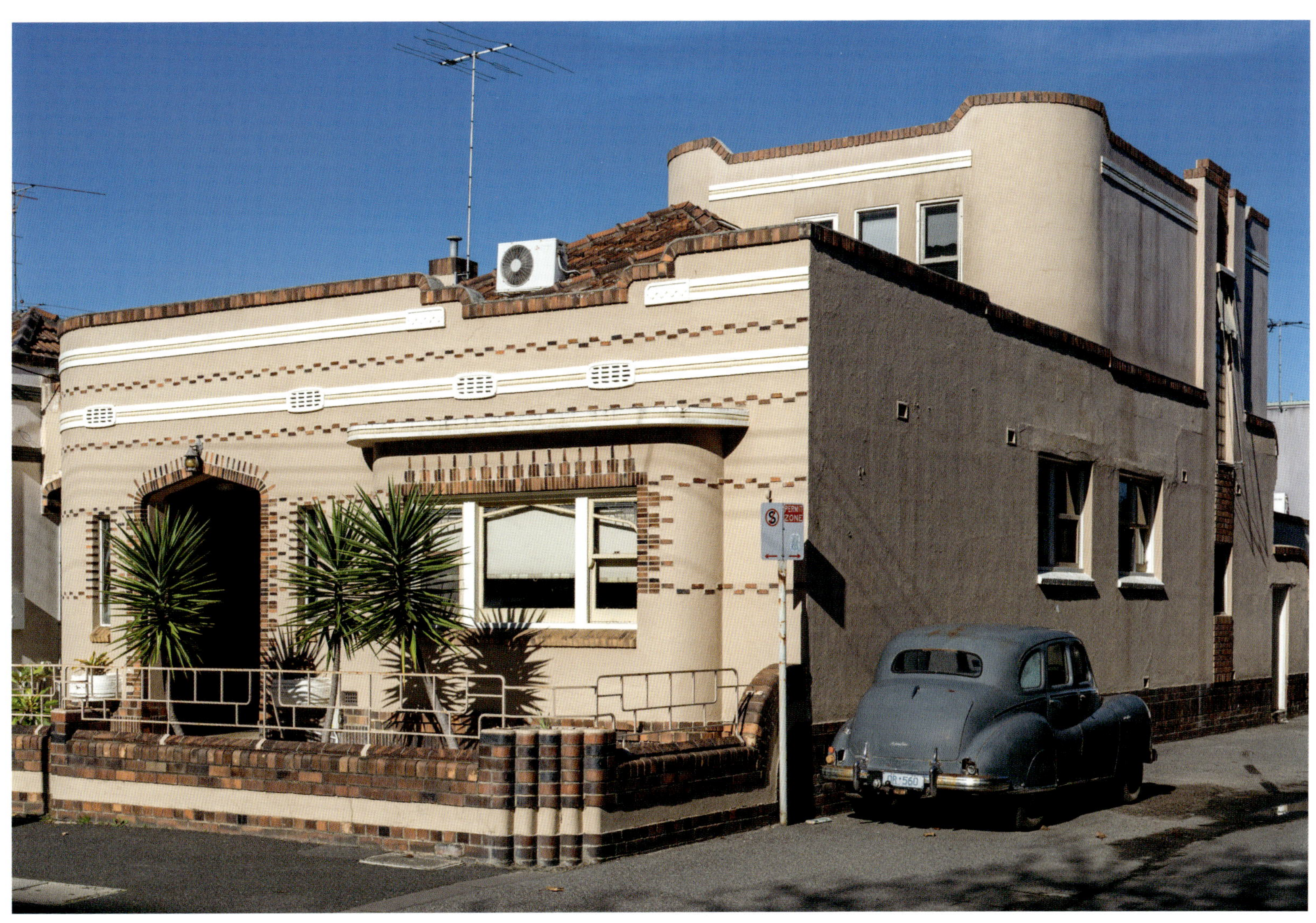

Princes Hill

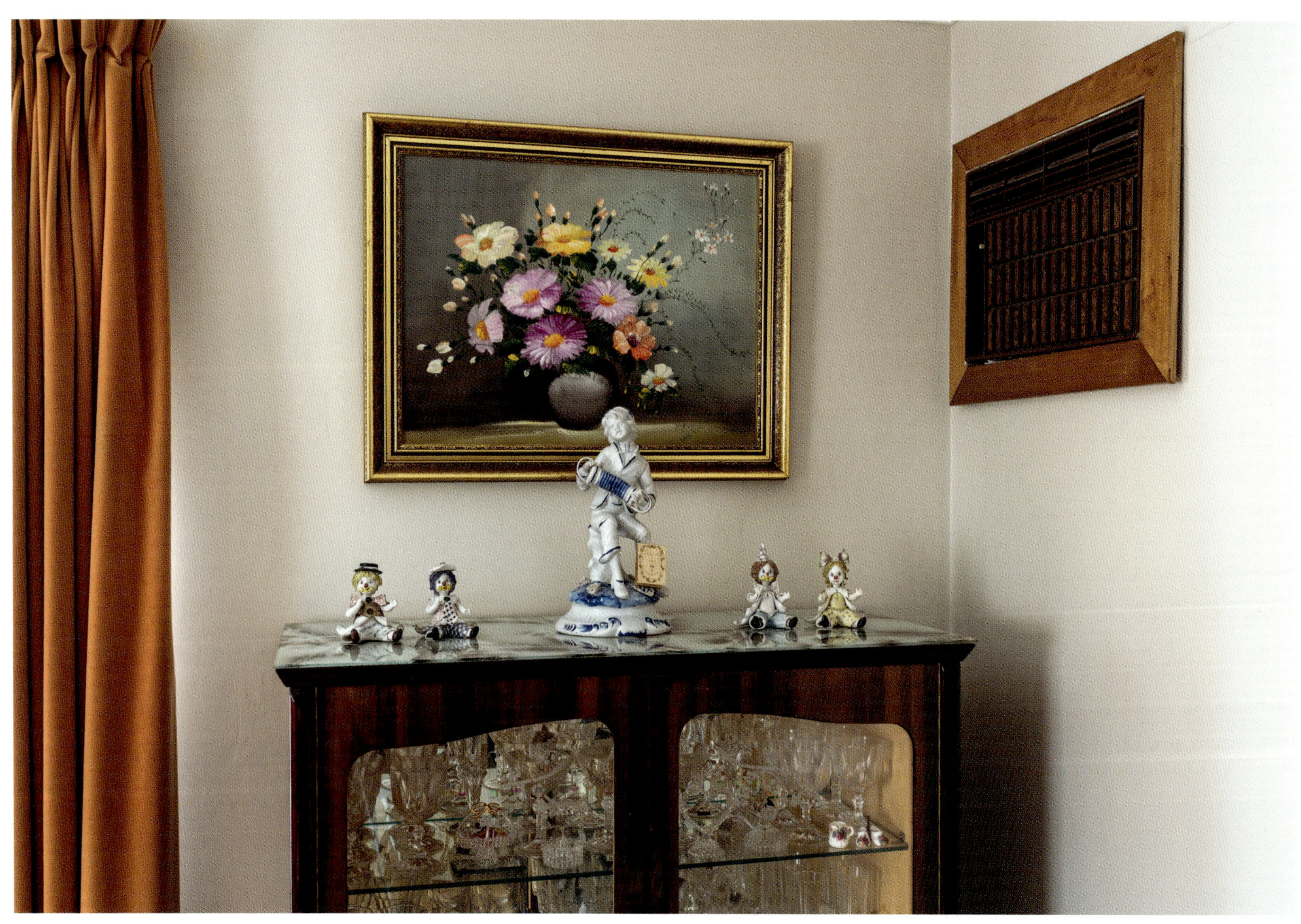

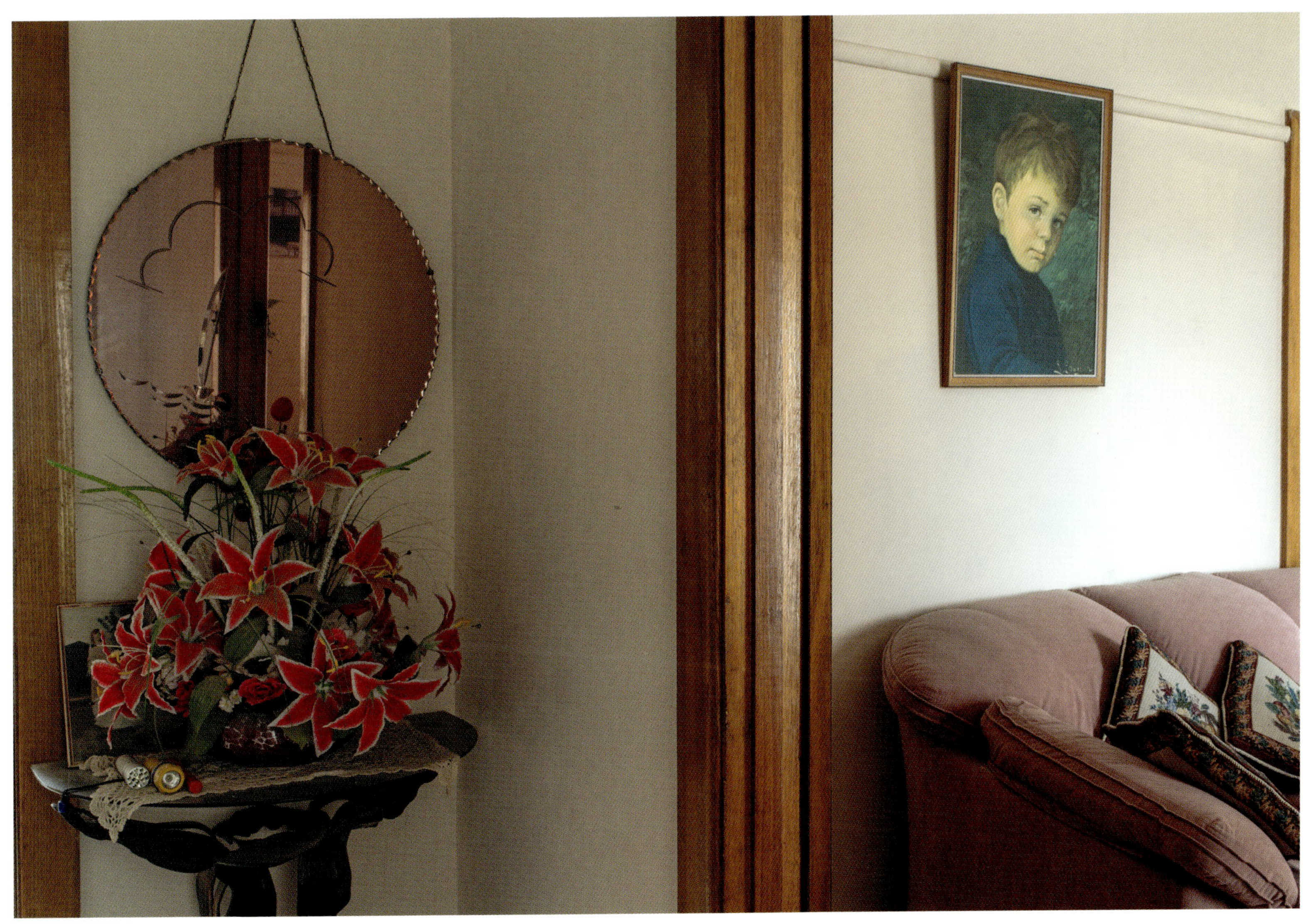

Reservoir

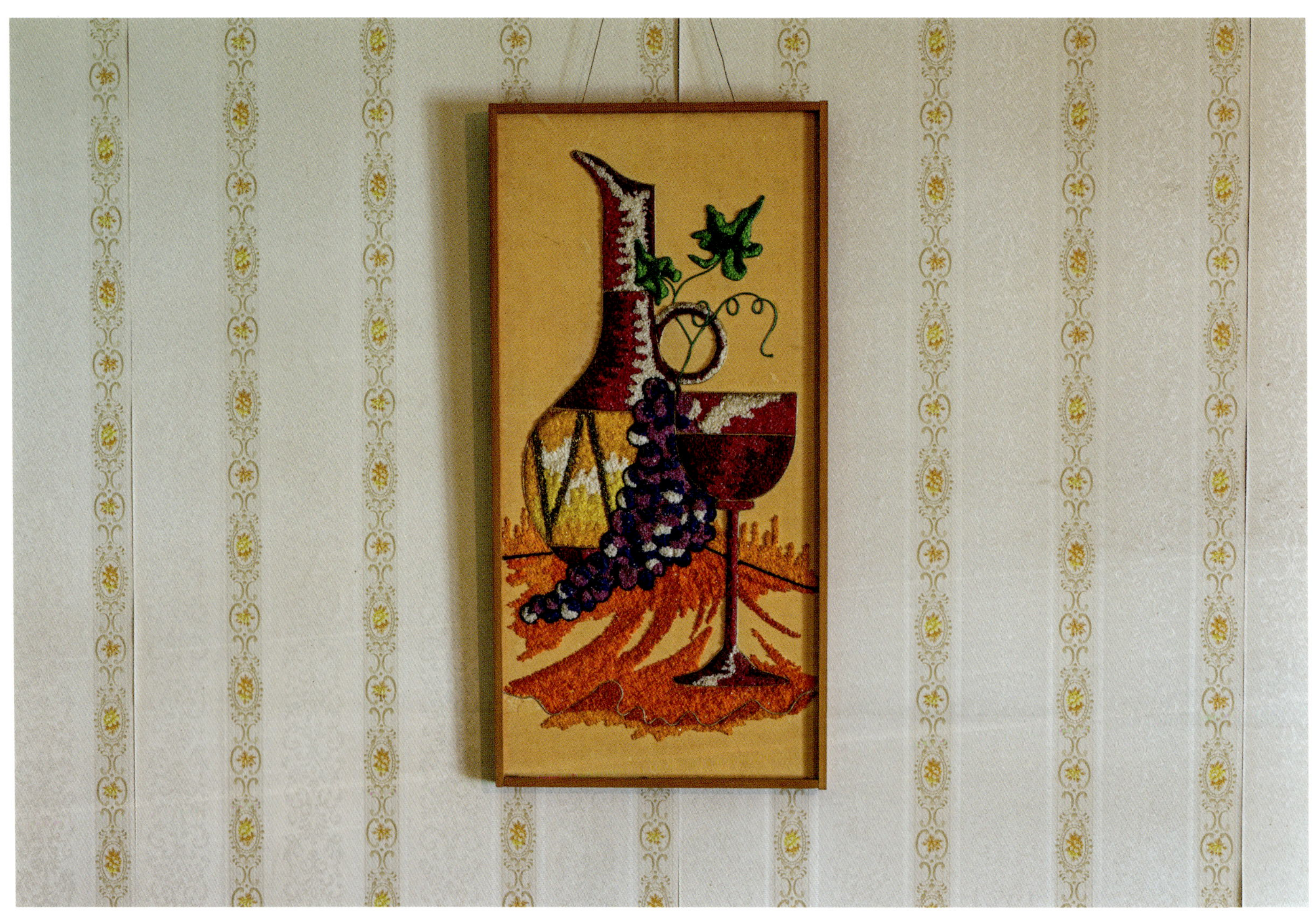

Carlton

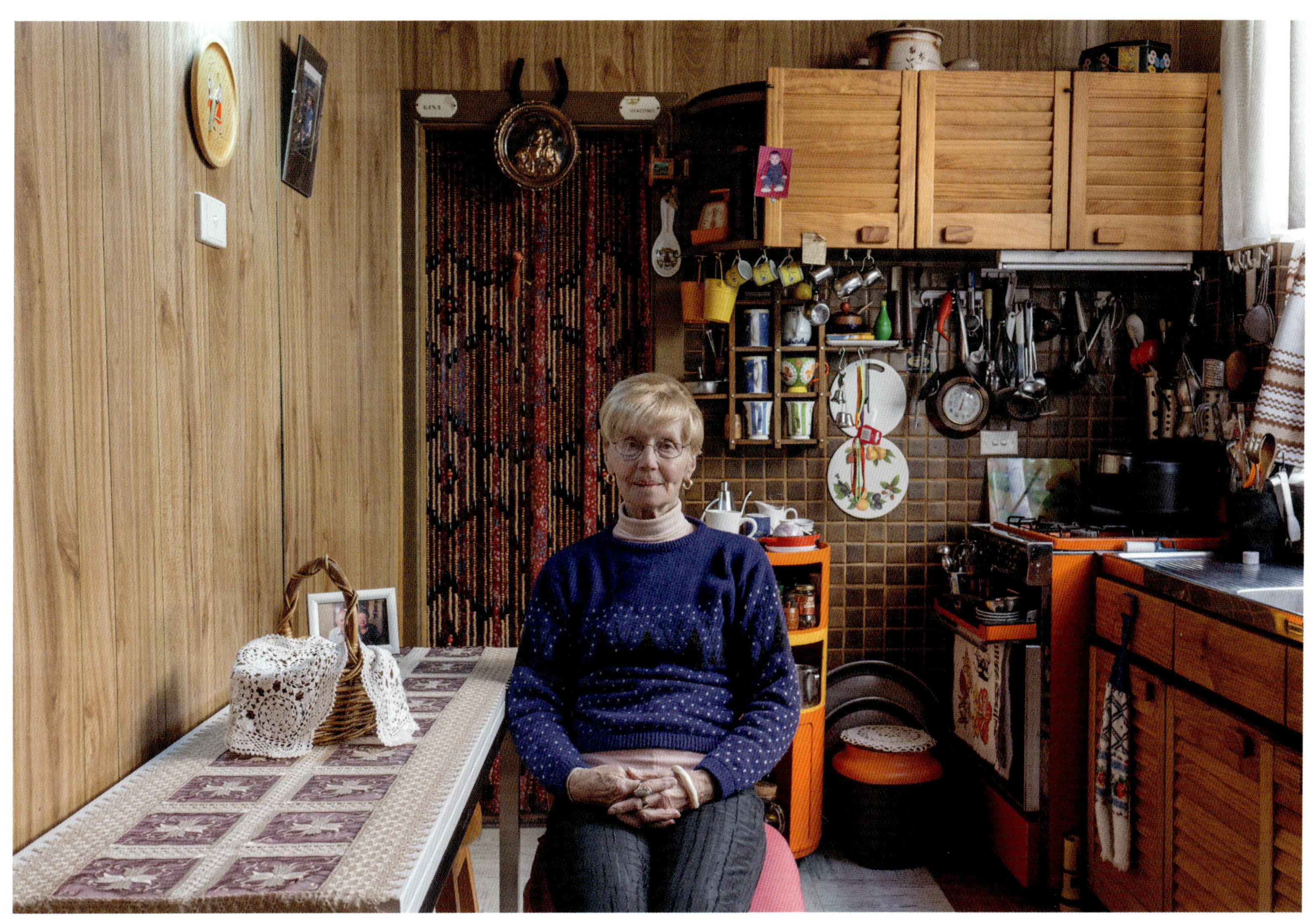

Carlton North

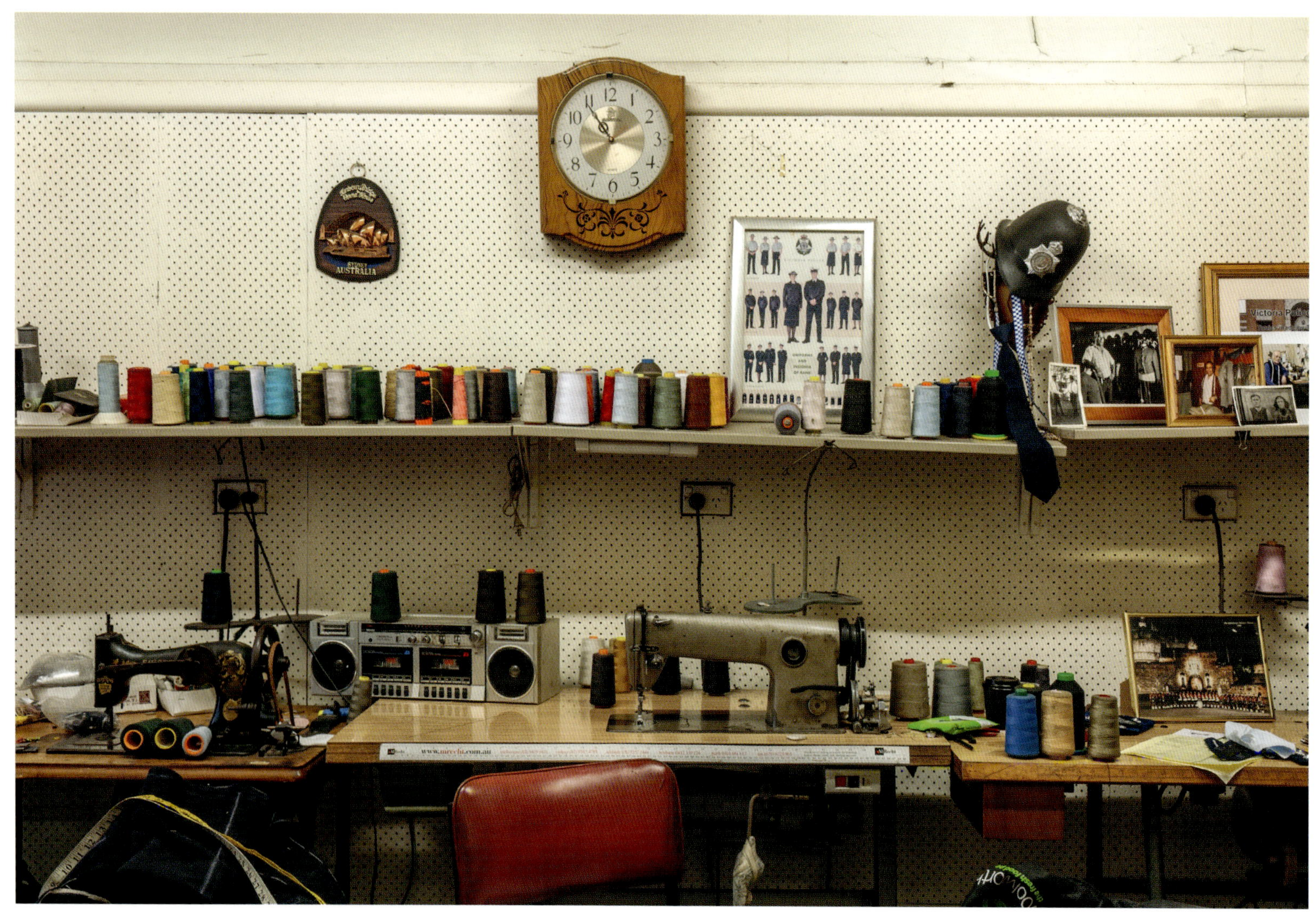

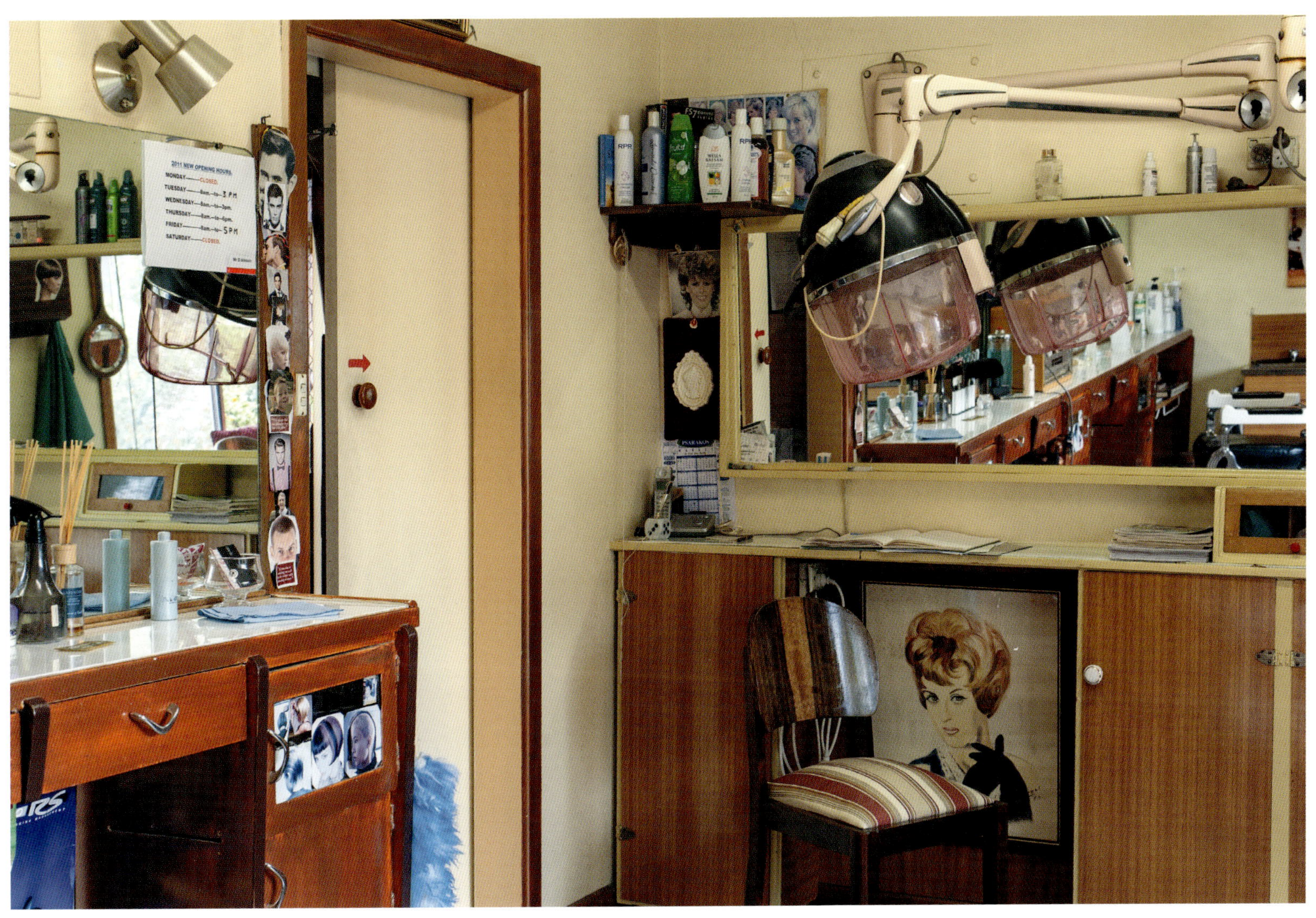

2011 NEW OPENING HOURS.
MONDAY———CLOSED.
TUESDAY———9am—to—3 PM
WEDNESDAY———9am—to—3pm.
THURSDAY———9am—to—4pm.
FRIDAY———9am—to—5PM
SATURDAY———CLOSED.

Thornbury

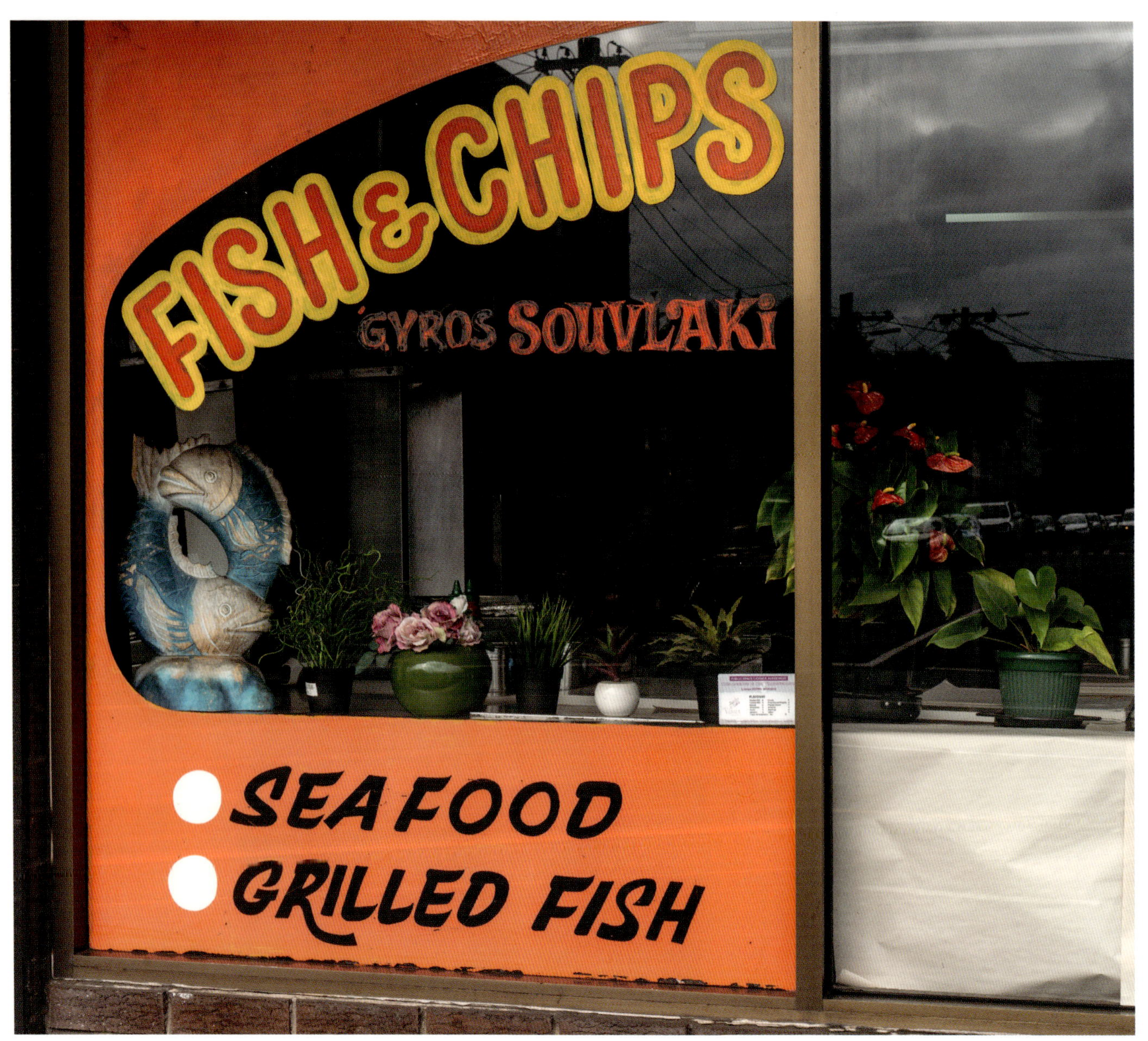

Abbotsford

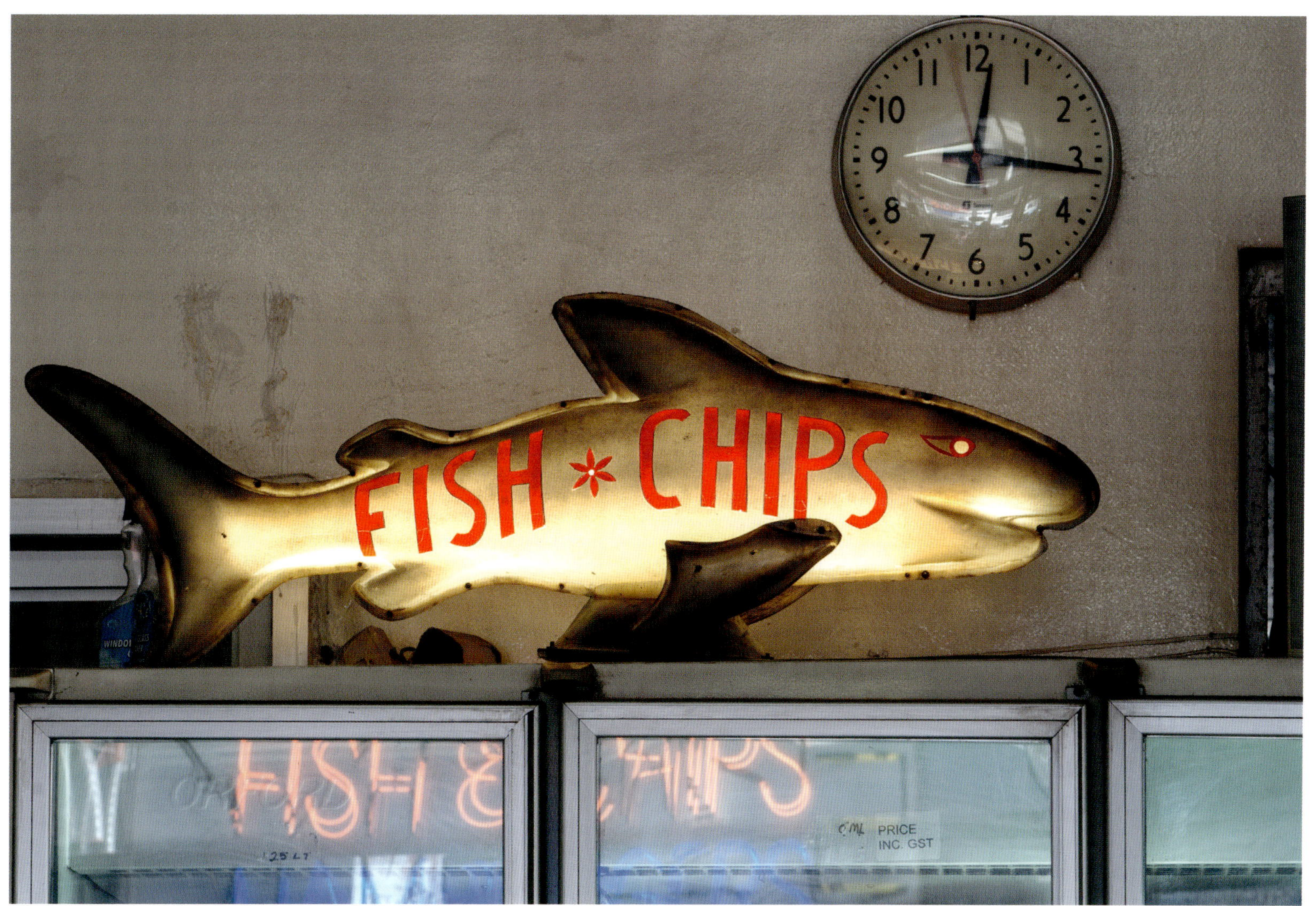

Northcote

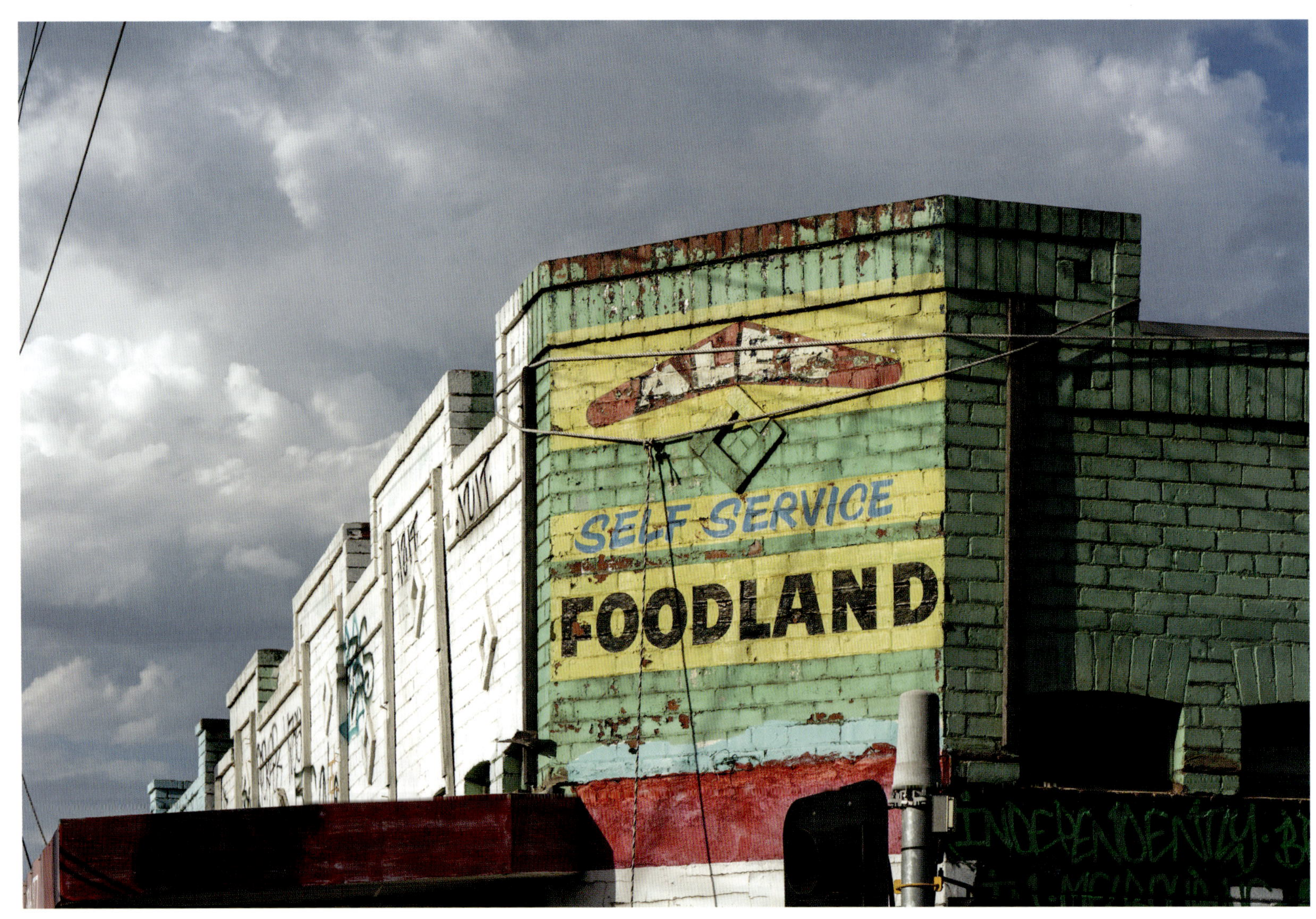

Brunswick West

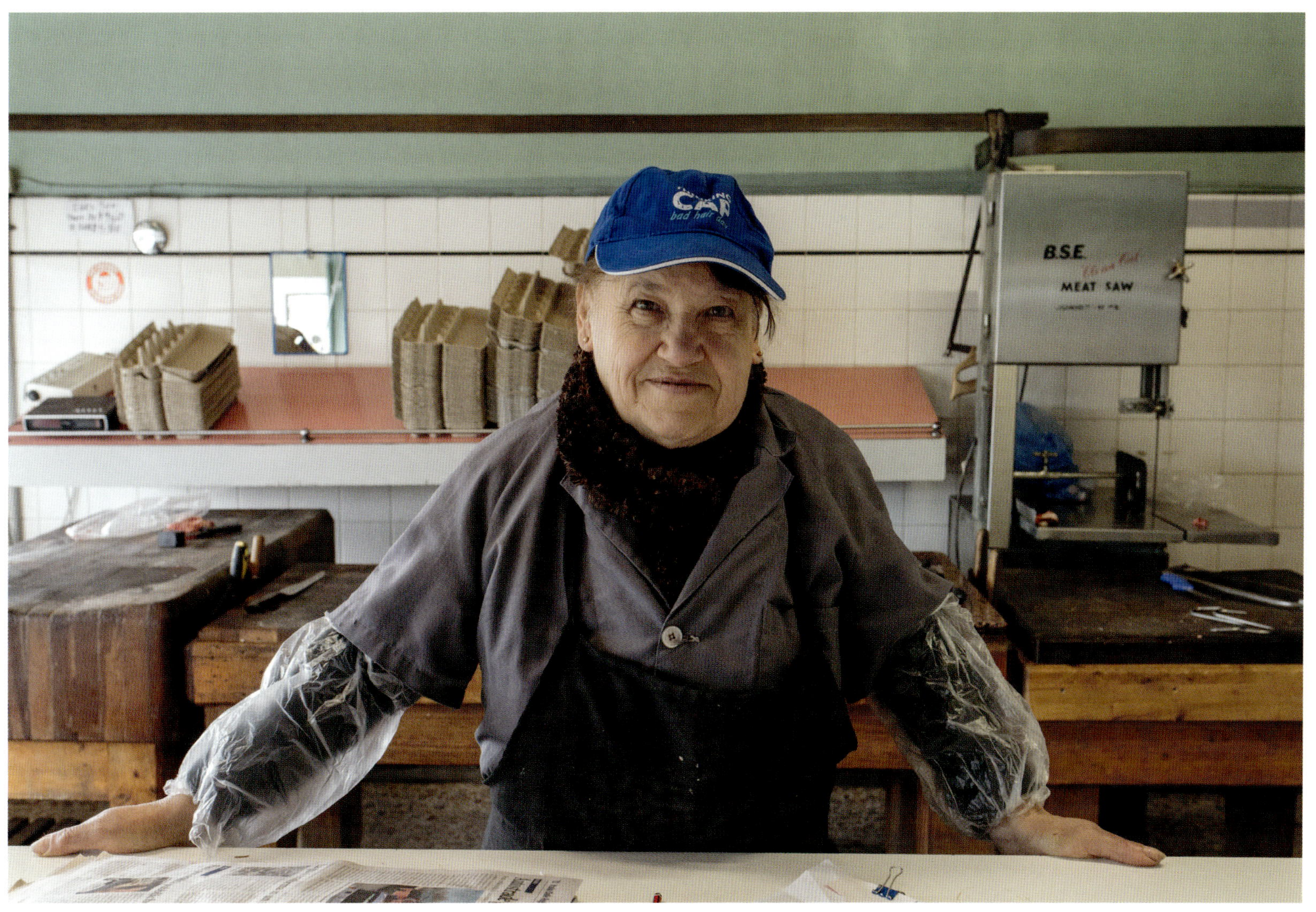

Northcote

MILK BAR
AUSTRALIAN Continental GROCERY
OPEN
Book Of Memories
VIVA
Quilton
Quilton
Sorbent
Enjoy
Coca-Cola
Coke
THE SUNDAY AGE
PICK CORNETTO
Streets

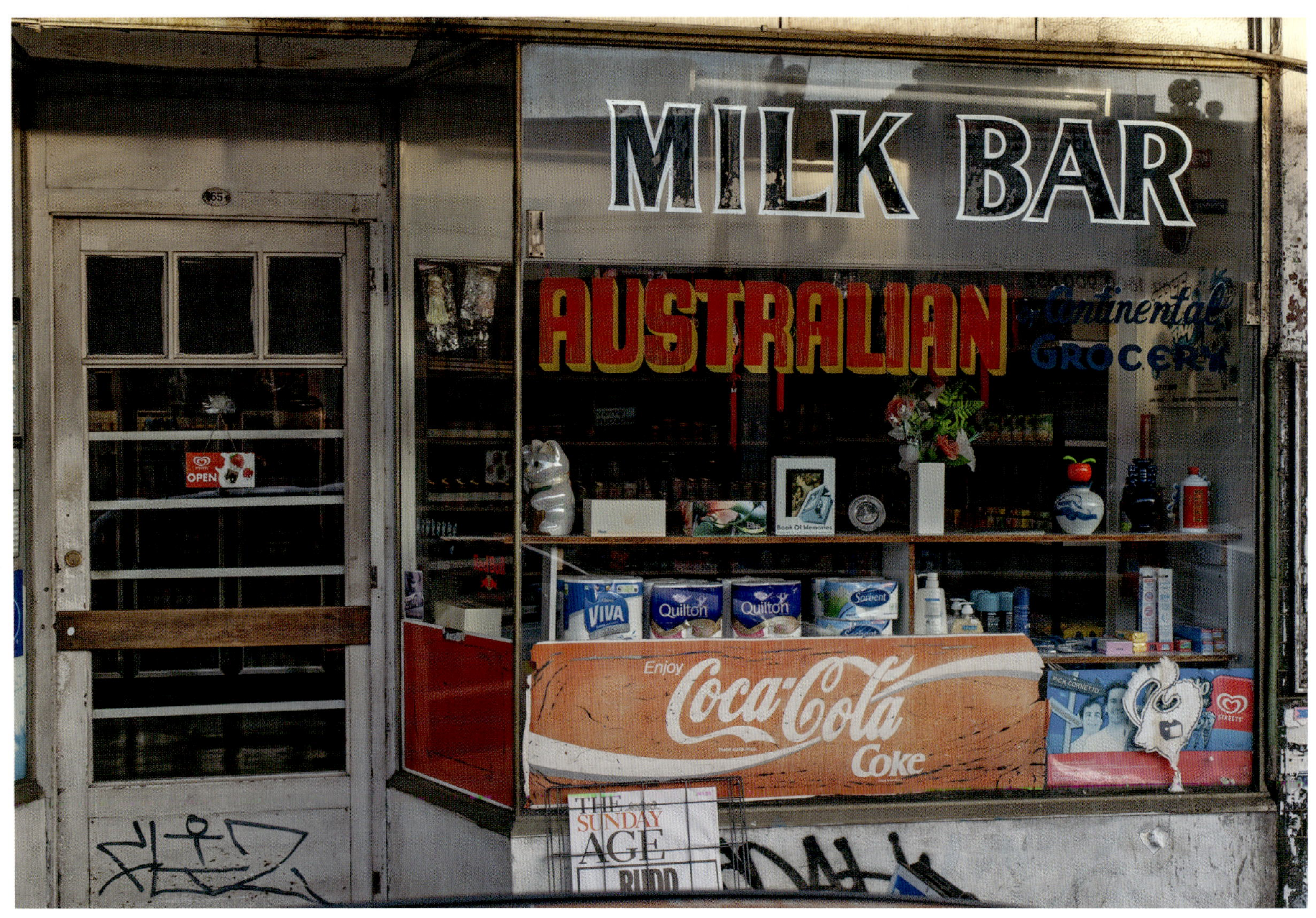

Northcote

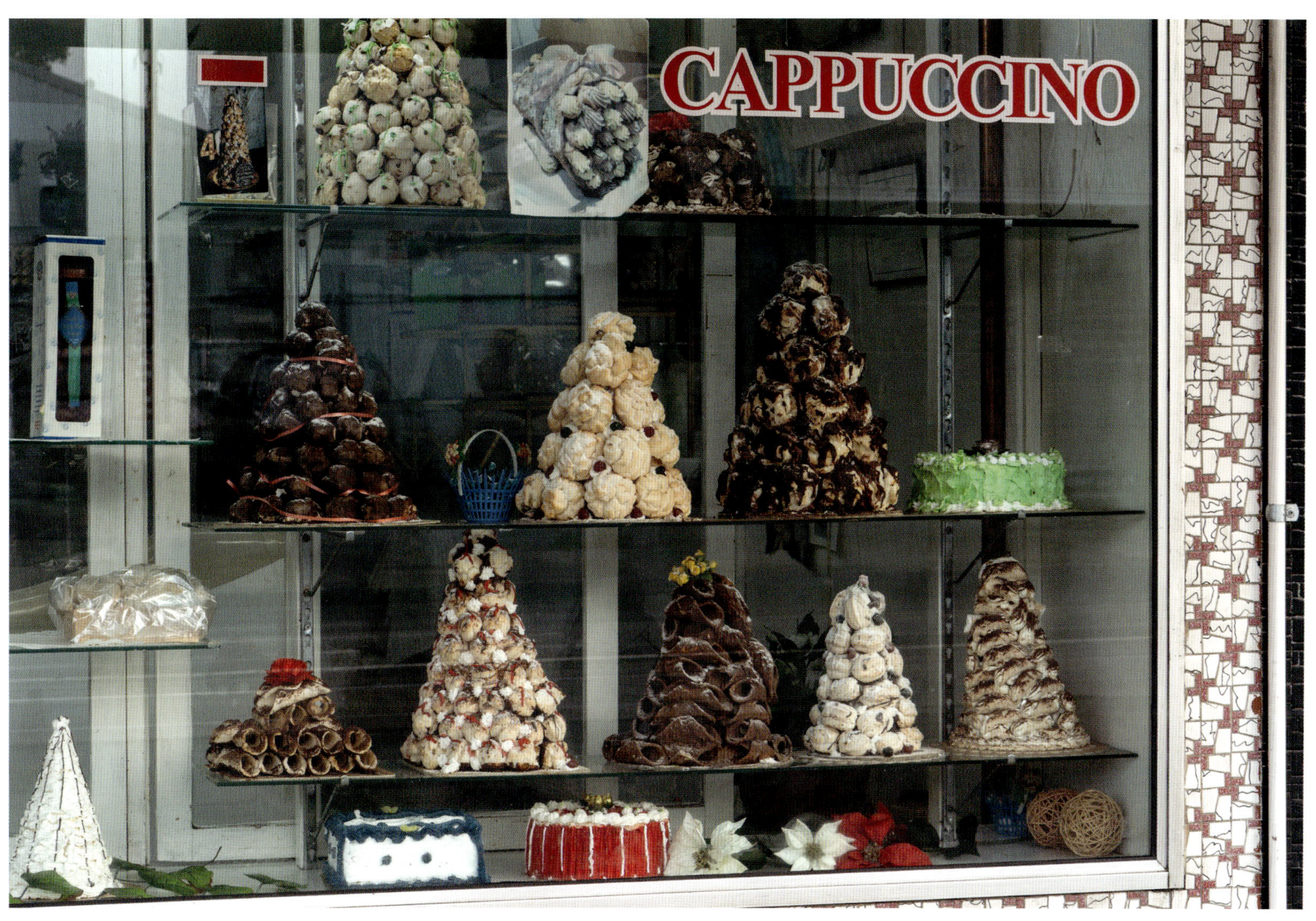

Thornbury

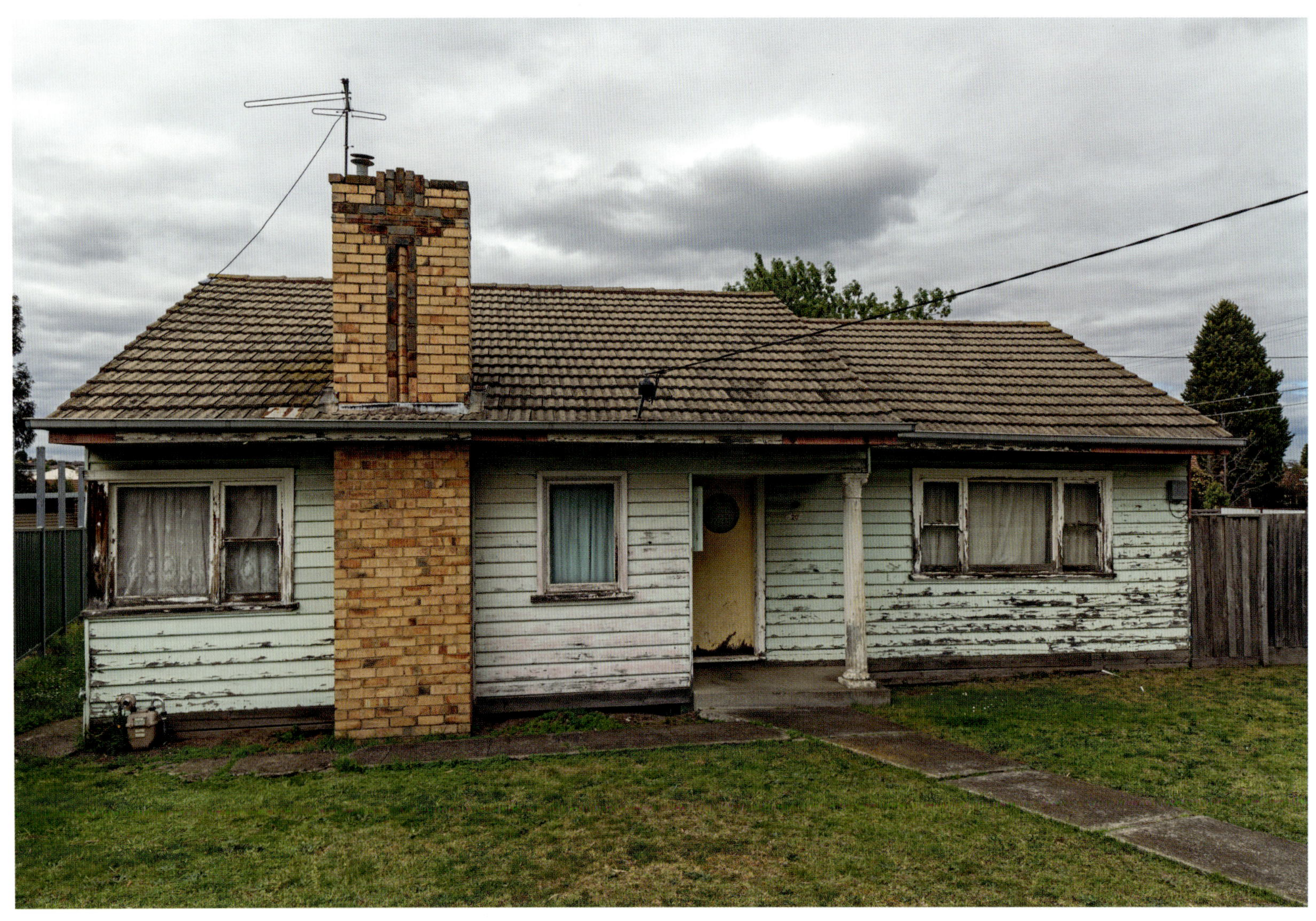

Reservoir

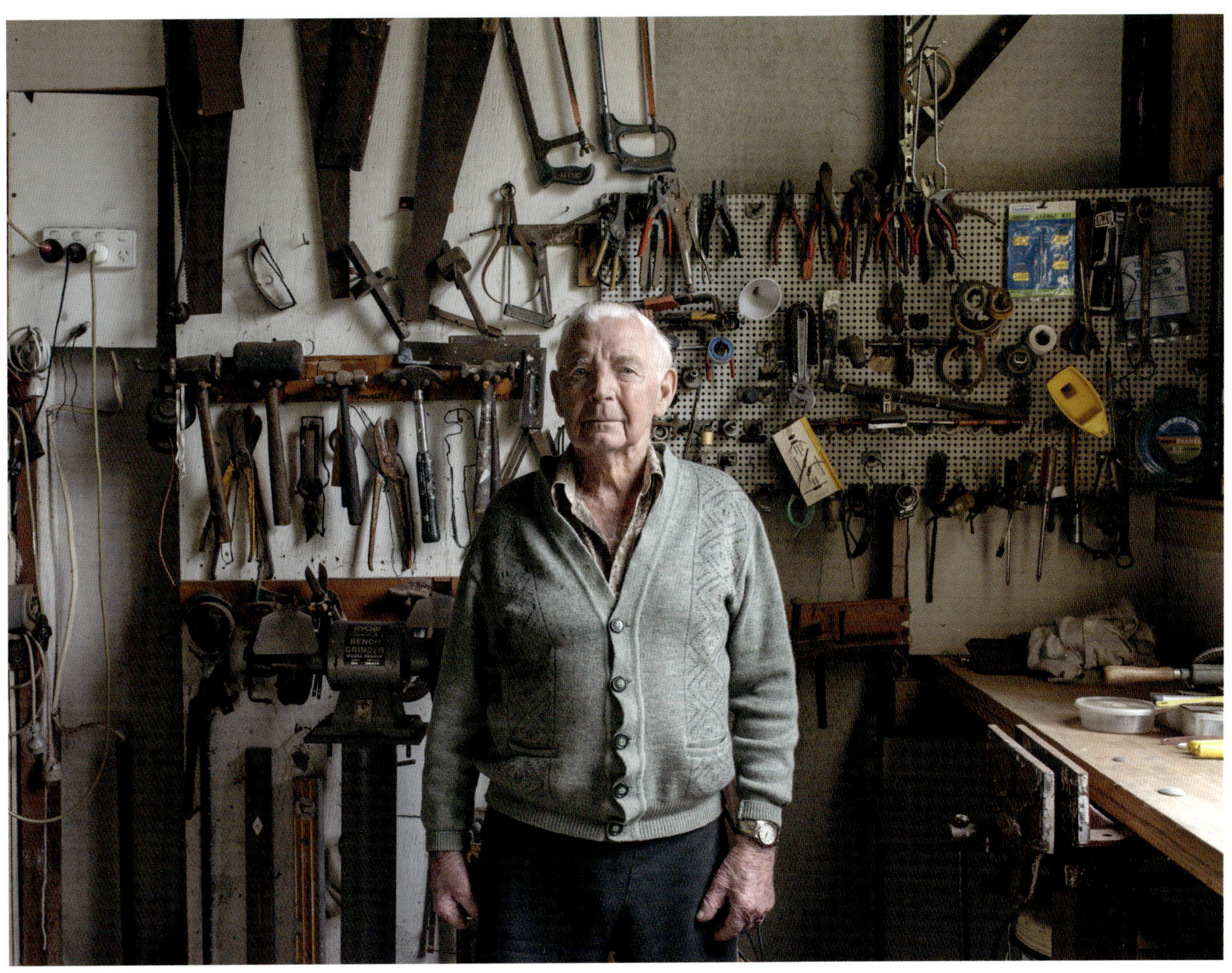

Reservoir

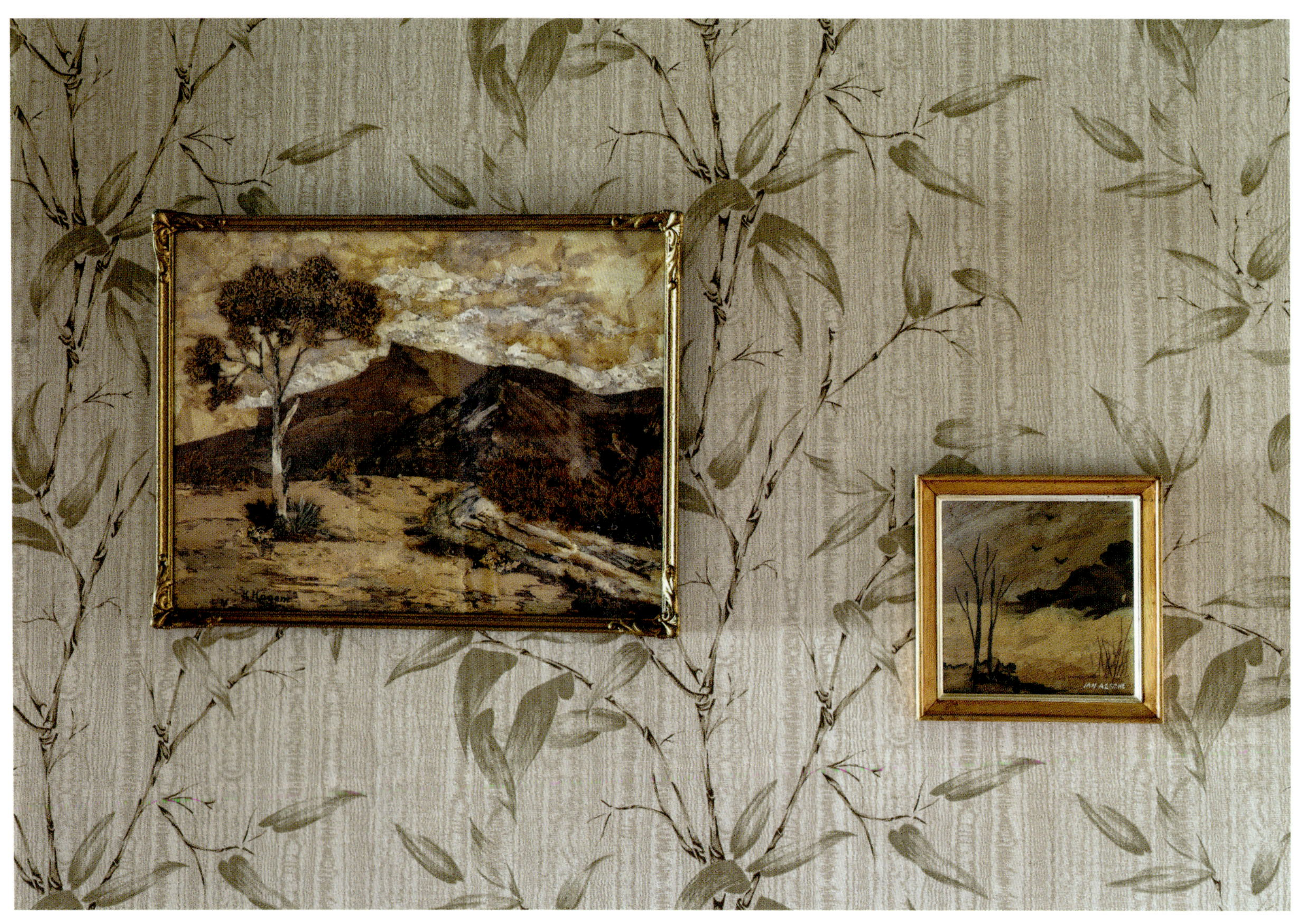

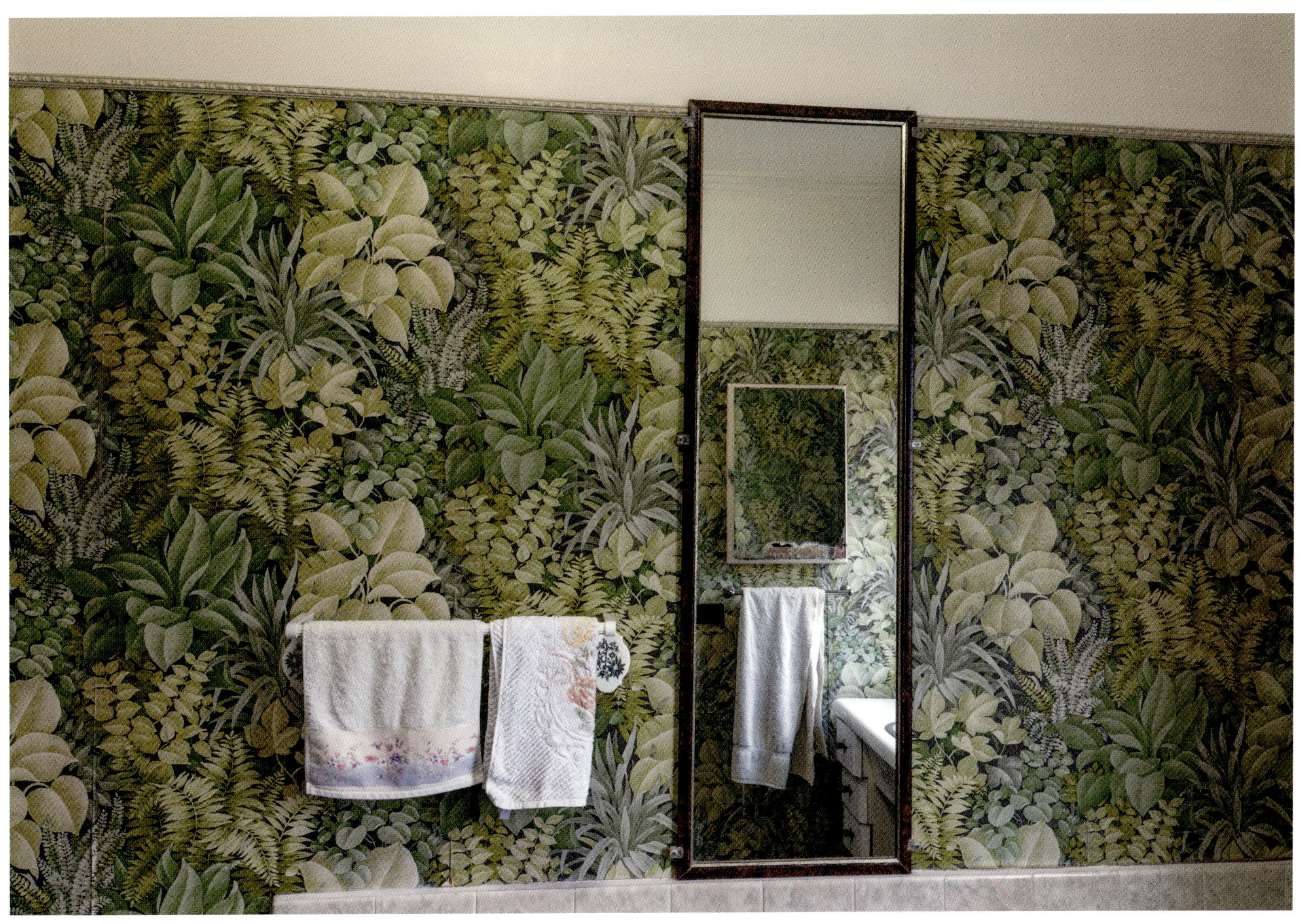

Oak Park

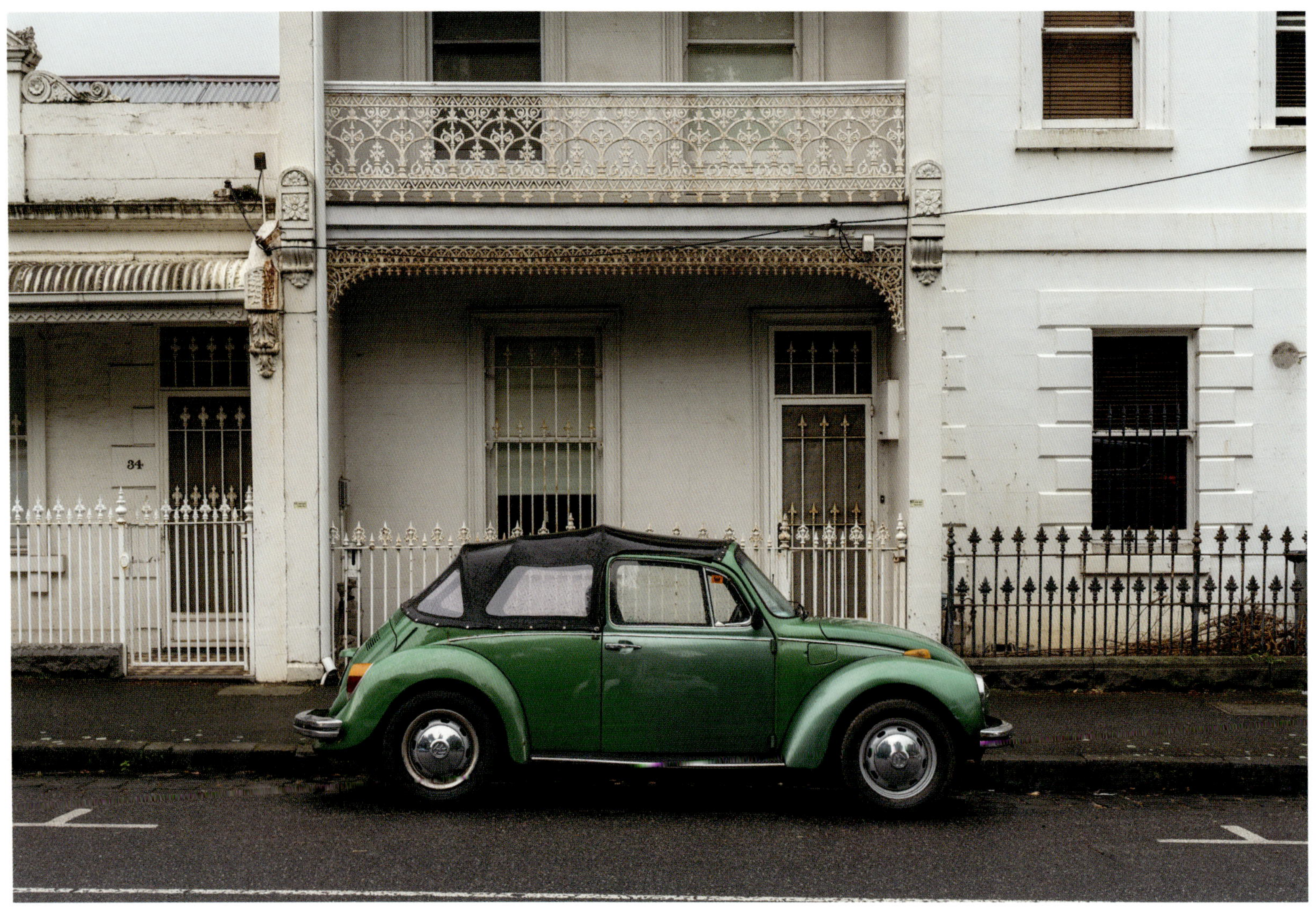

Carlton

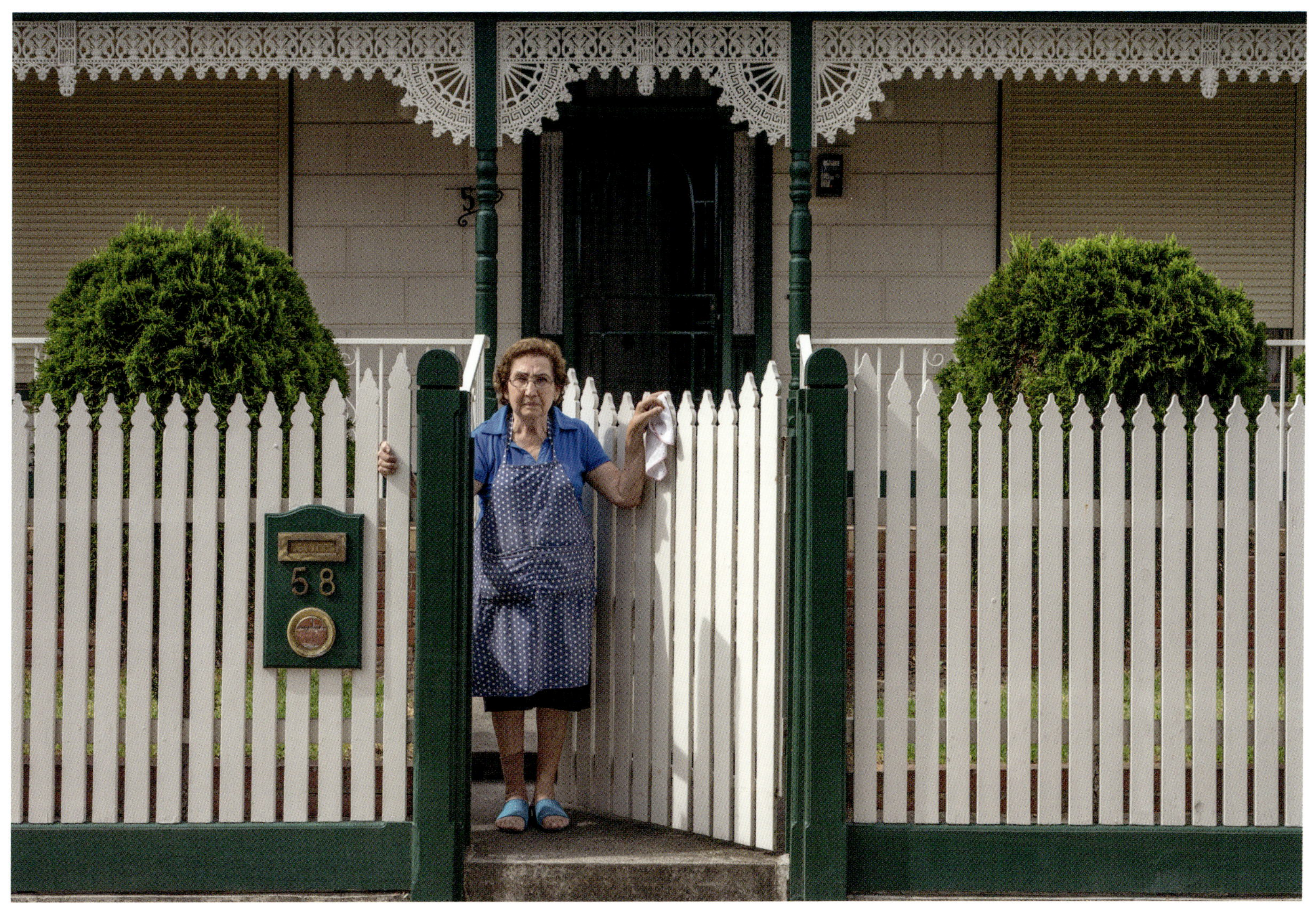

Brunswick

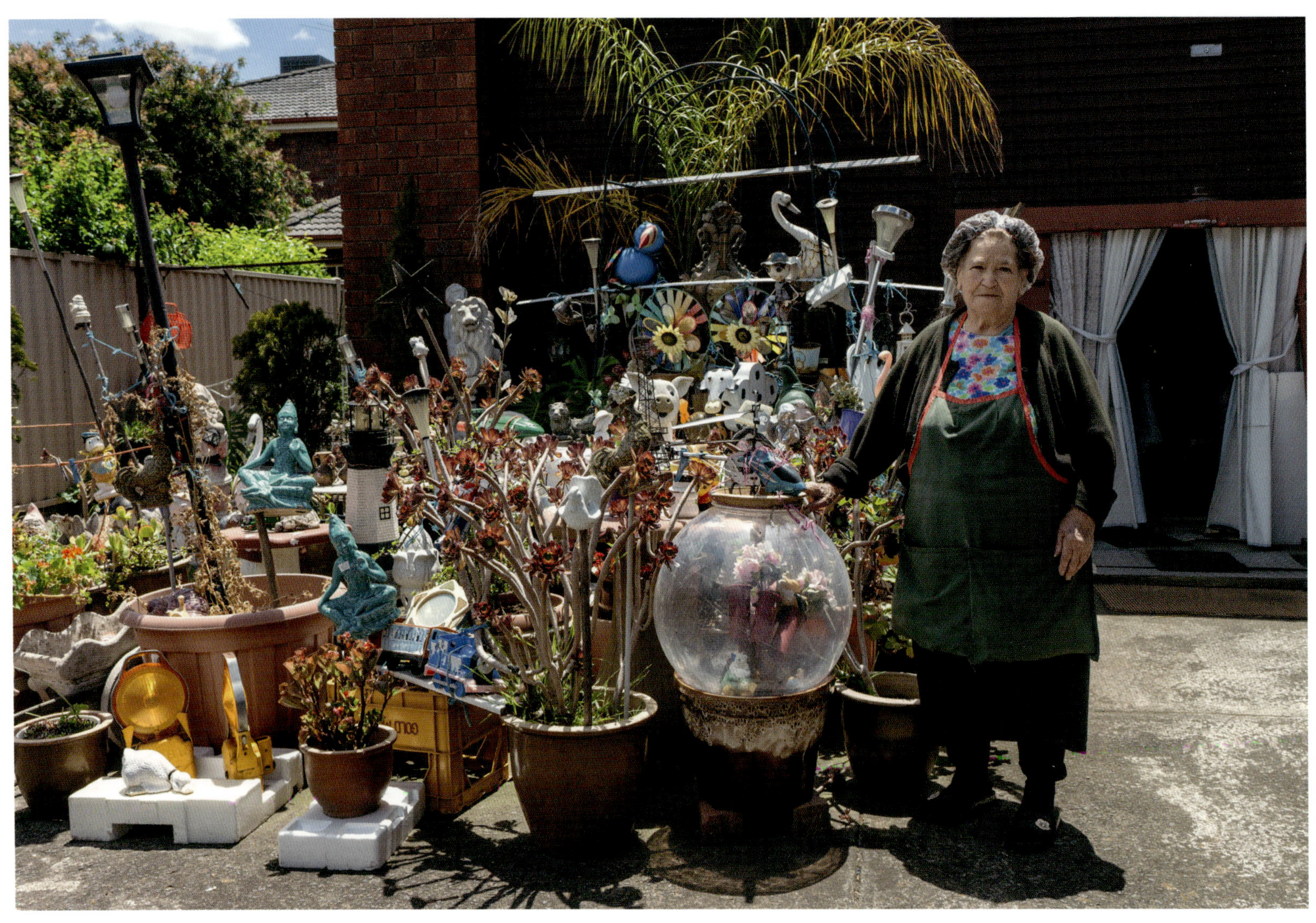

Coburg North

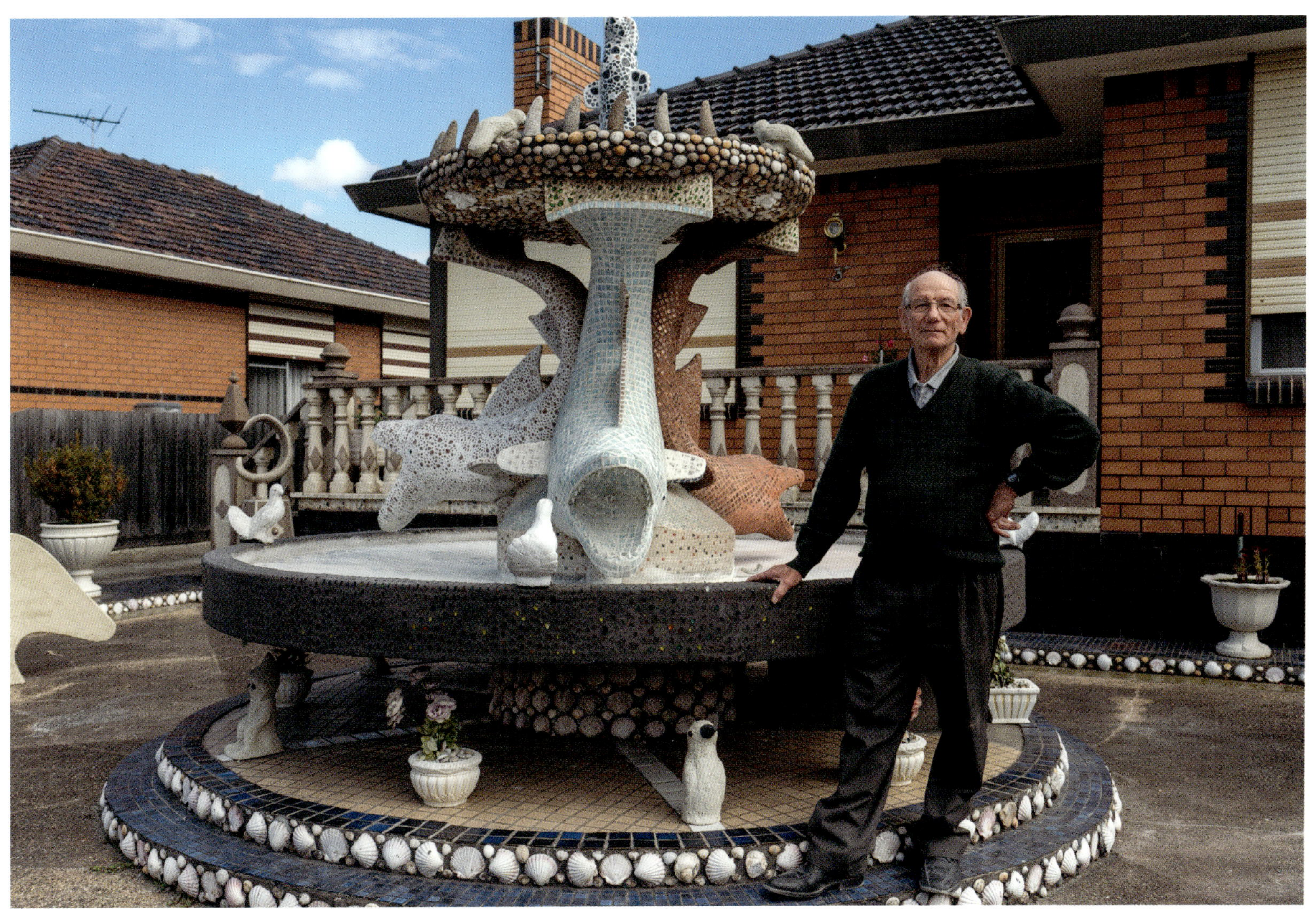

Reservoir

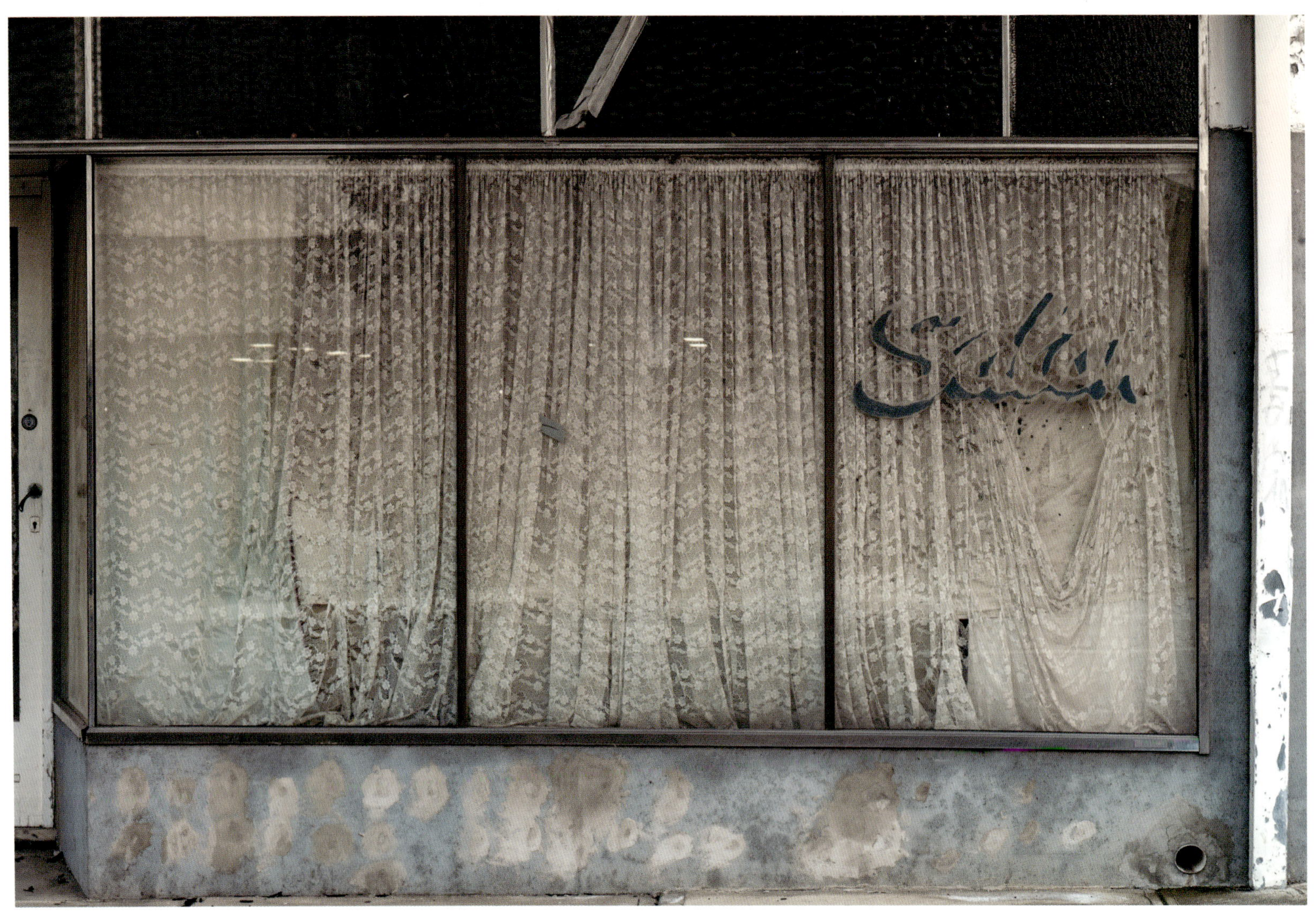

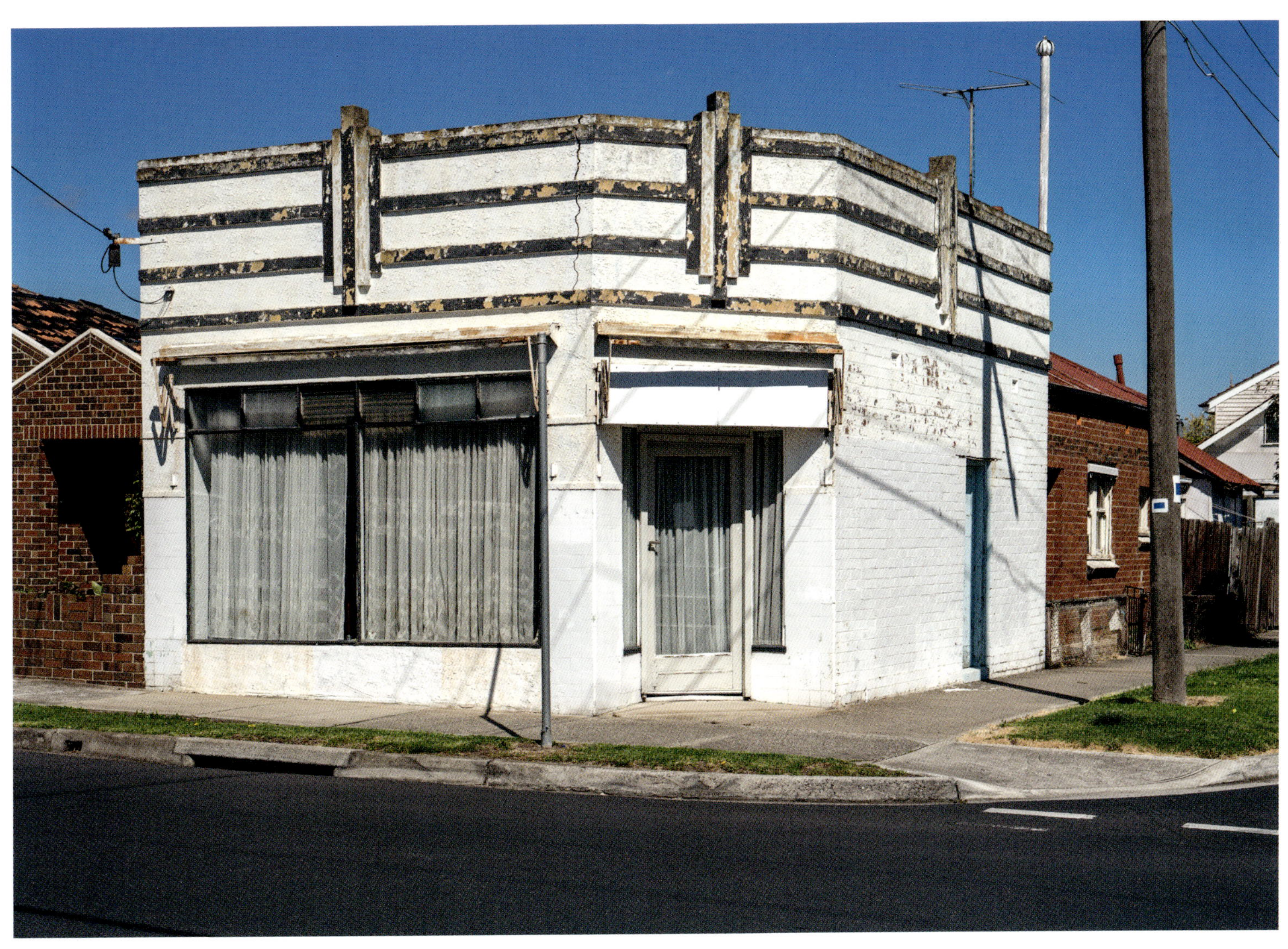

Pascoe Vale South

71

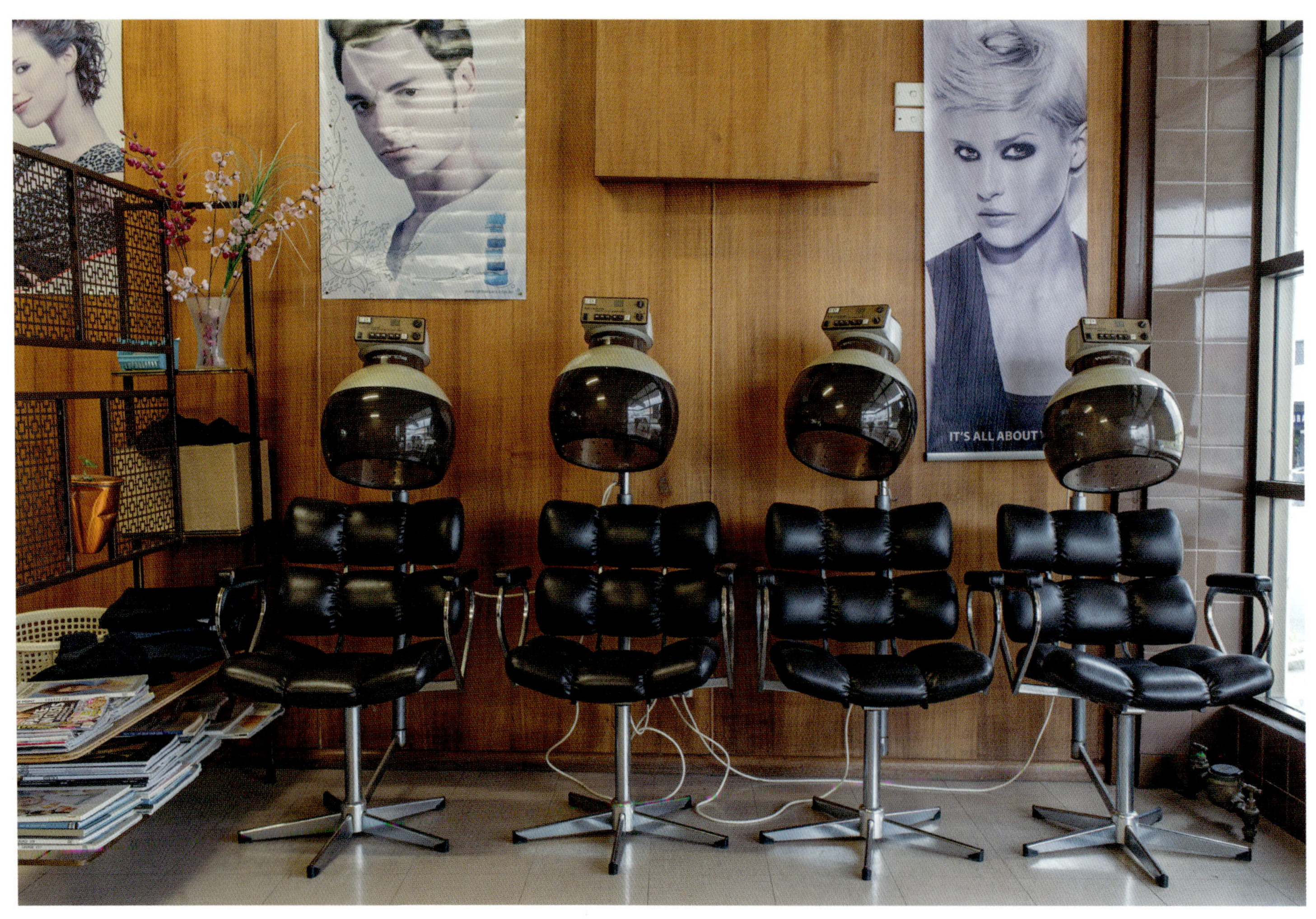

Preston

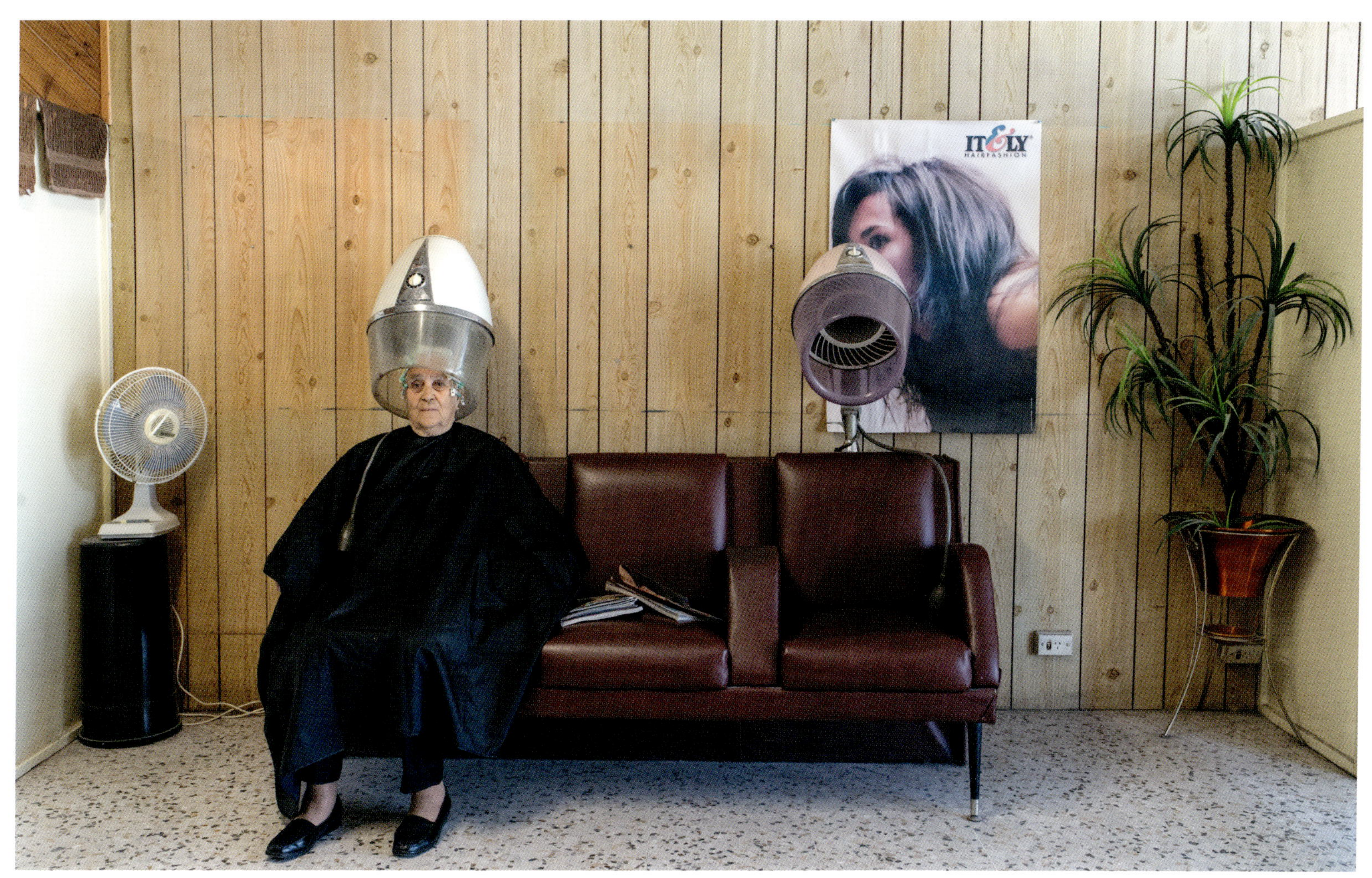

Reservoir

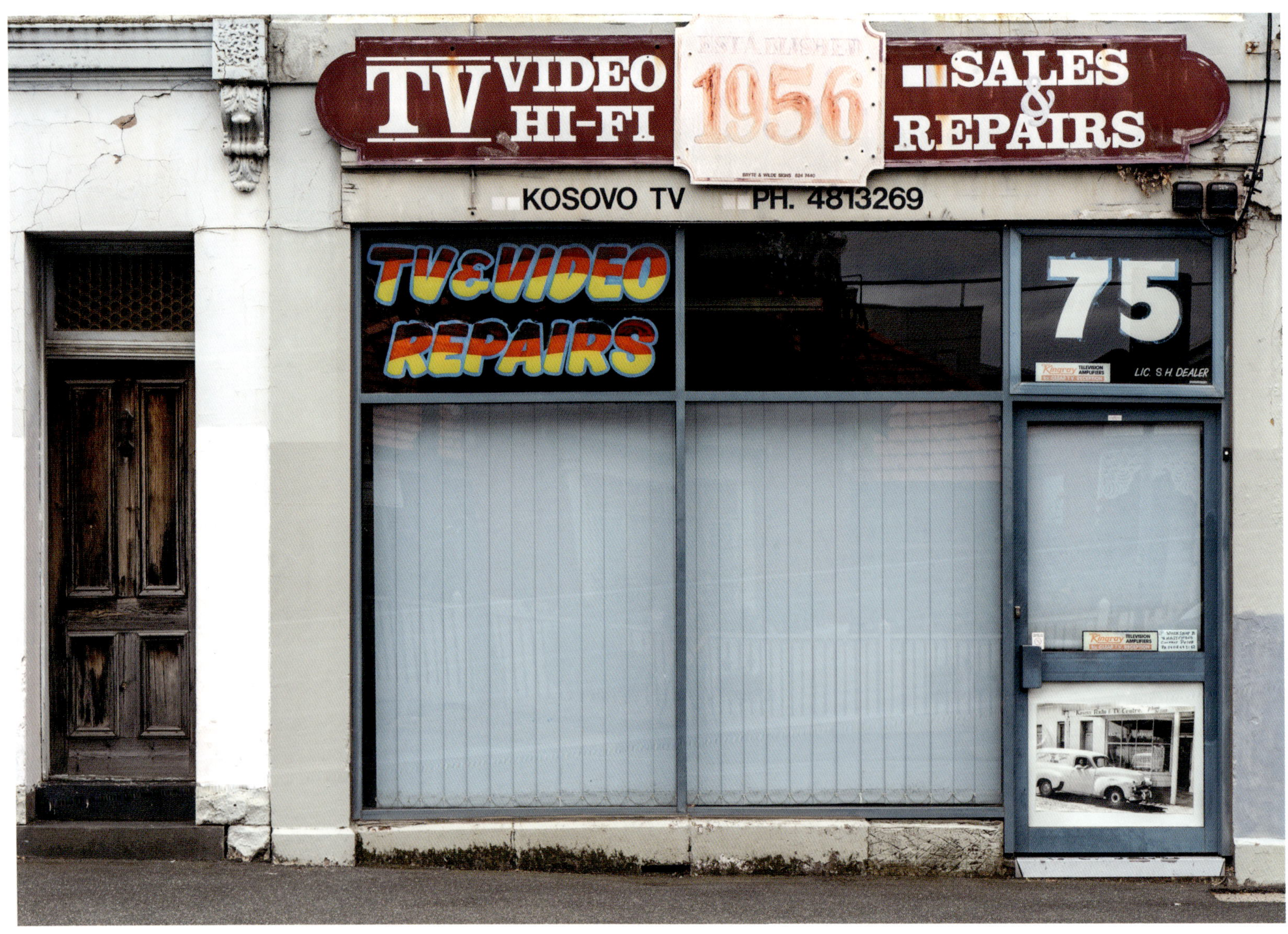

TV VIDEO HI-FI
ESTABLISHED 1956
SALES & REPAIRS
KOSOVO TV   PH. 4813269
TV & VIDEO REPAIRS
75
LIC. S.H. DEALER

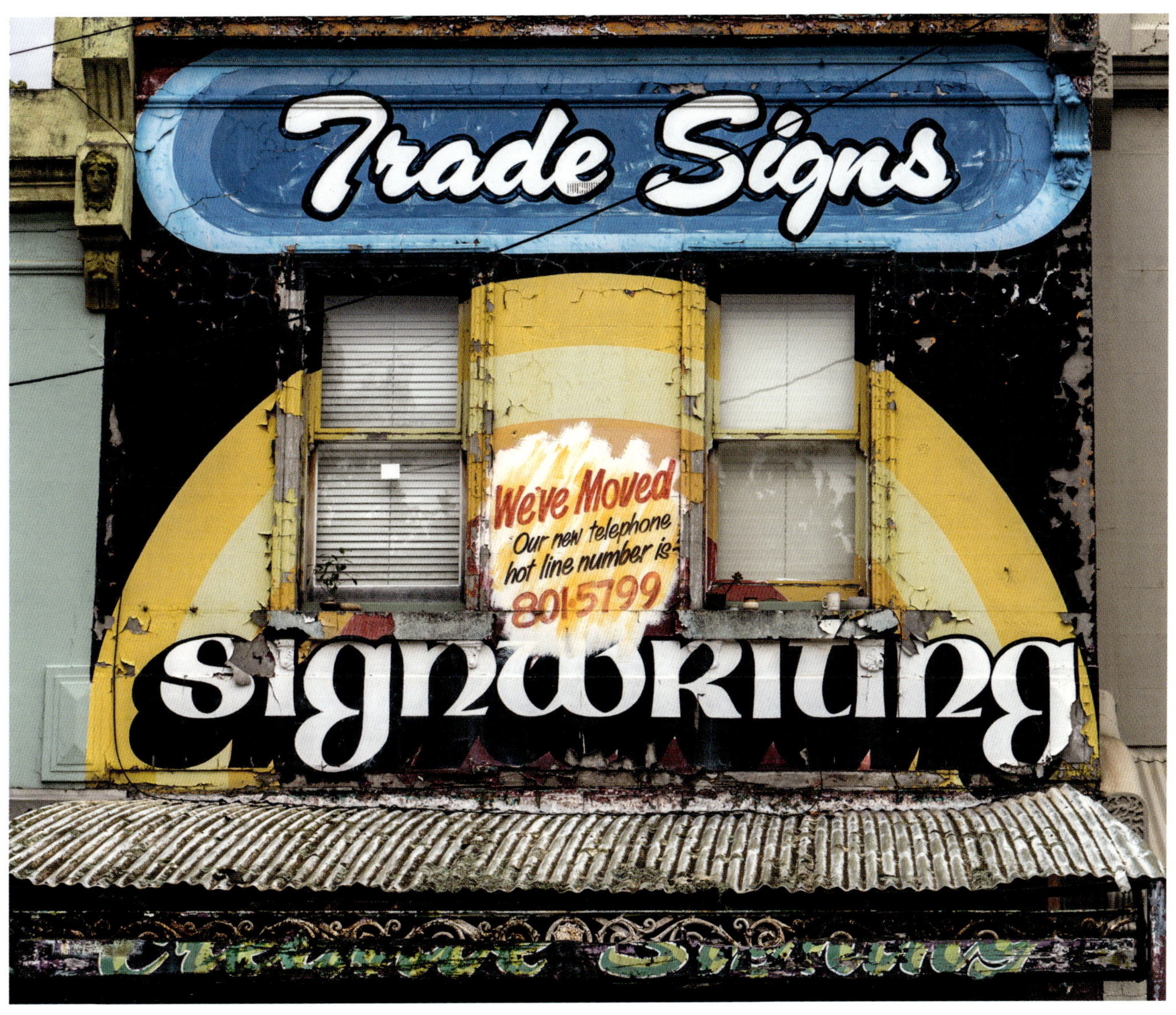

North Melbourne

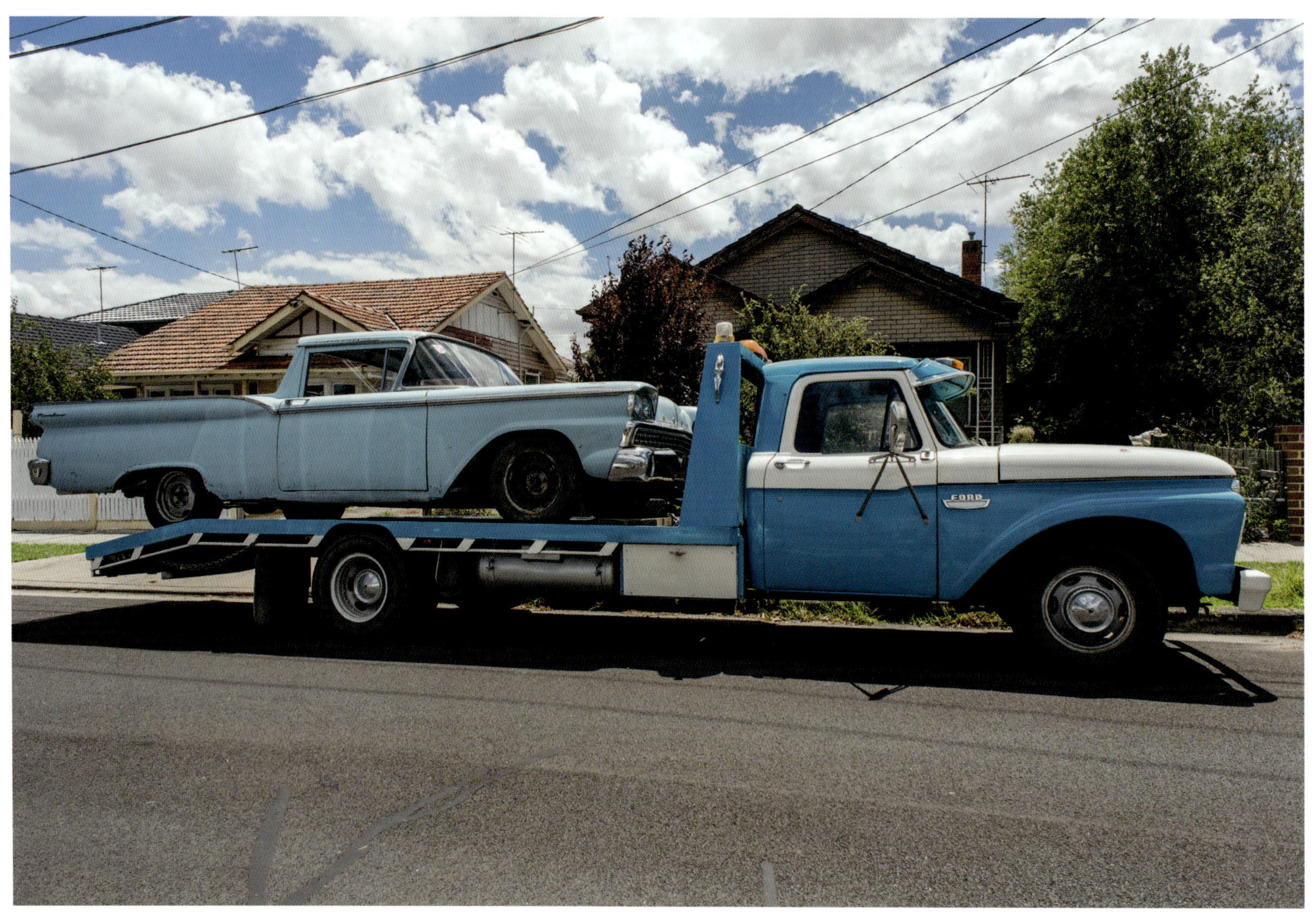

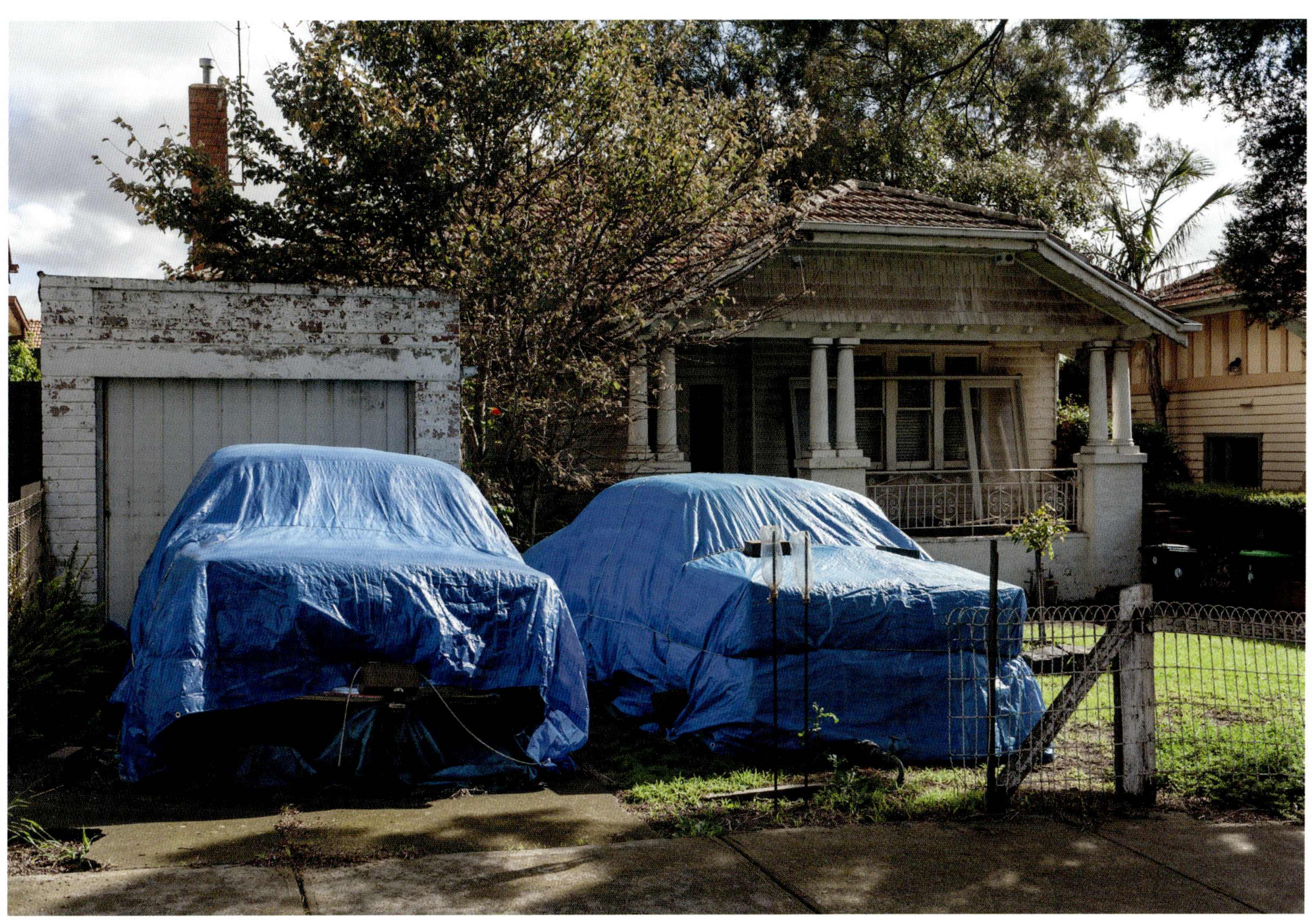

Brunswick West

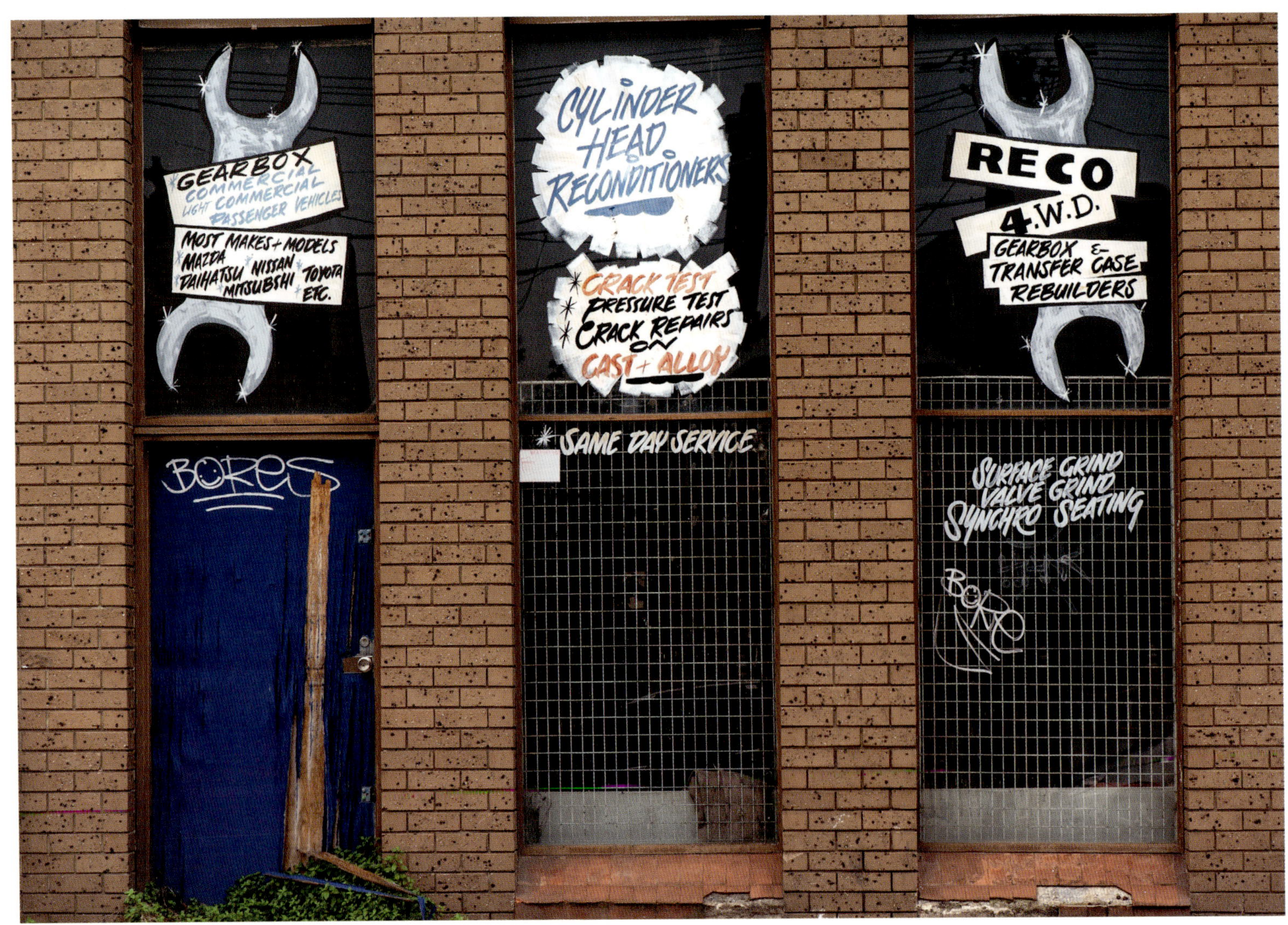
GEARBOX
COMMERCIAL
LIGHT COMMERCIAL
PASSENGER VEHICLES
MOST MAKES + MODELS
MAZDA
DAIHATSU NISSAN
MITSUBSHI TOYOTA
ETC.
CYLINDER HEAD RECONDITIONERS
CRACK TEST
PRESSURE TEST
CRACK REPAIRS ON
CAST + ALLOY
SAME DAY SERVICE
RECO
4.W.D.
GEARBOX &
TRANSFER CASE
REBUILDERS
SURFACE GRIND
VALVE GRIND
SYNCHRO SEATING

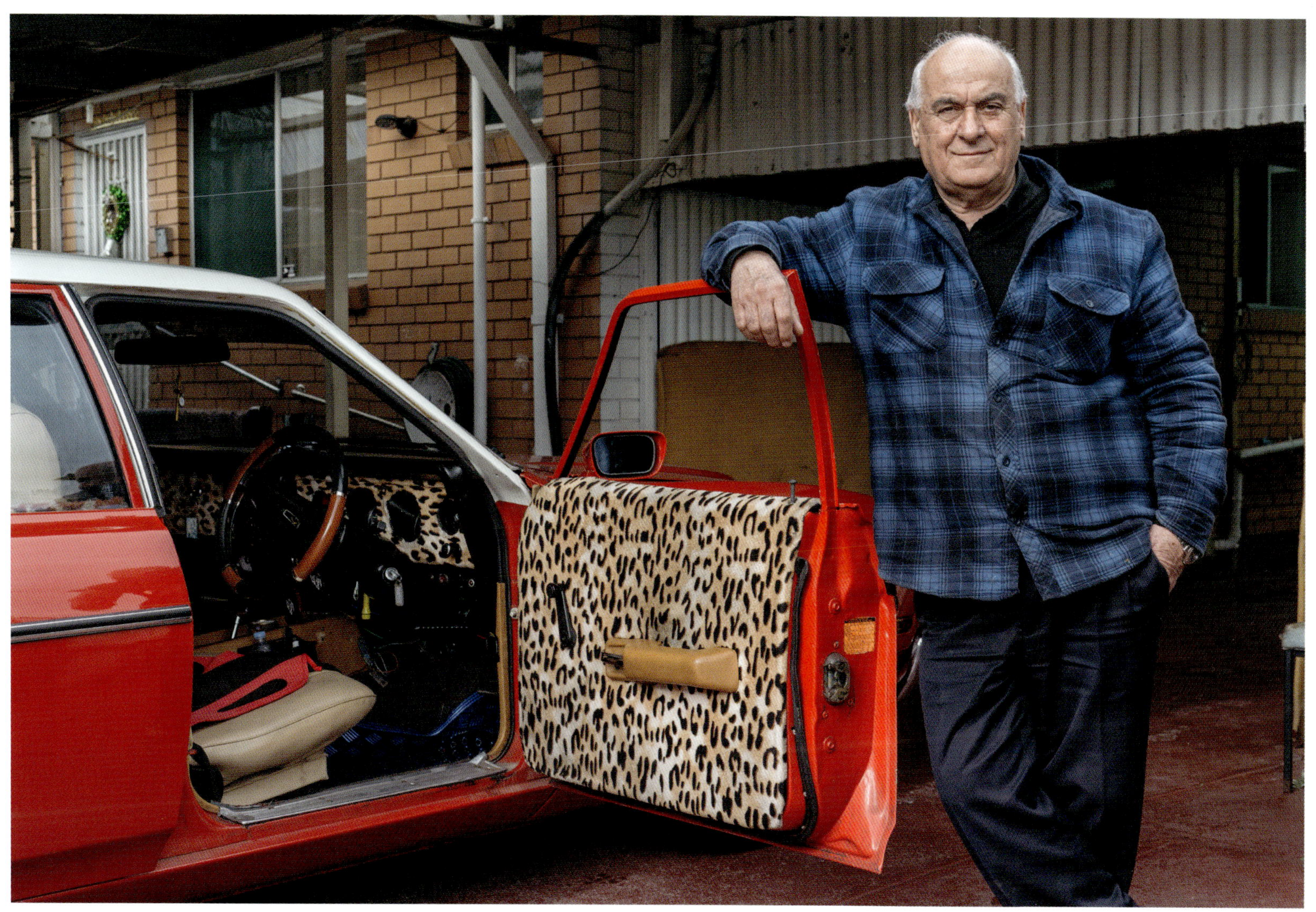

Campbellfield

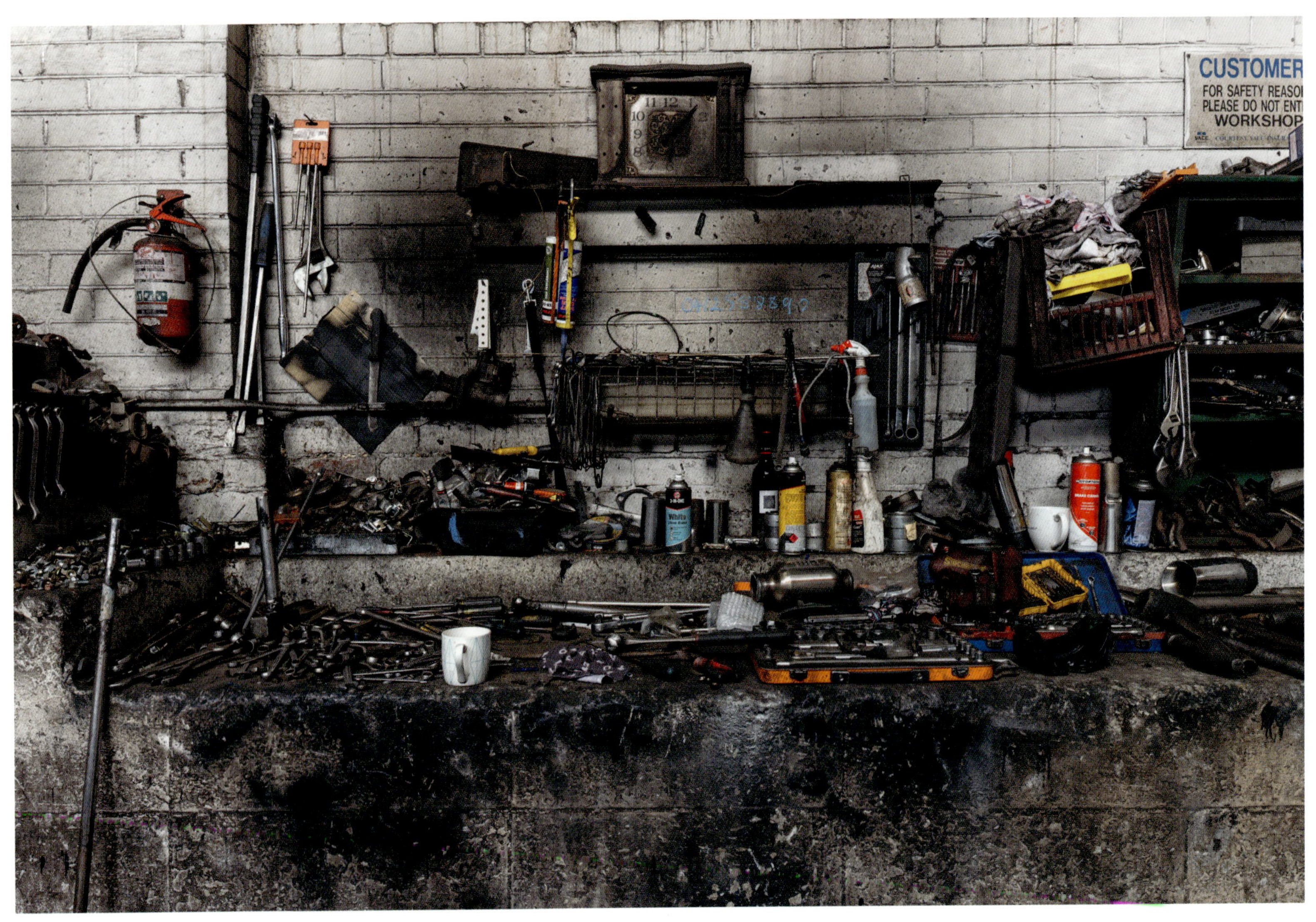

Alphington

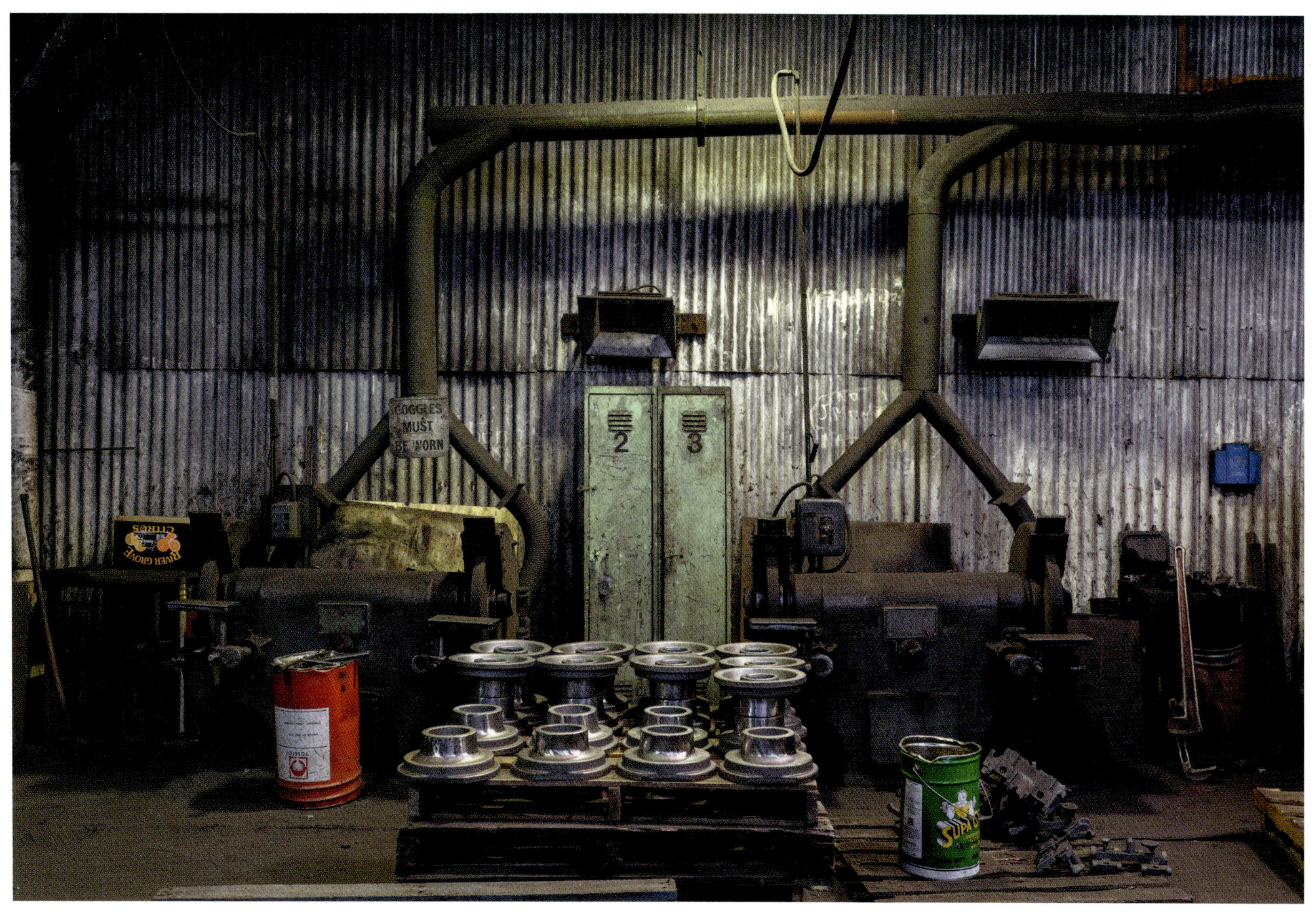

Coburg North

R.H. GRIERSON & CO. PTY. LTD.
OFFICE · STATIONERY · FURNITURE
PRESTON 4781244
"OFFICE"
"FURNITURE"
New & Used,
Bought & Sold
R.H. GRIERSON
& CO. PTY. LTD.
506 HIGH ST. PRESTON
Ph. 4781244

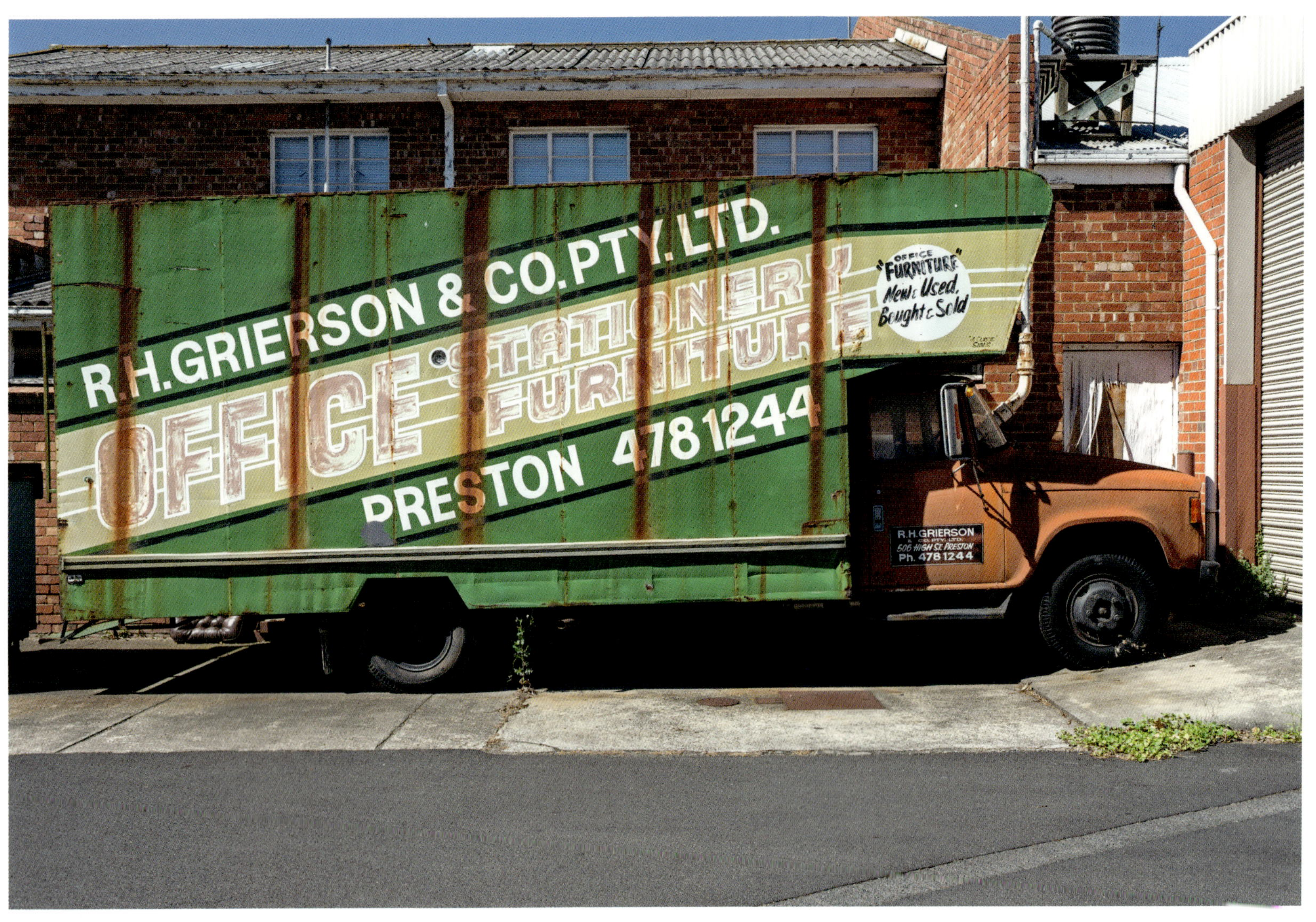

Preston

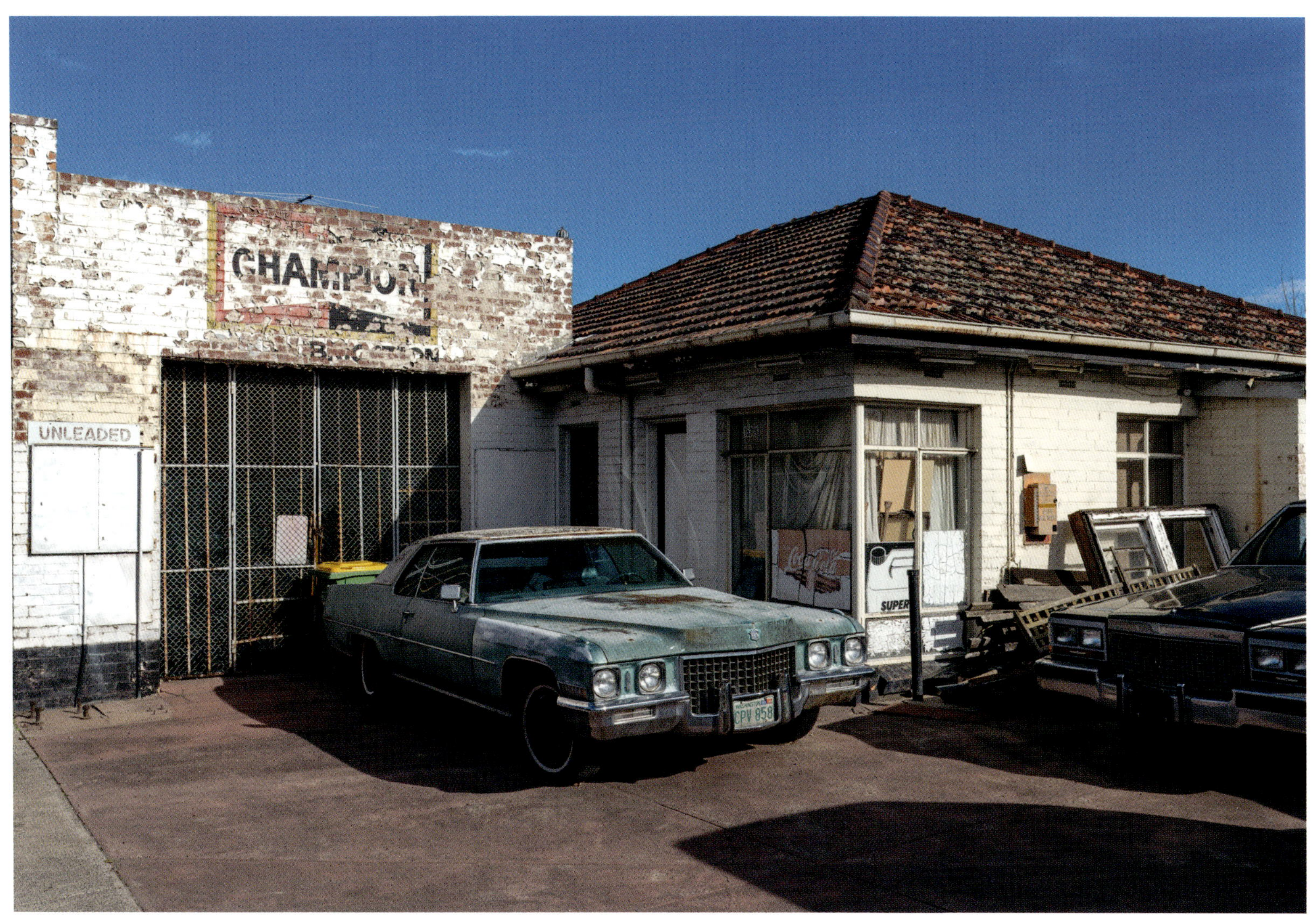

83

Reservoir

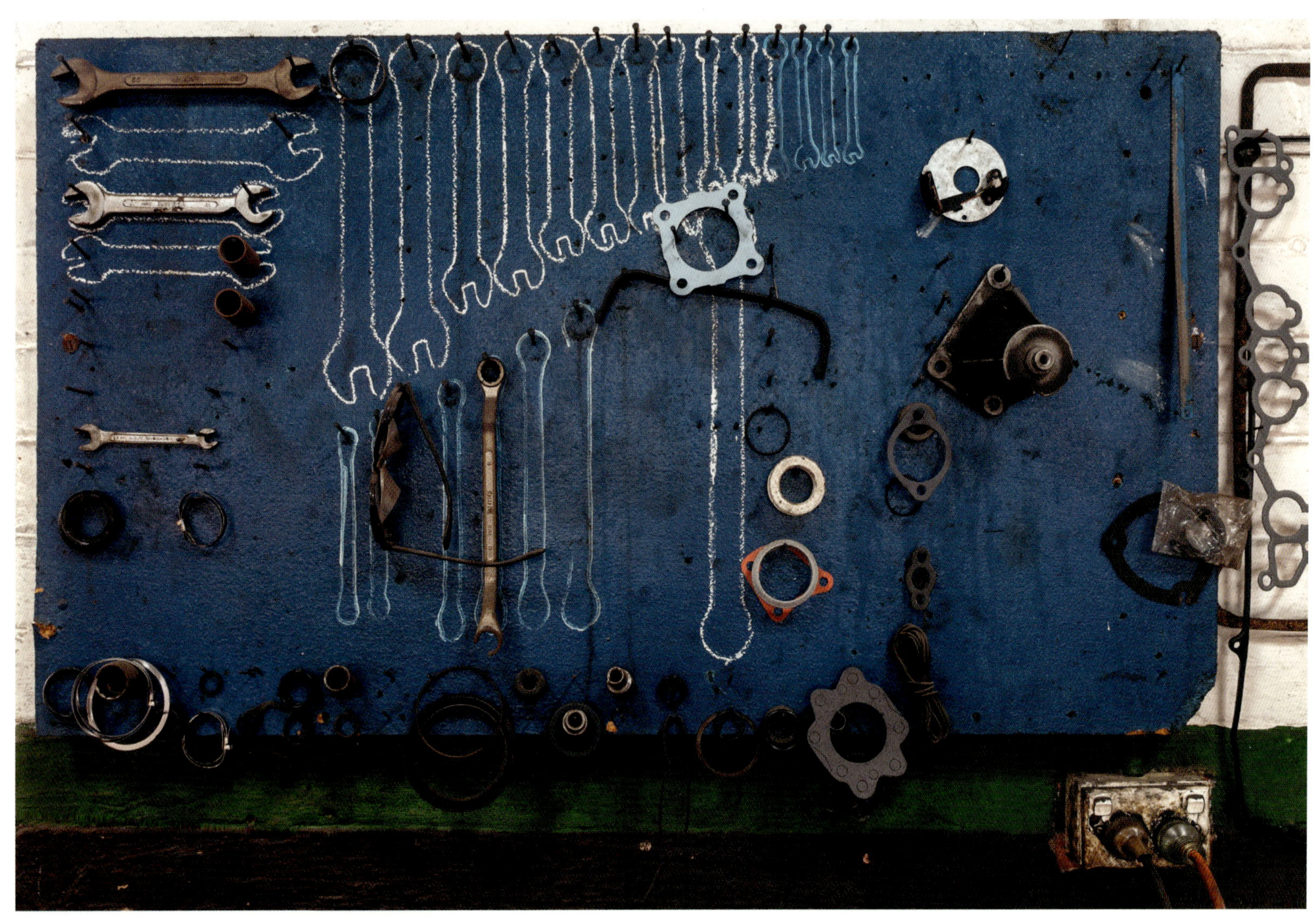

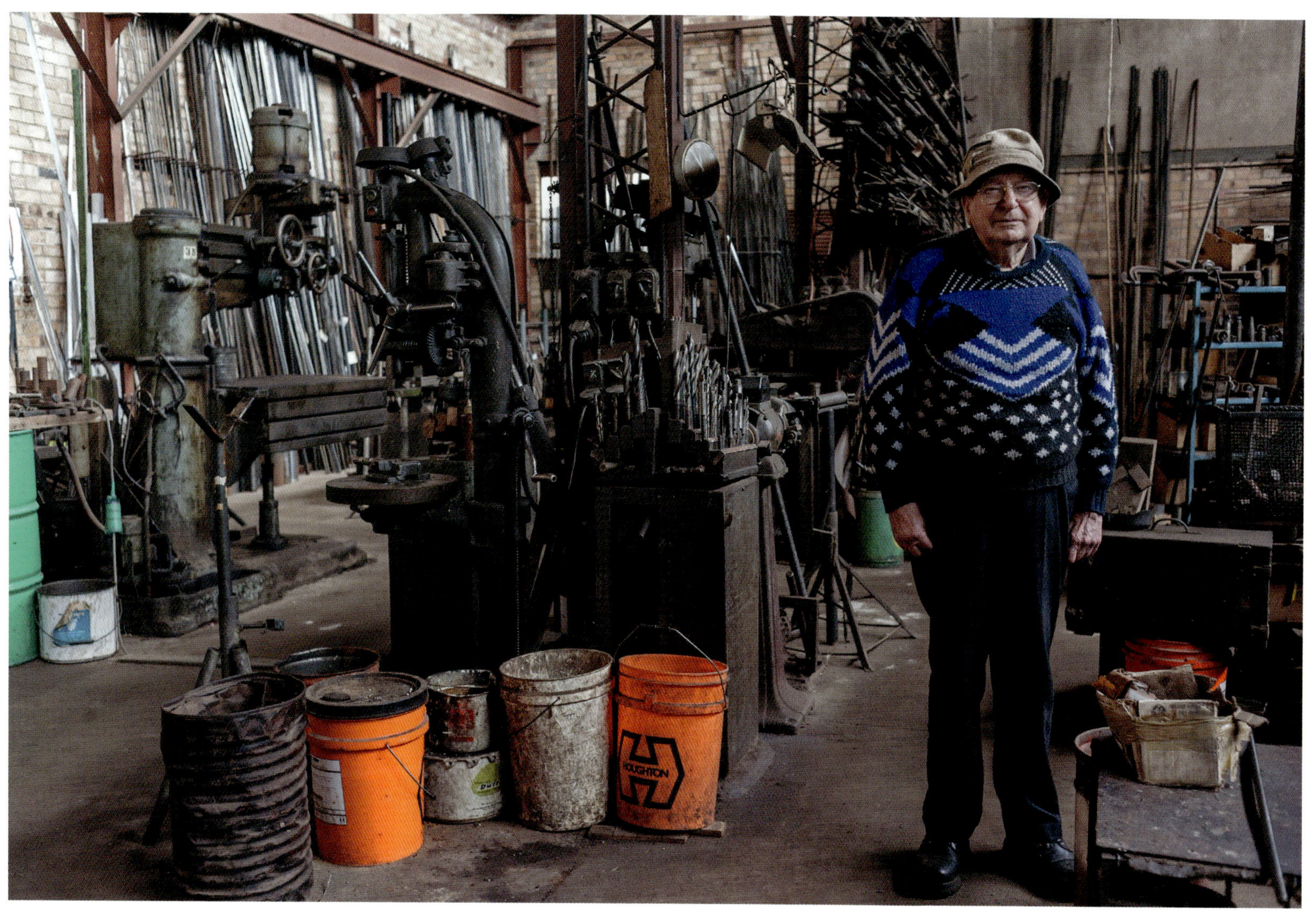

Coburg North

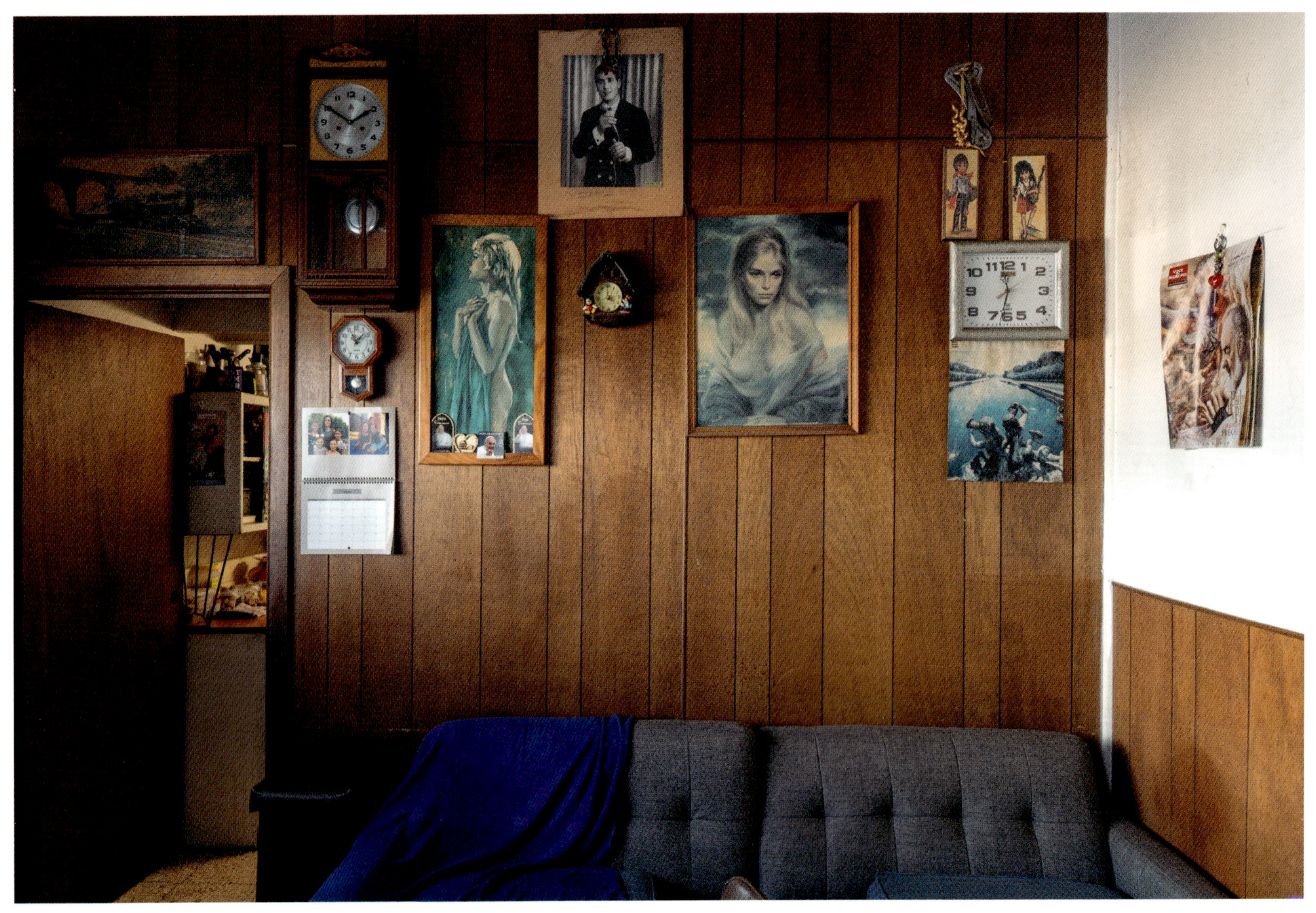

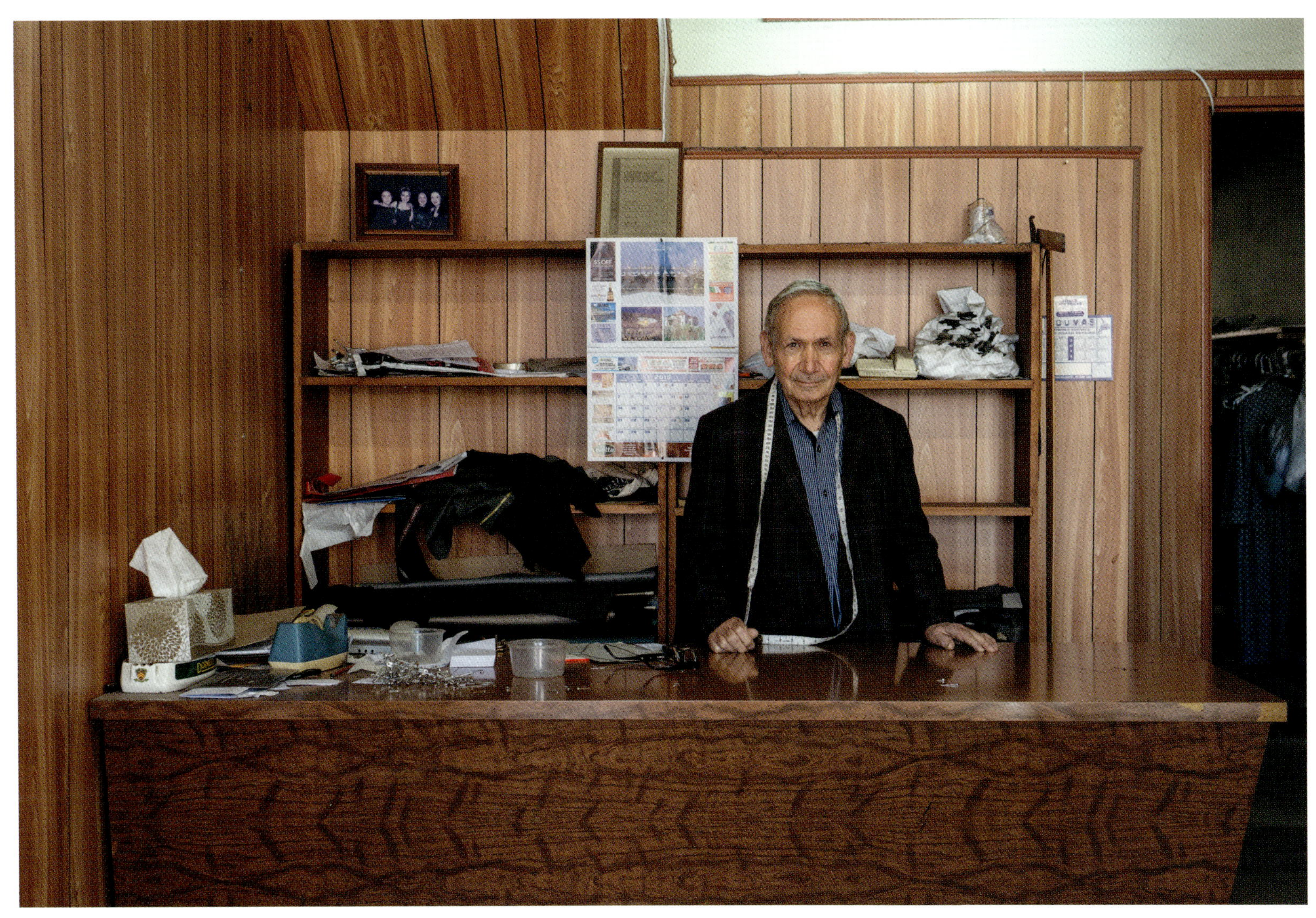

Carlton

AUTOMOTIVE ELECTRICAL SUPPLIES REPAIRS
ELECTRIC DRILLS
VACUUM CLEANERS
FLOOR POLISHERS
FOOD MIXERS
ELECTRIC MOTOR REPAIRS
HOUSE WIRING

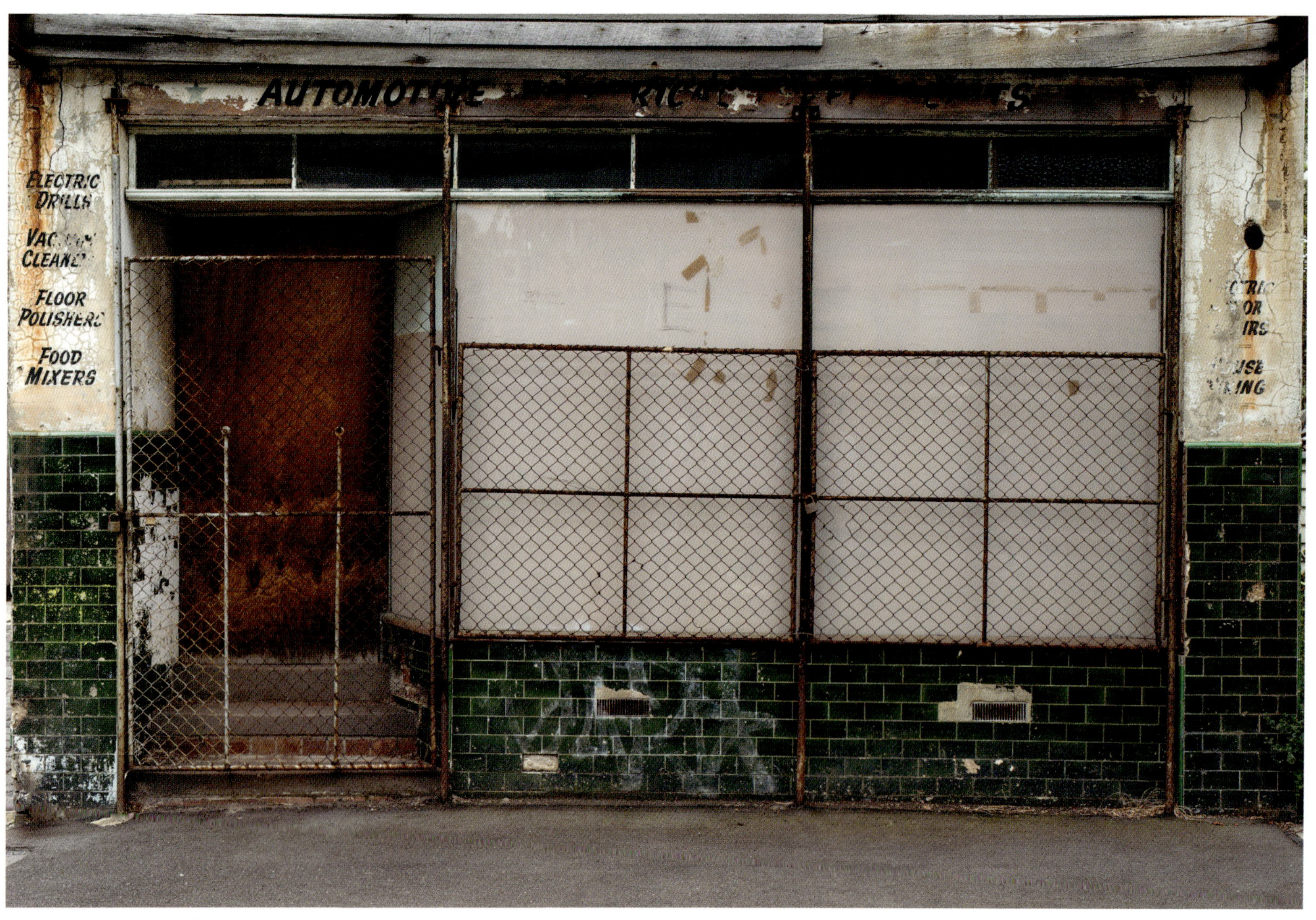

Brunswick

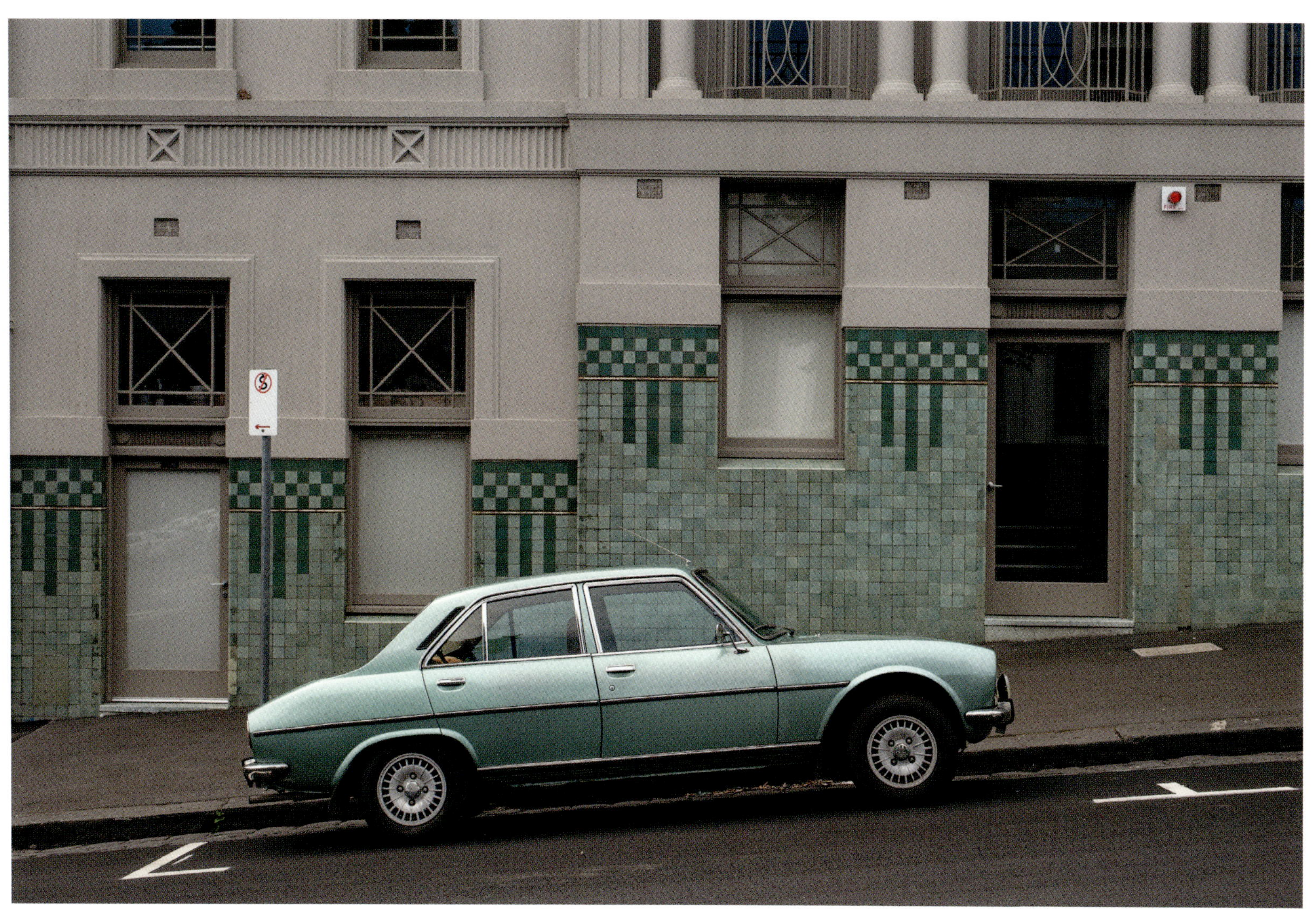

North Melbourne

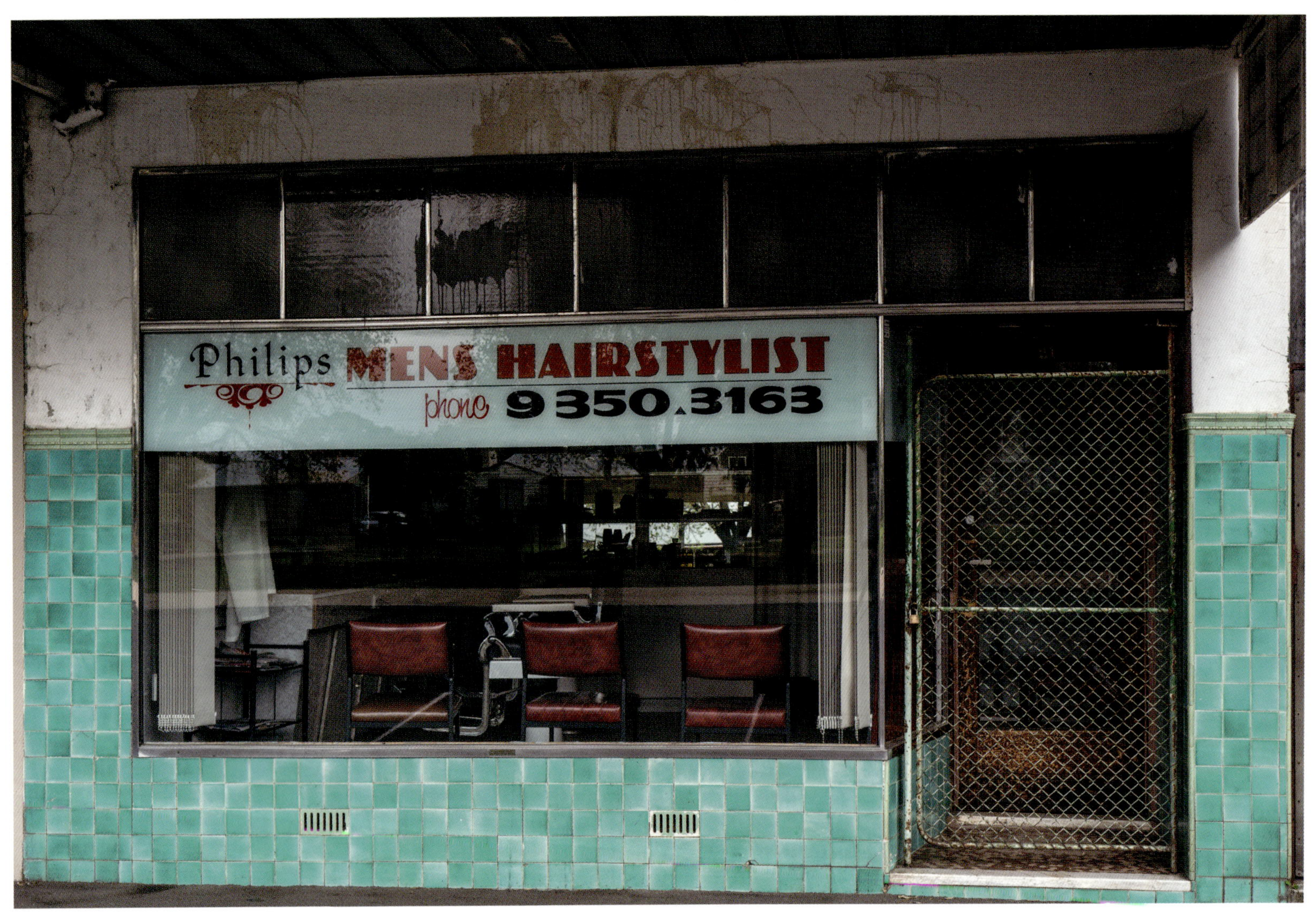

Philips MENS HAIRSTYLIST
phone 9 350.3163

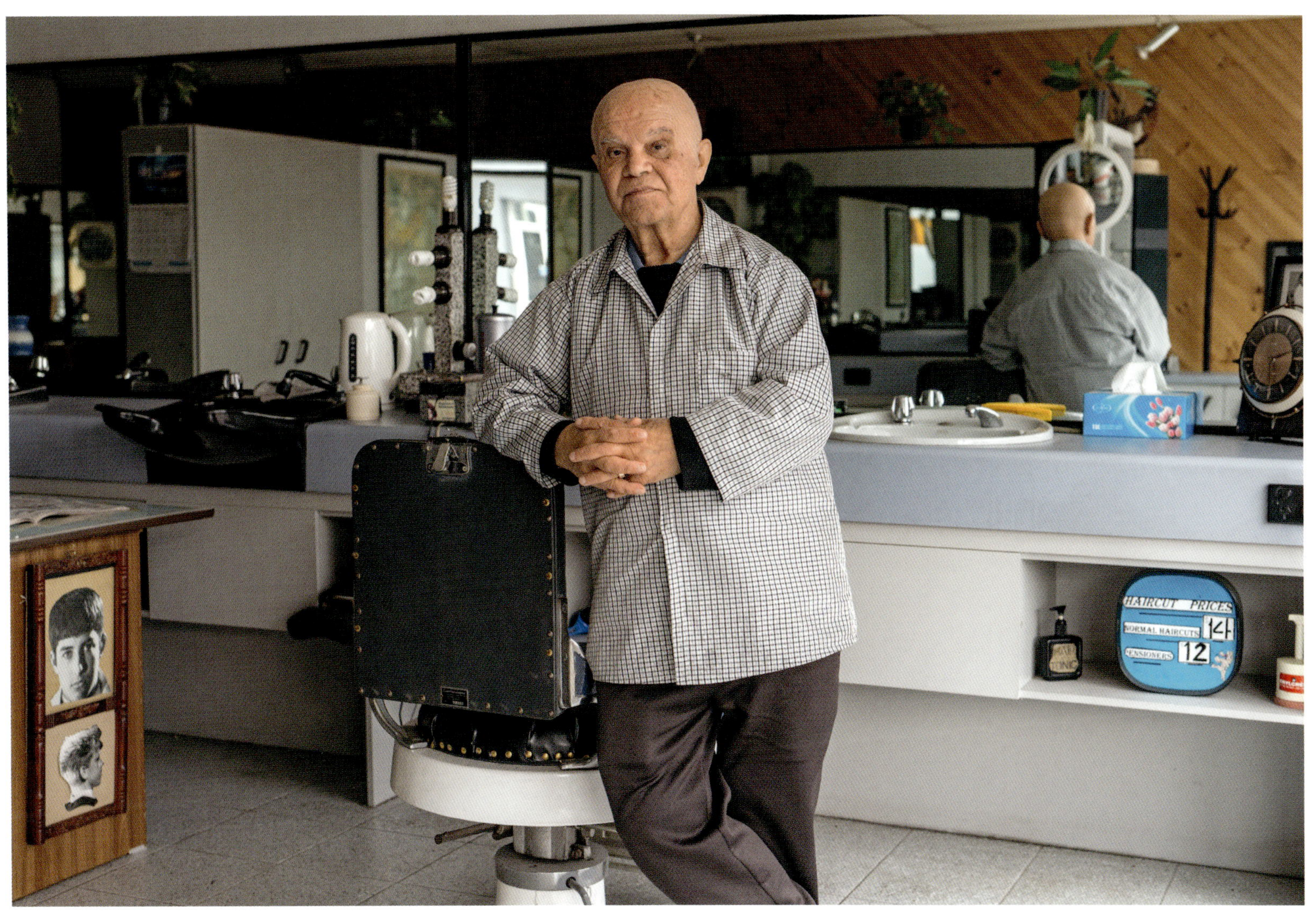

Preston

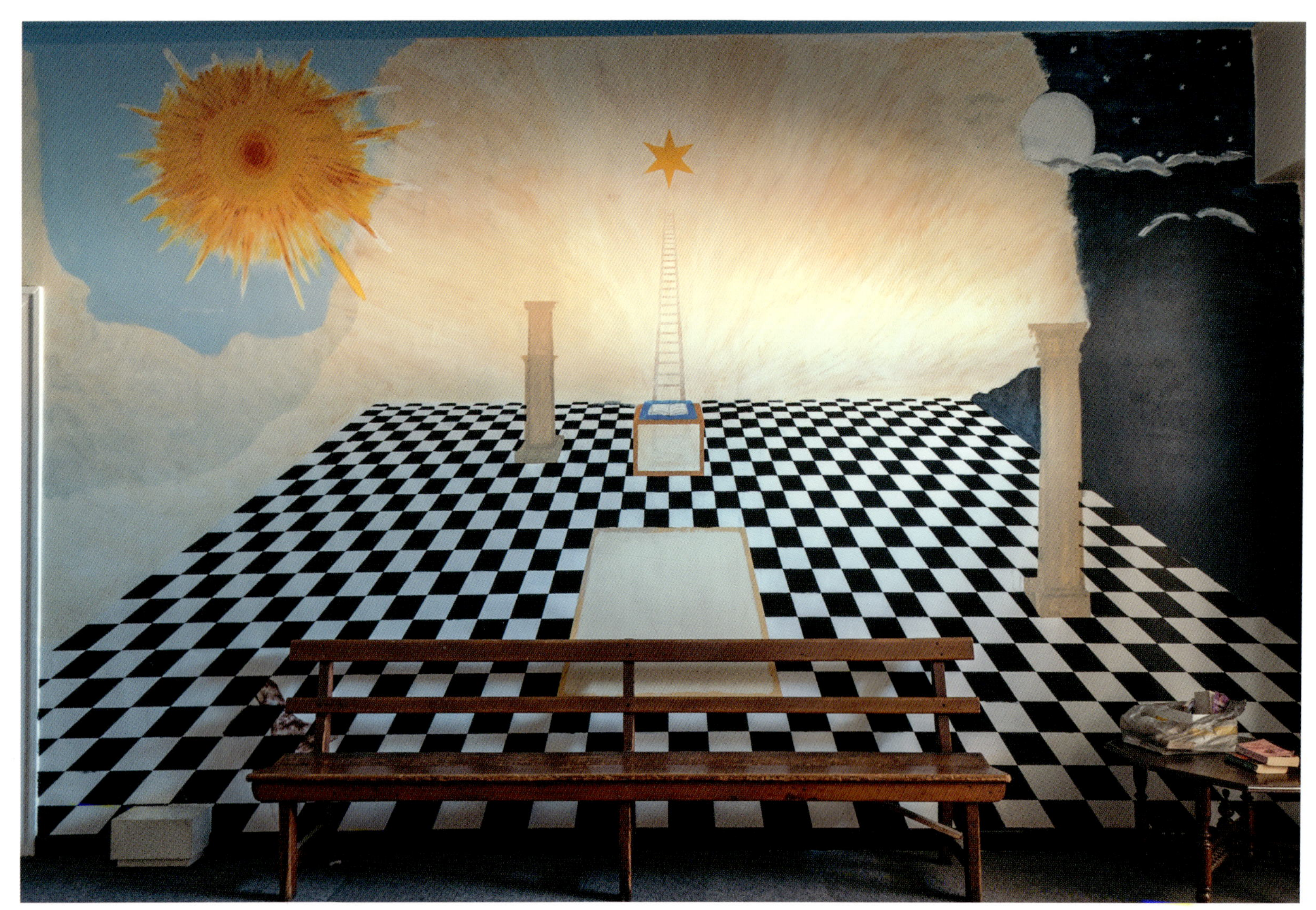

Preston

92

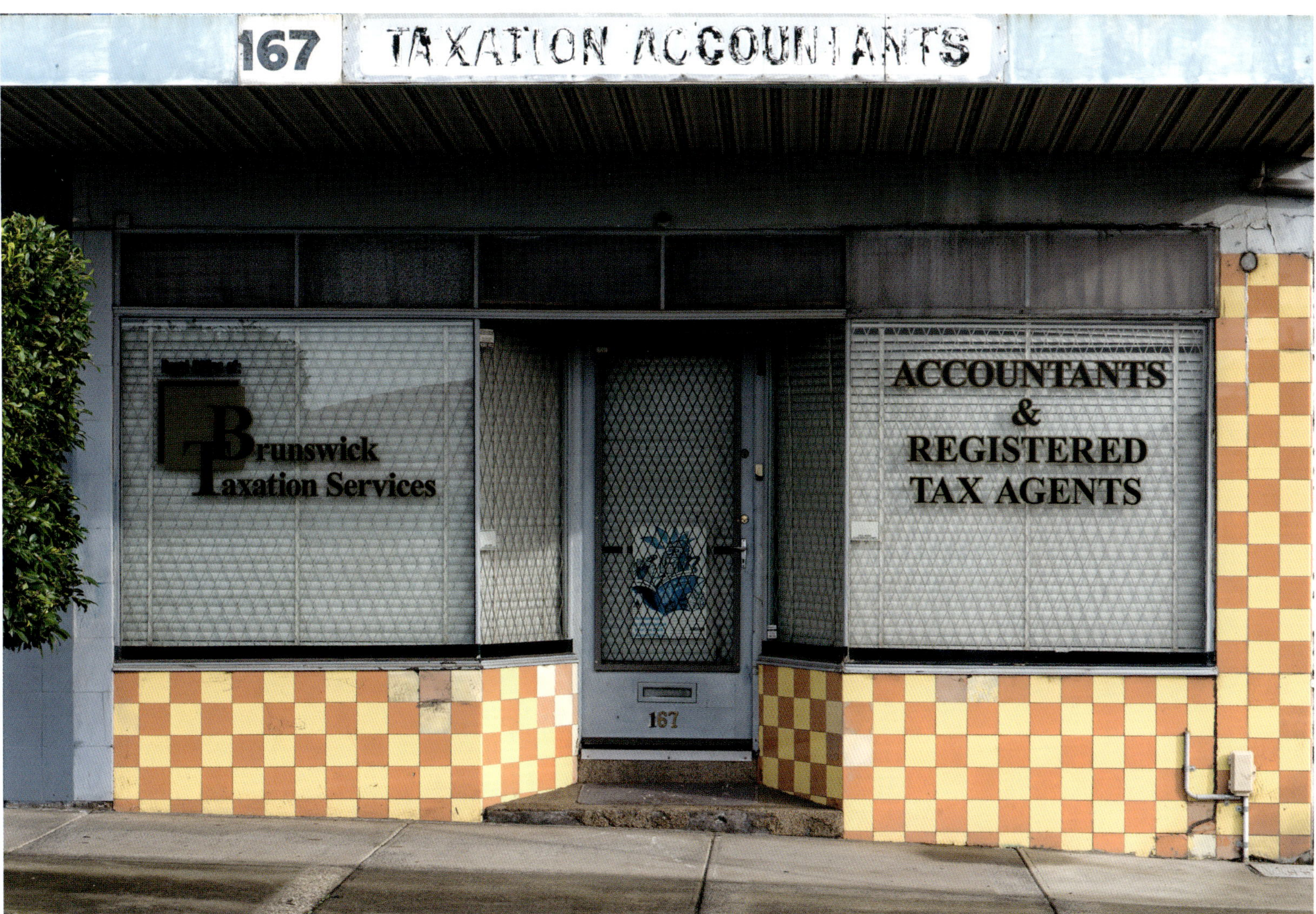

Brunswick West

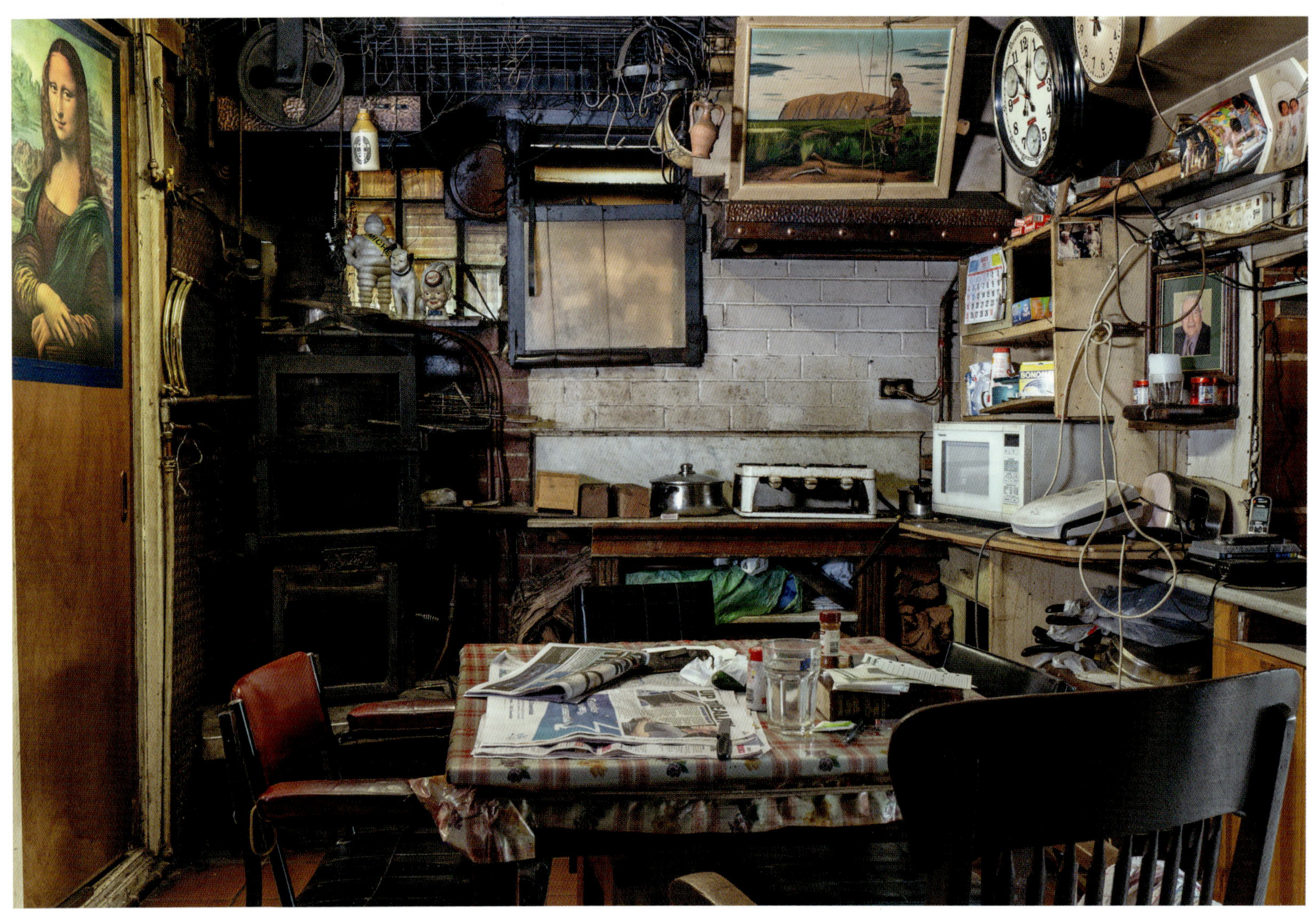

Brunswick

94

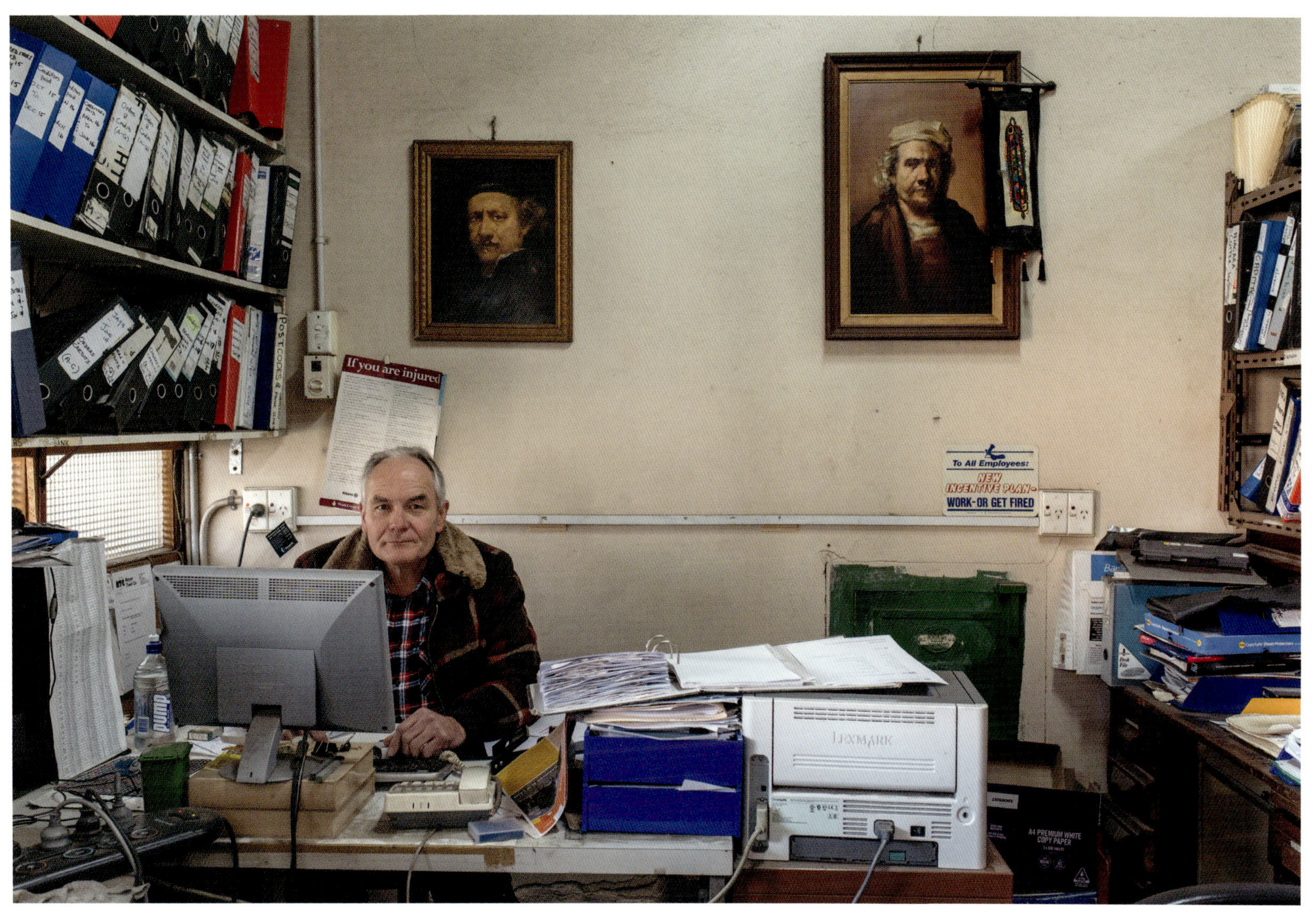

Preston

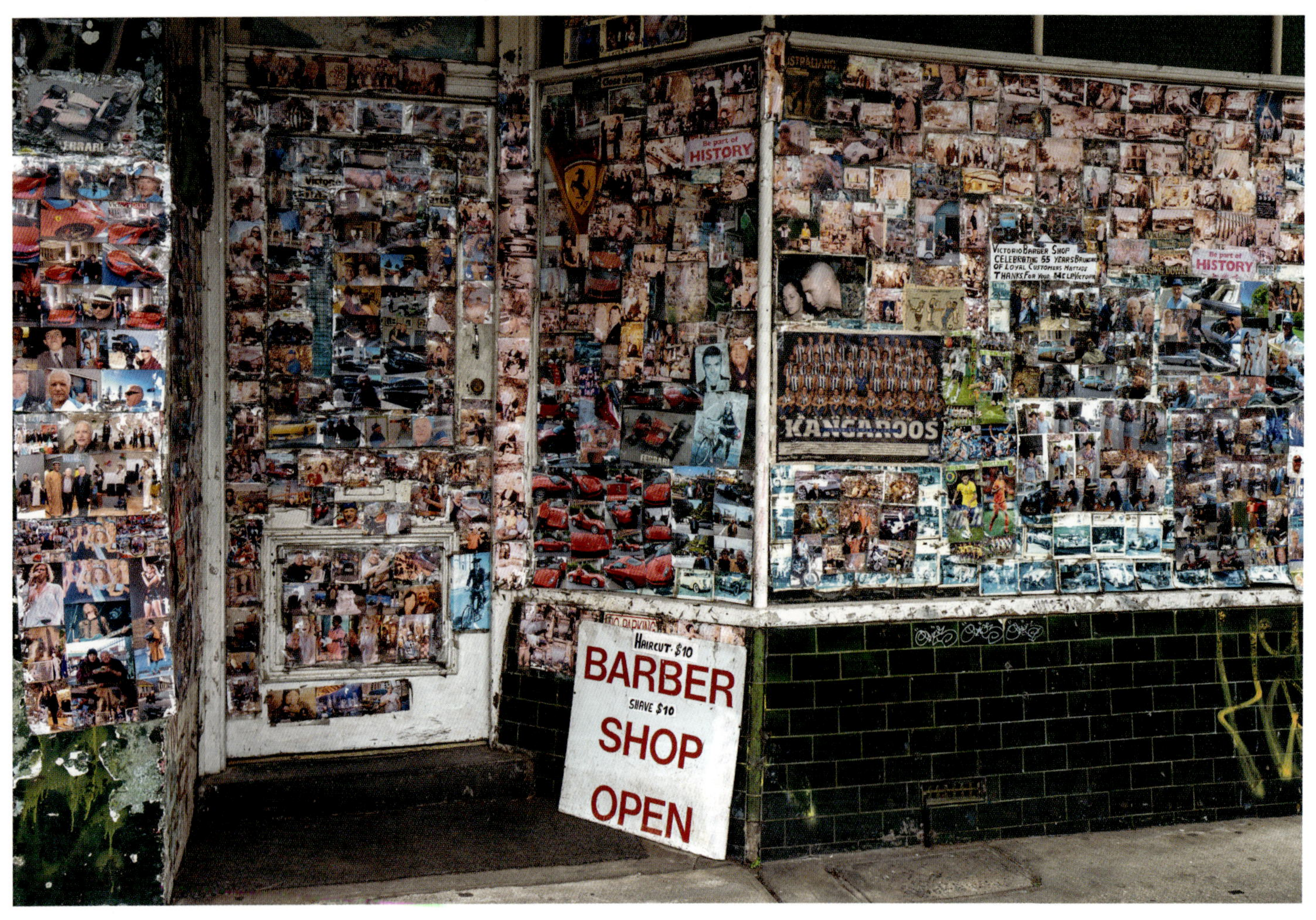

Brunswick

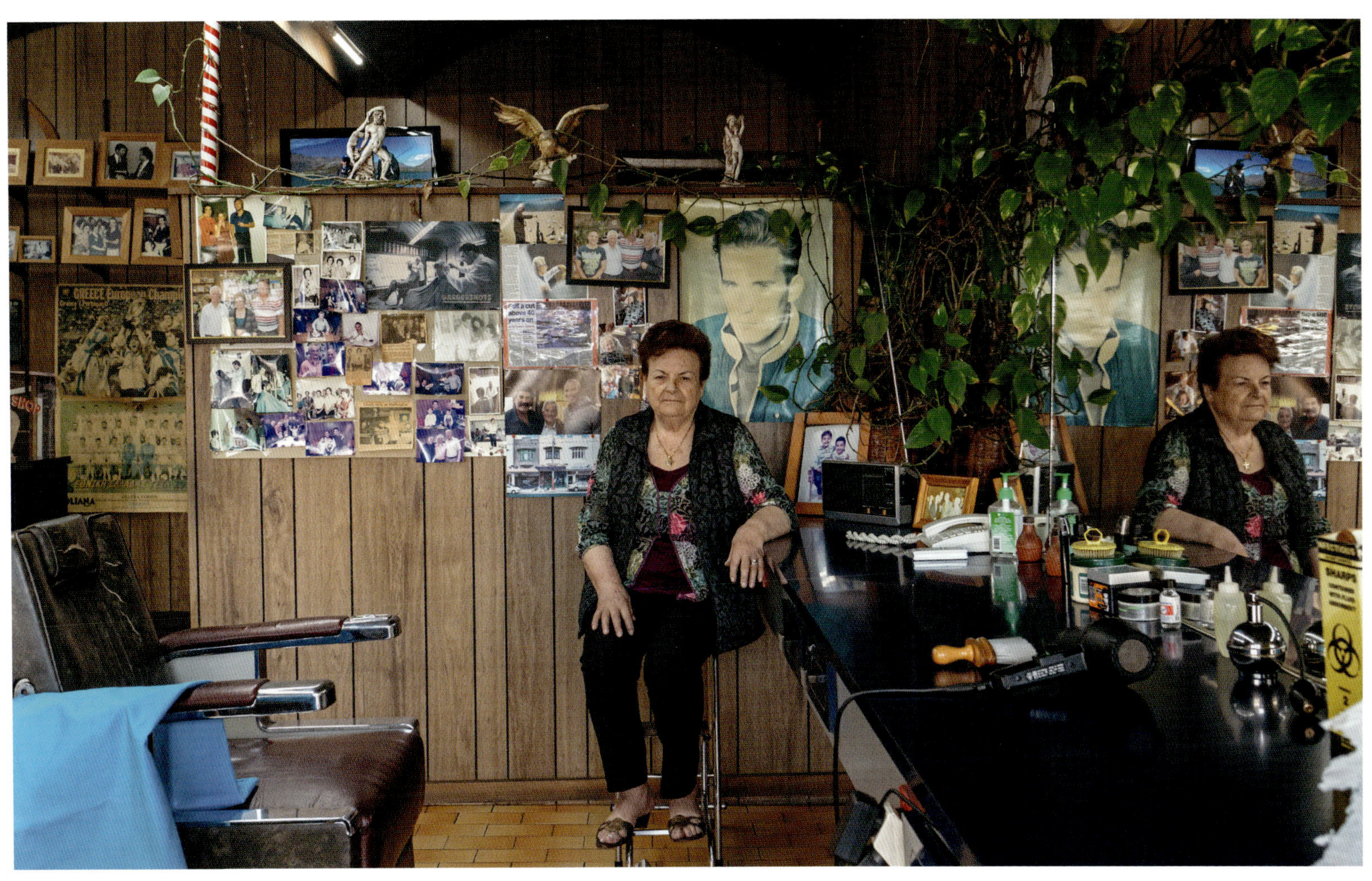

Northcote

35 BINGO! CALL 24
1 11 21 31 41 51 61 71 81
2 12 22 32 42 52 62 72 82
3 13 23 33 43 53 63 73 83
4 14 24 34 44 54 64 74 84
5 15 25 35 45 55 65 75 85
6 16 26 36 46 56 66 76 86
7 17 27 37 47 57 67 77 87
8 18 28 38 48 58 68 78 88
9 19 29 39 49 59 69 79 89
10 20 30 40 50 60 70 80 90
Enjoy Your Melita Bingo Day
MELITA SOCIAL CLUB

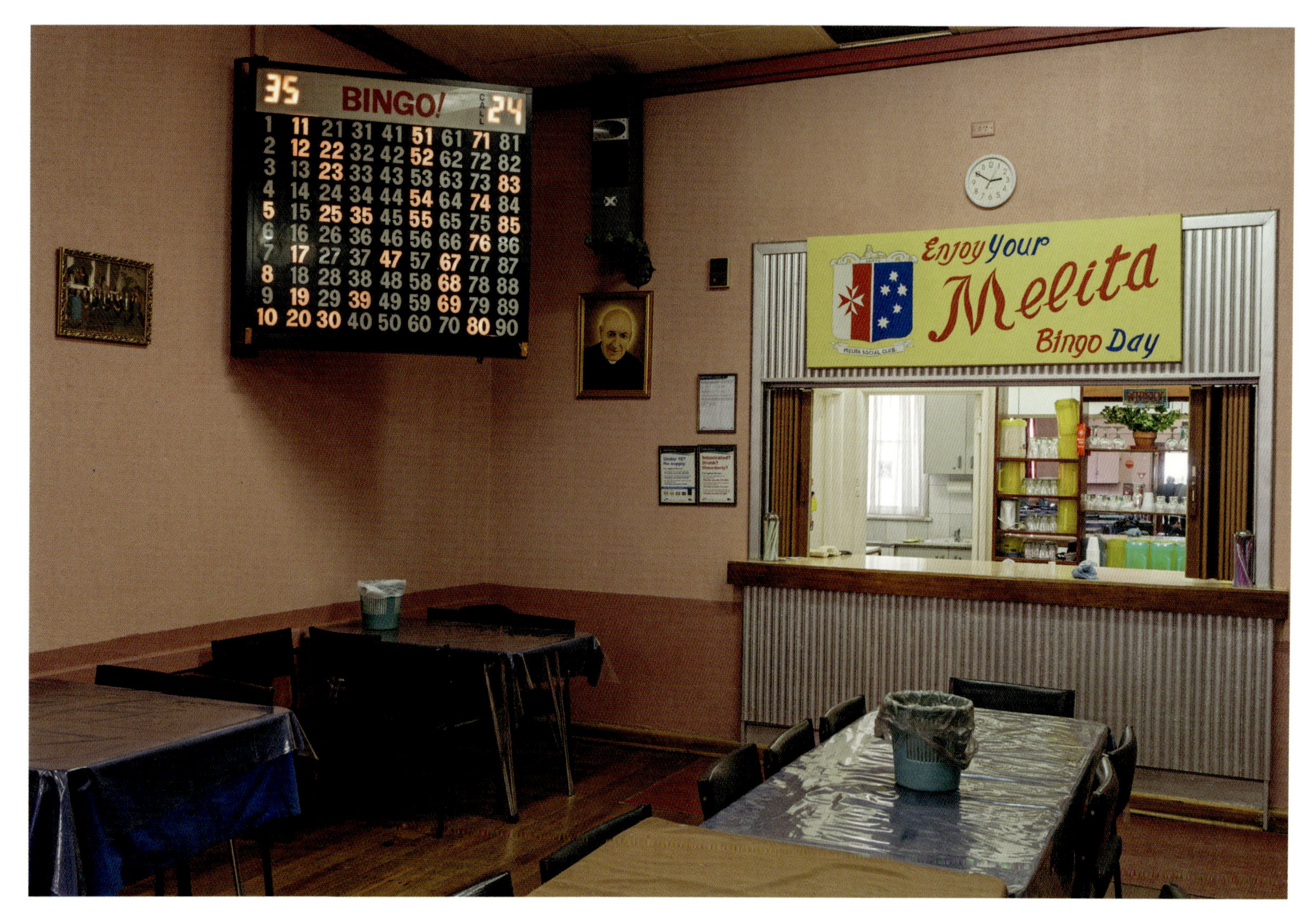

Coburg

RAOB
R A O B
MEADOW-GLEN
LODGE
CITY
TYLER
No 278
G.L.E.
MEADOW-GLEN
No 27
STRICT ORDER
R.A.O.B.
MEADOW-GLEN
LODGE
CM
No 278
G.L.E
G.L.V

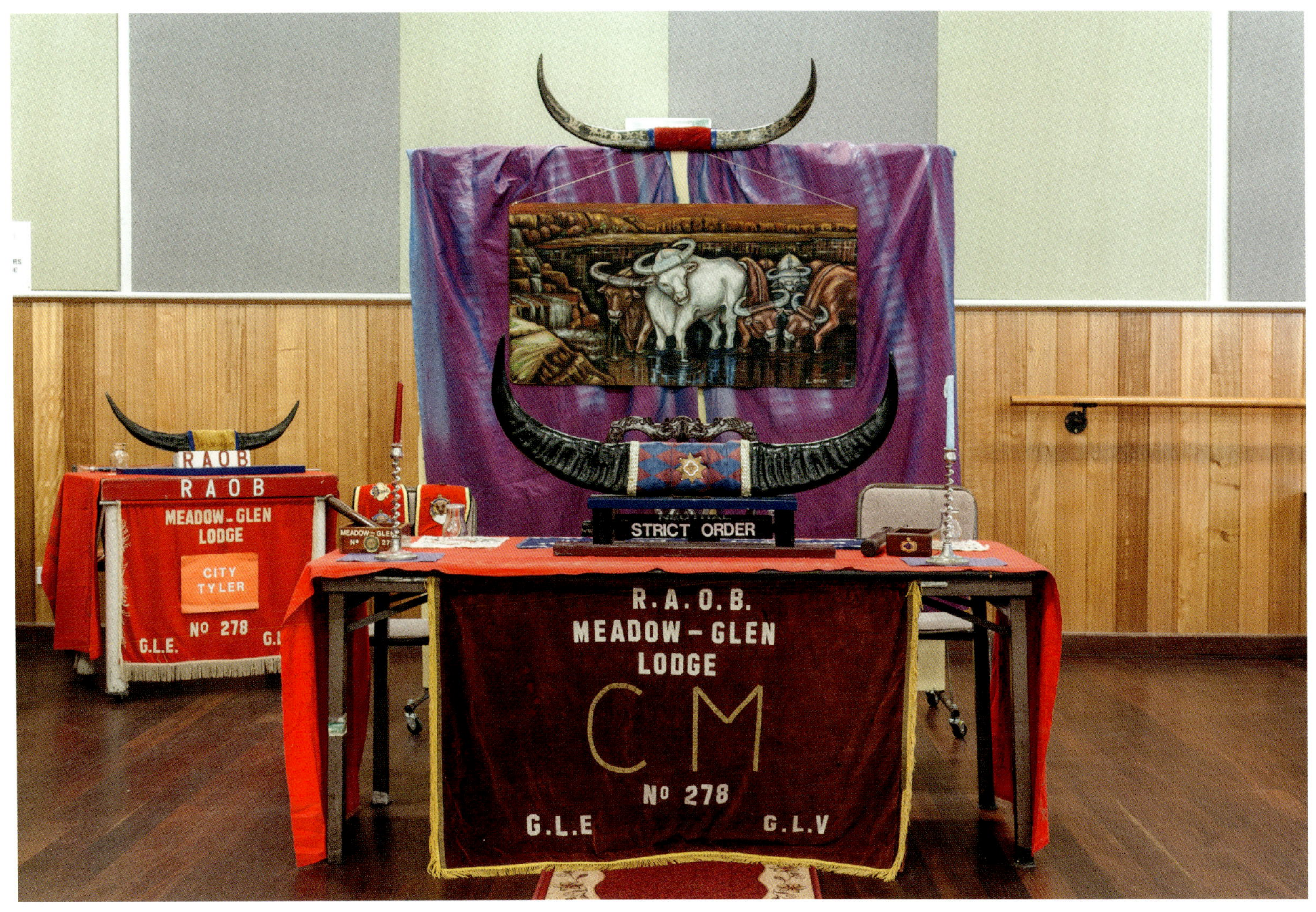

Glenroy

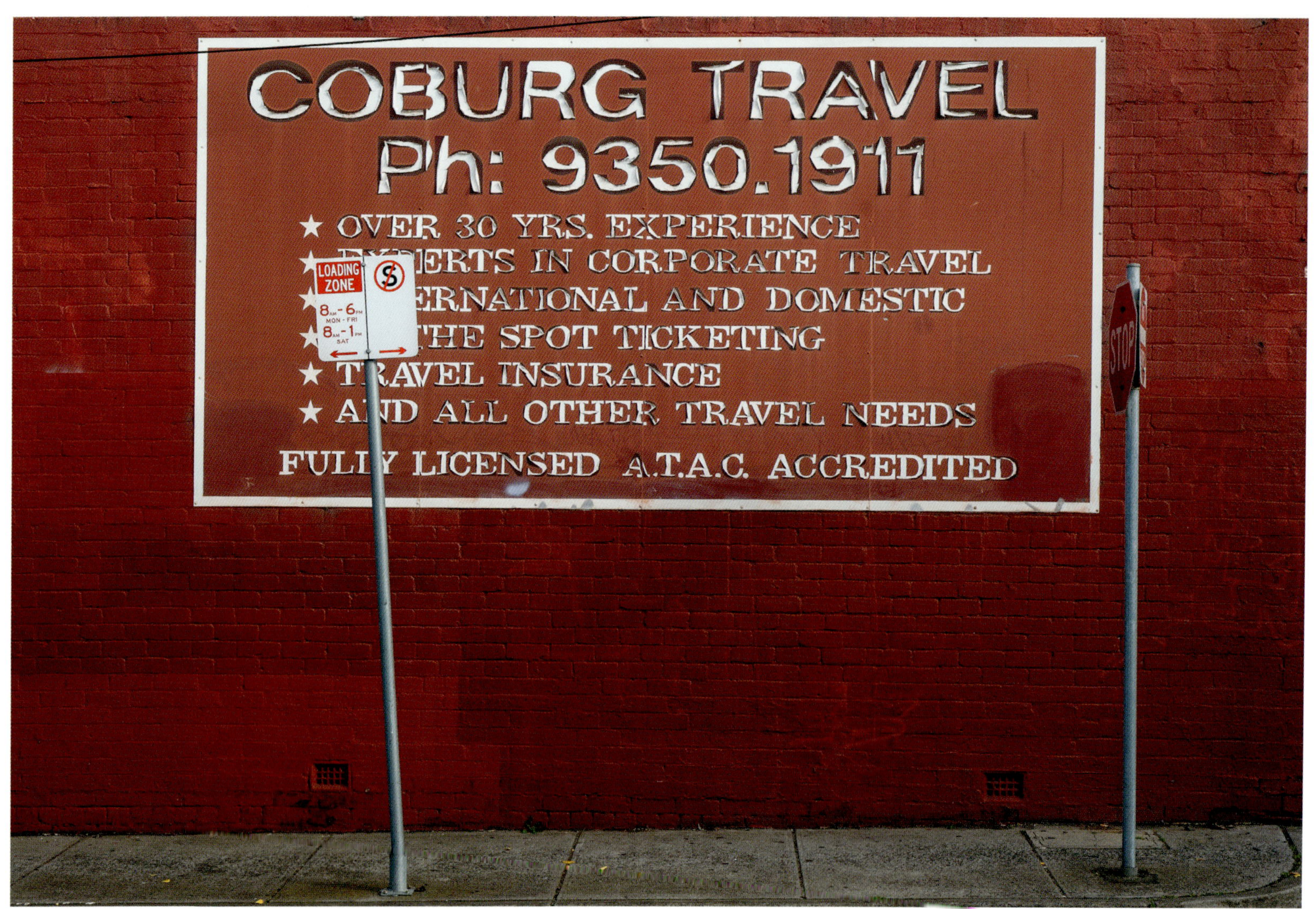
COBURG TRAVEL
Ph: 9350.1911
★ OVER 30 YRS. EXPERIENCE
EXPERTS IN CORPORATE TRAVEL
INTERNATIONAL AND DOMESTIC
ON THE SPOT TICKETING
★ TRAVEL INSURANCE
★ AND ALL OTHER TRAVEL NEEDS
FULLY LICENSED A.T.A.C. ACCREDITED
LOADING ZONE
8AM - 6PM
MON - FRI
8AM - 1PM
SAT
STOP

AUSTRALIAN ARTIFICIAL EYE SERVICES
169
AUSTRALIAN ARTIFICIAL
EYE SERVICES
MR. G. RUSSELL
DENTAL TECHNICIAN
PHONE: 9482 1013
MR. G. RUSSELL
169

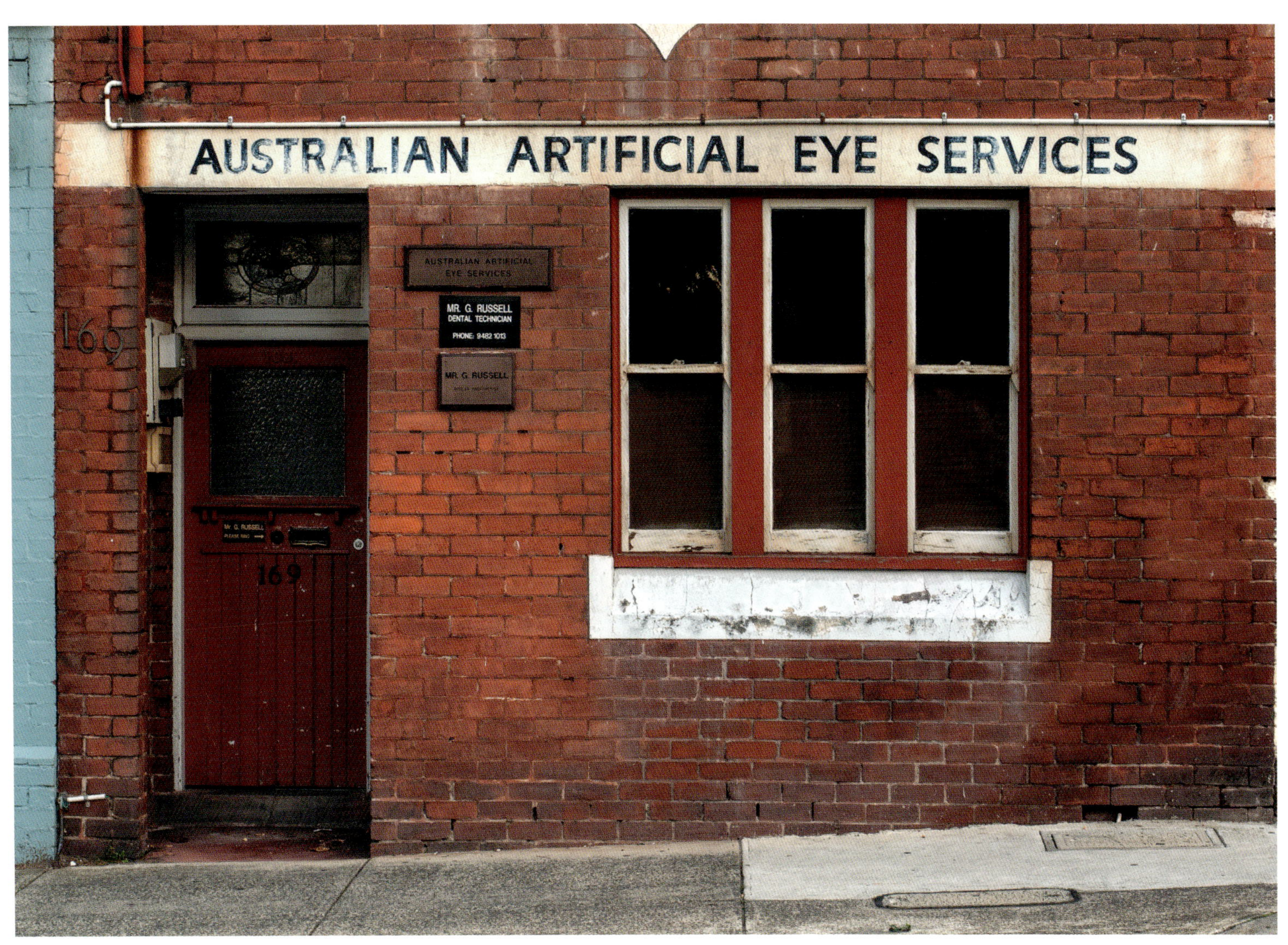

Northcote

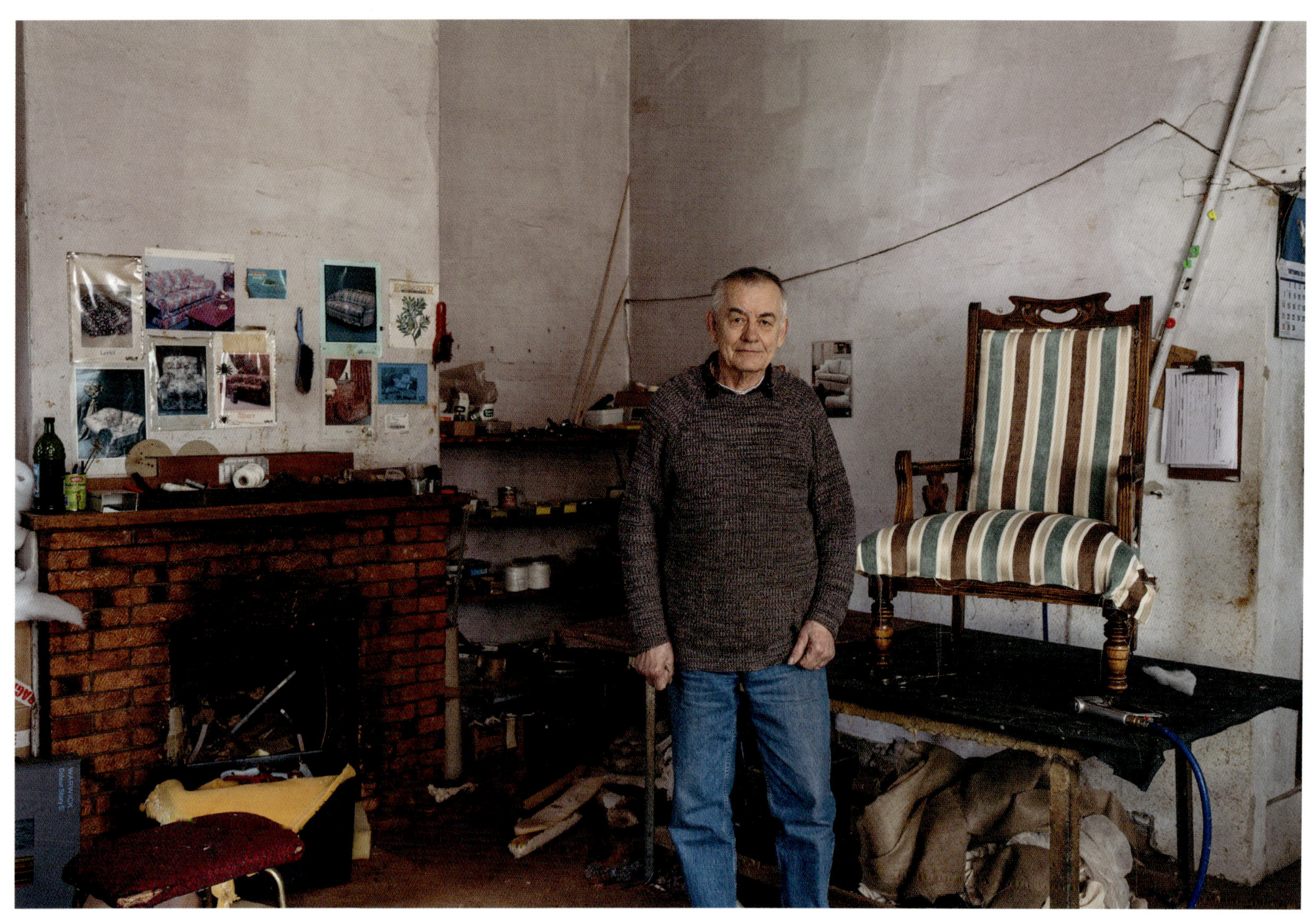

Brunswick East

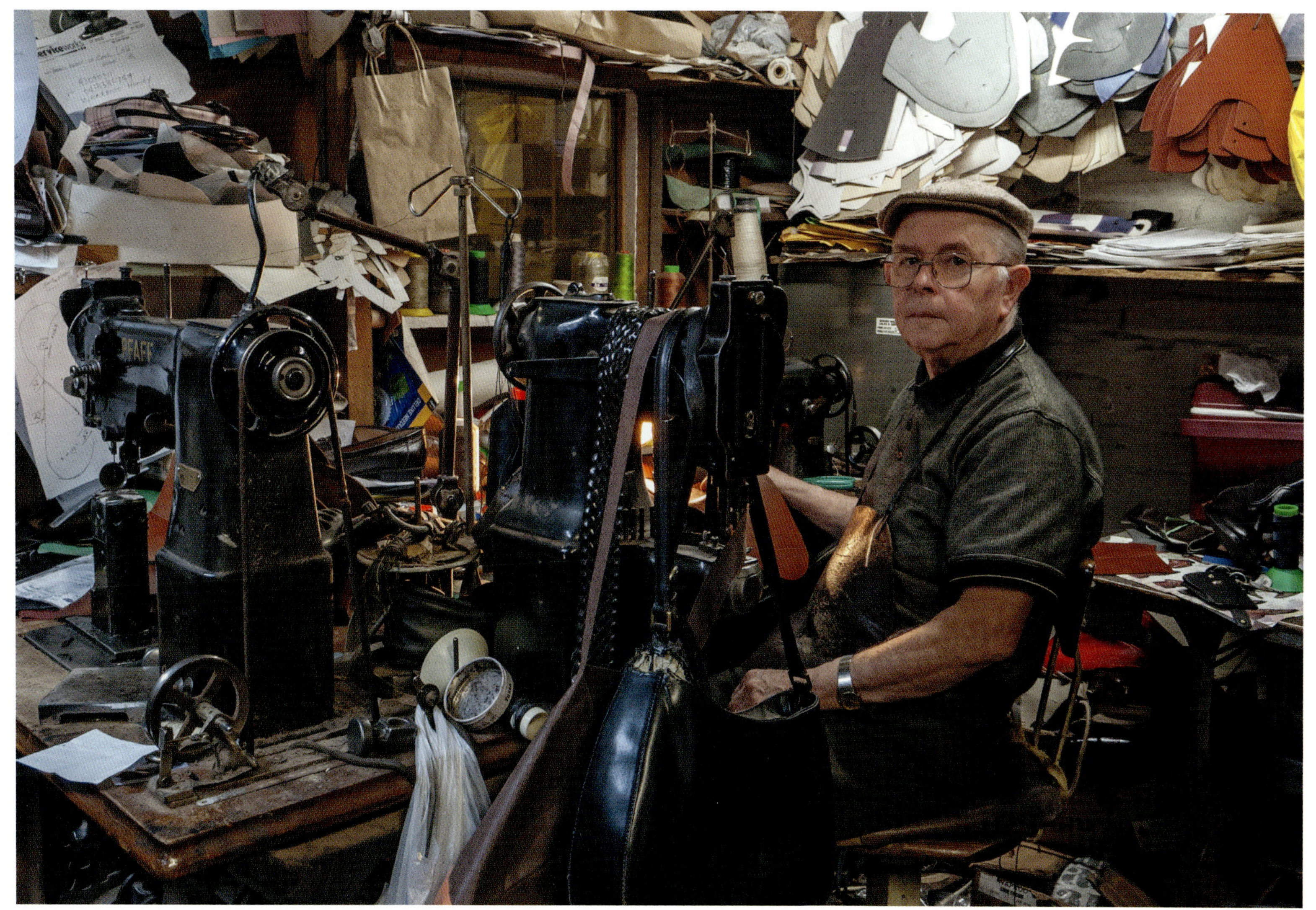

Brunswick East

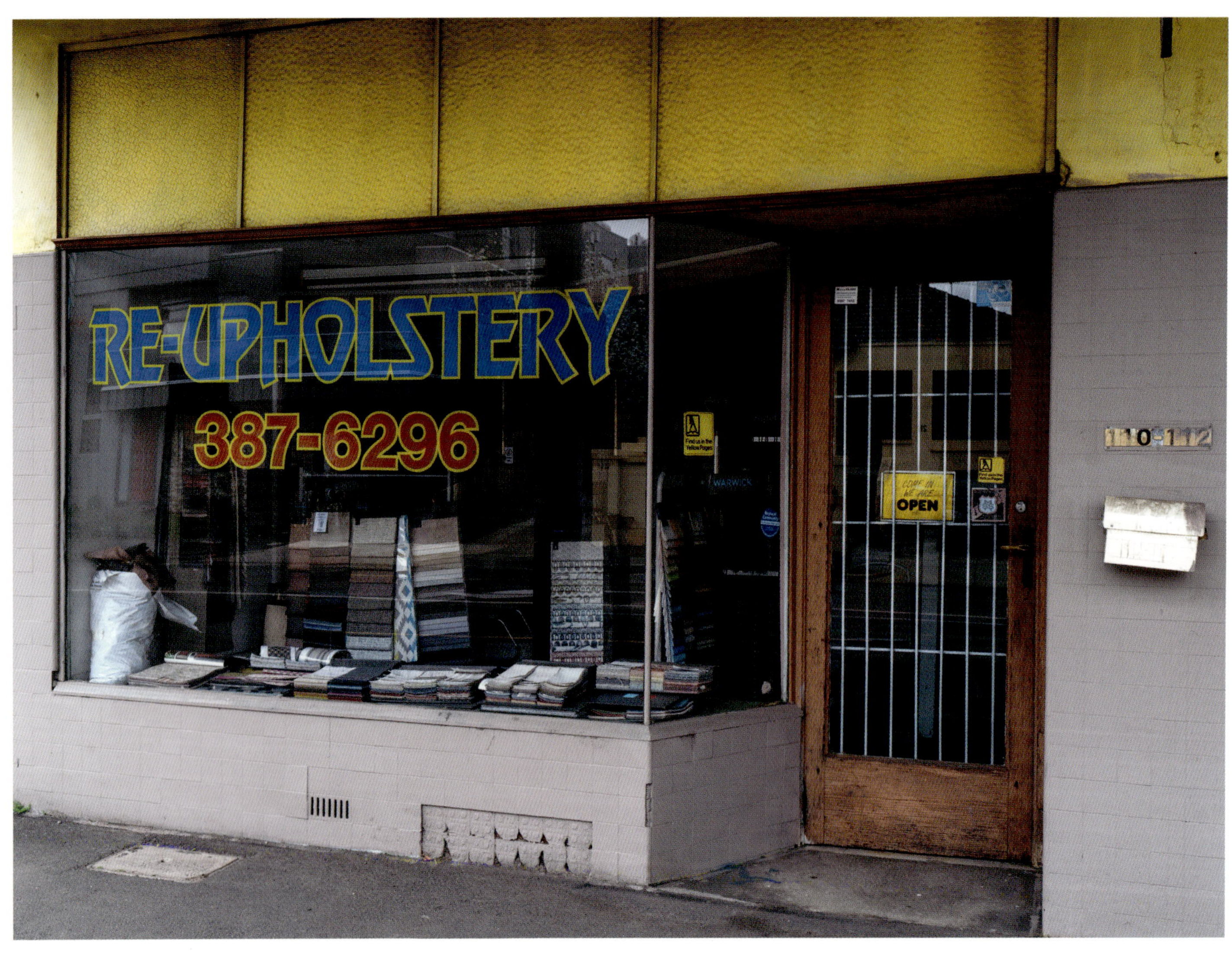

Brunswick East

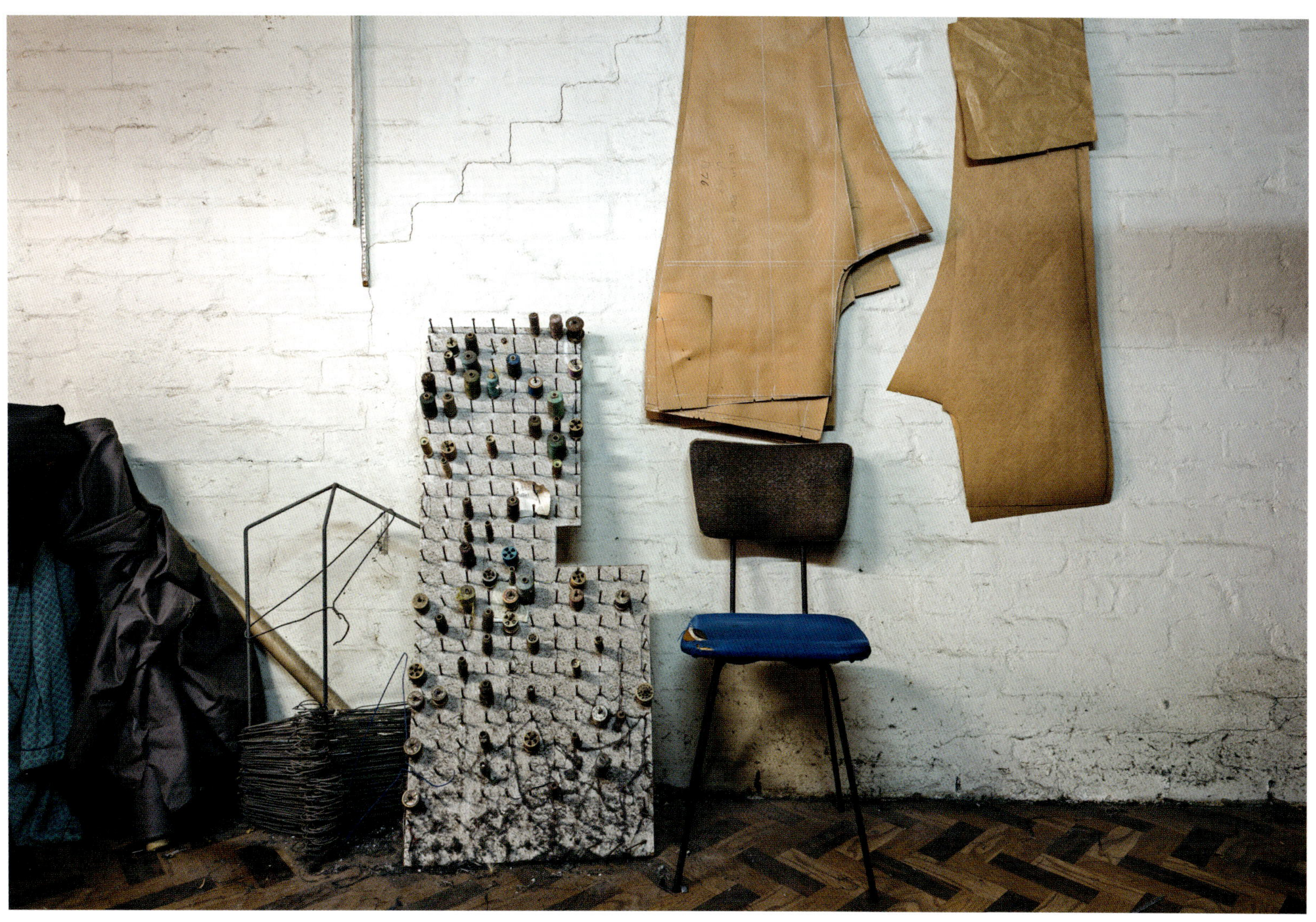

Carlton

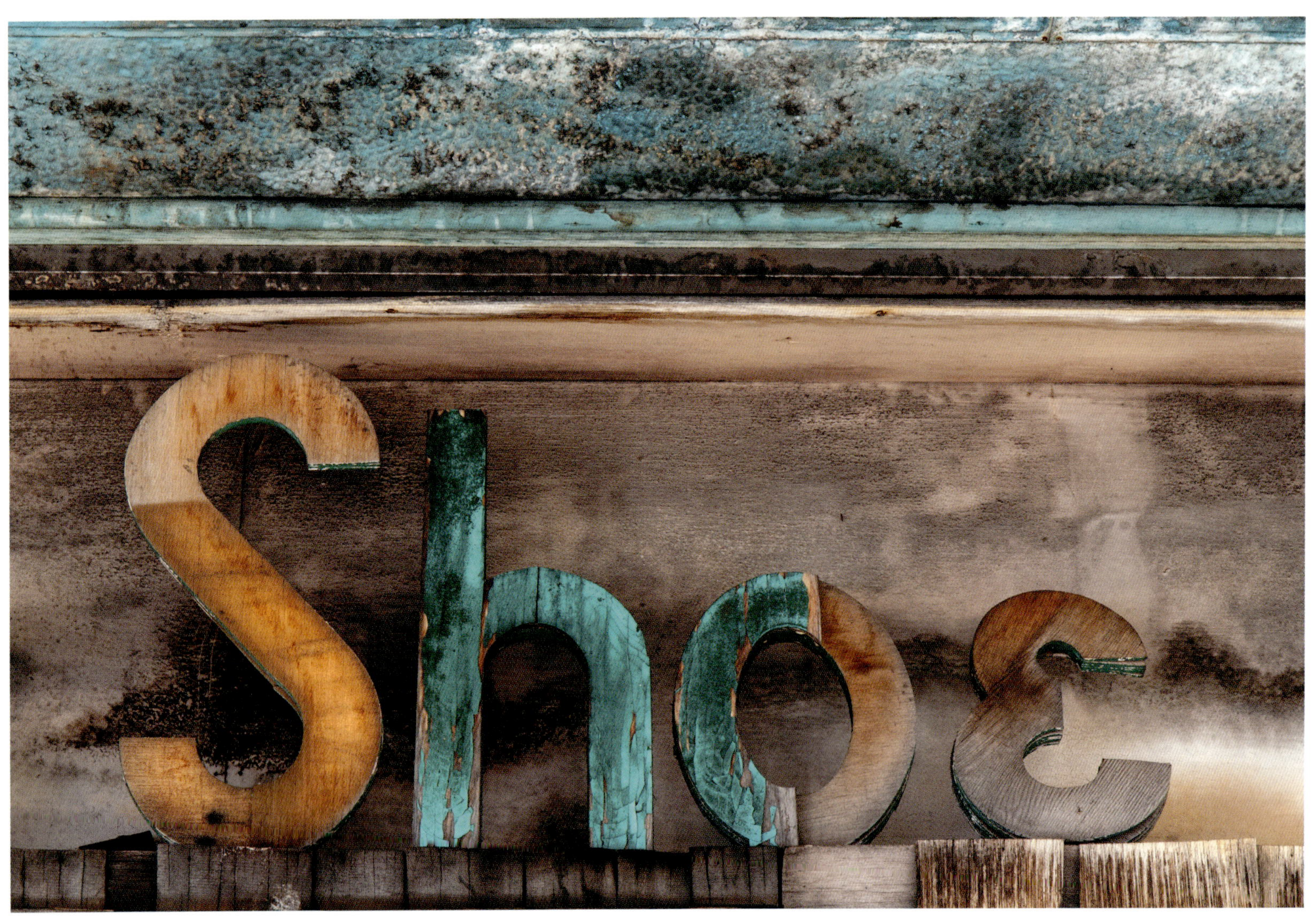
Shoe

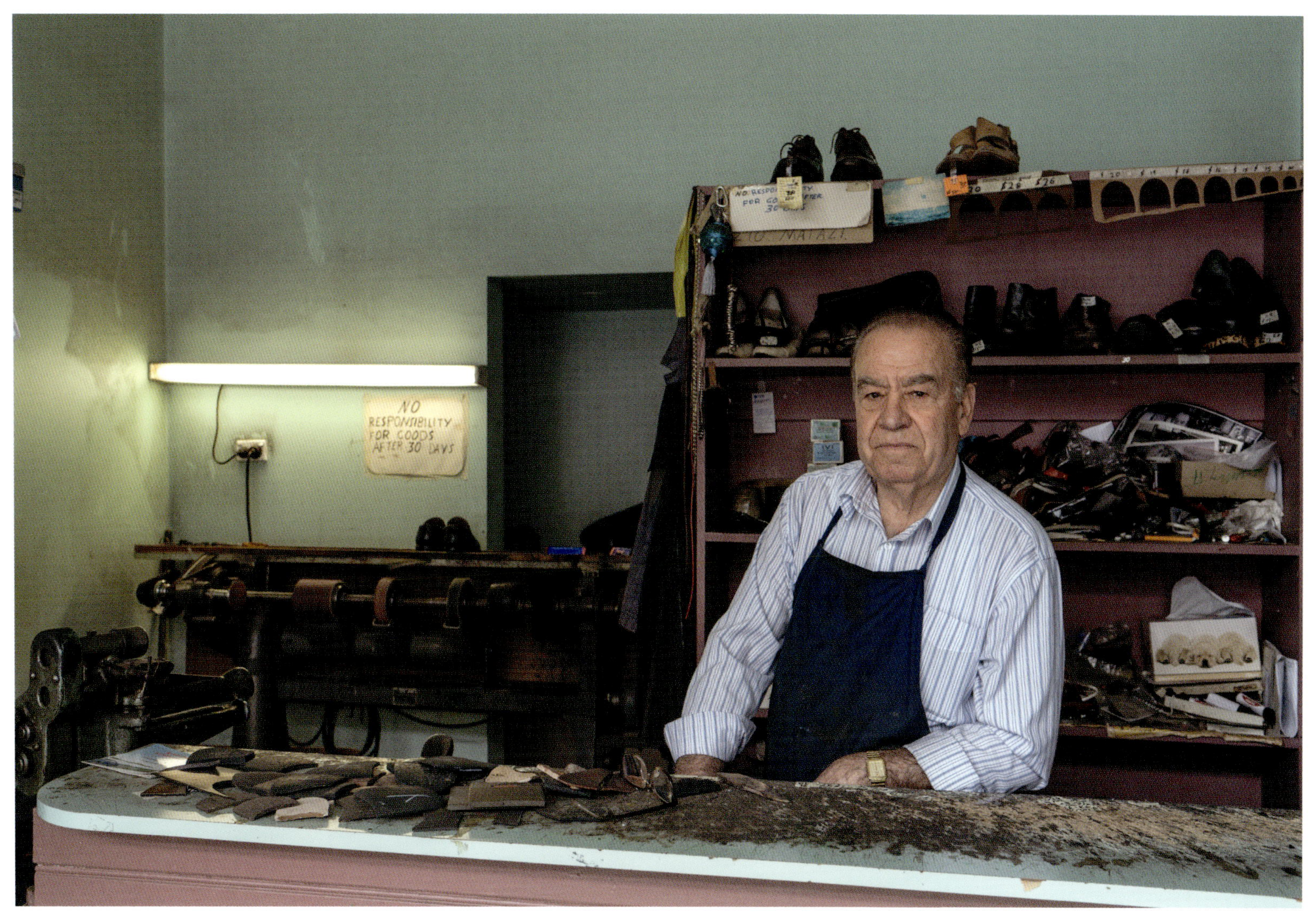

Brunswick

V·M·R·Rossi (CO) P/L.
CANVAS GOODS
TARPOULINS, ANNEXES, BLINDS AND TENTS .....
REPAIR WORK·ALTERATIONS
9460·3932
ah 9434~6779
V·M·R·Rossi (CO) P/L
CANVAS GOODS 166

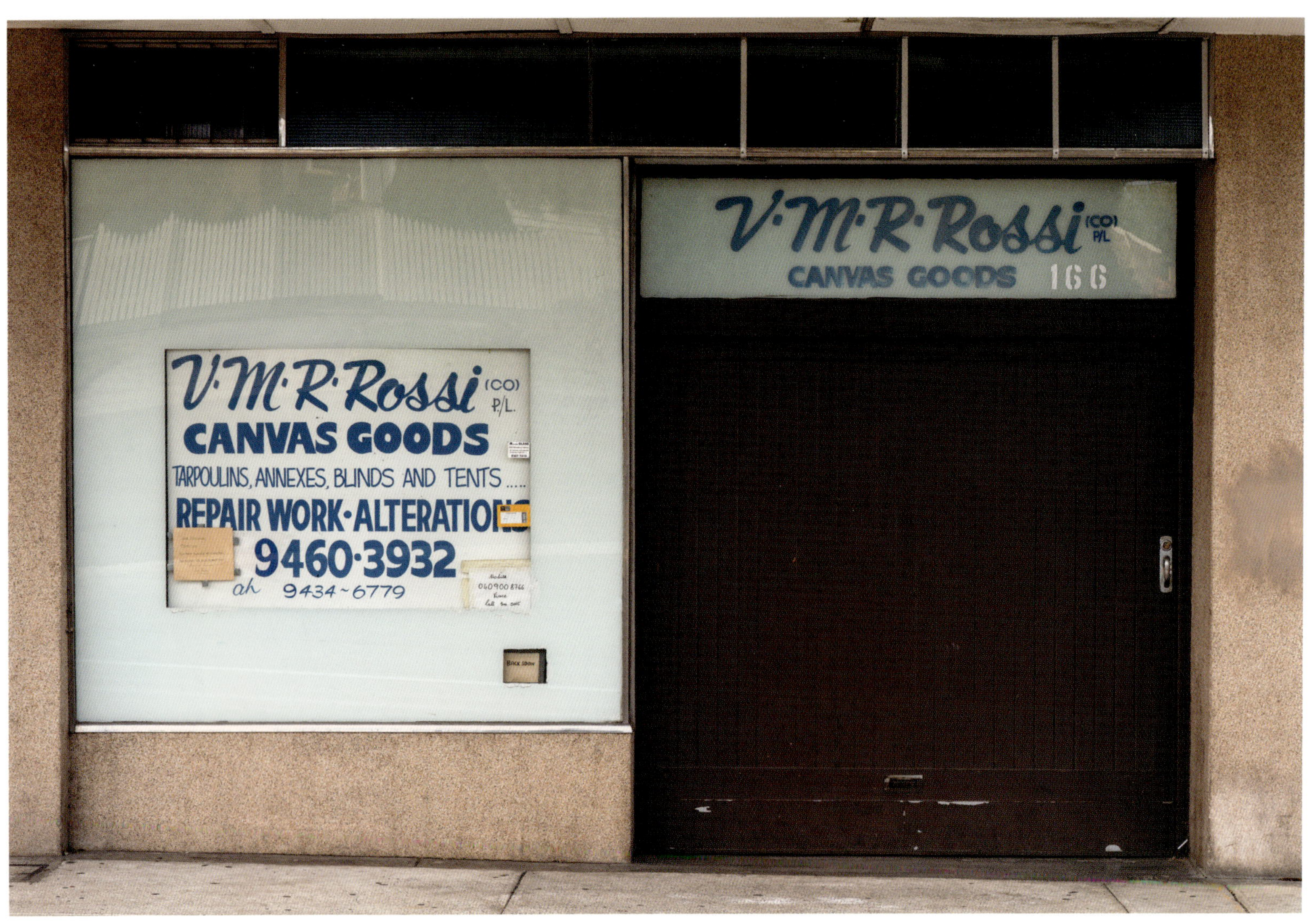

Reservoir

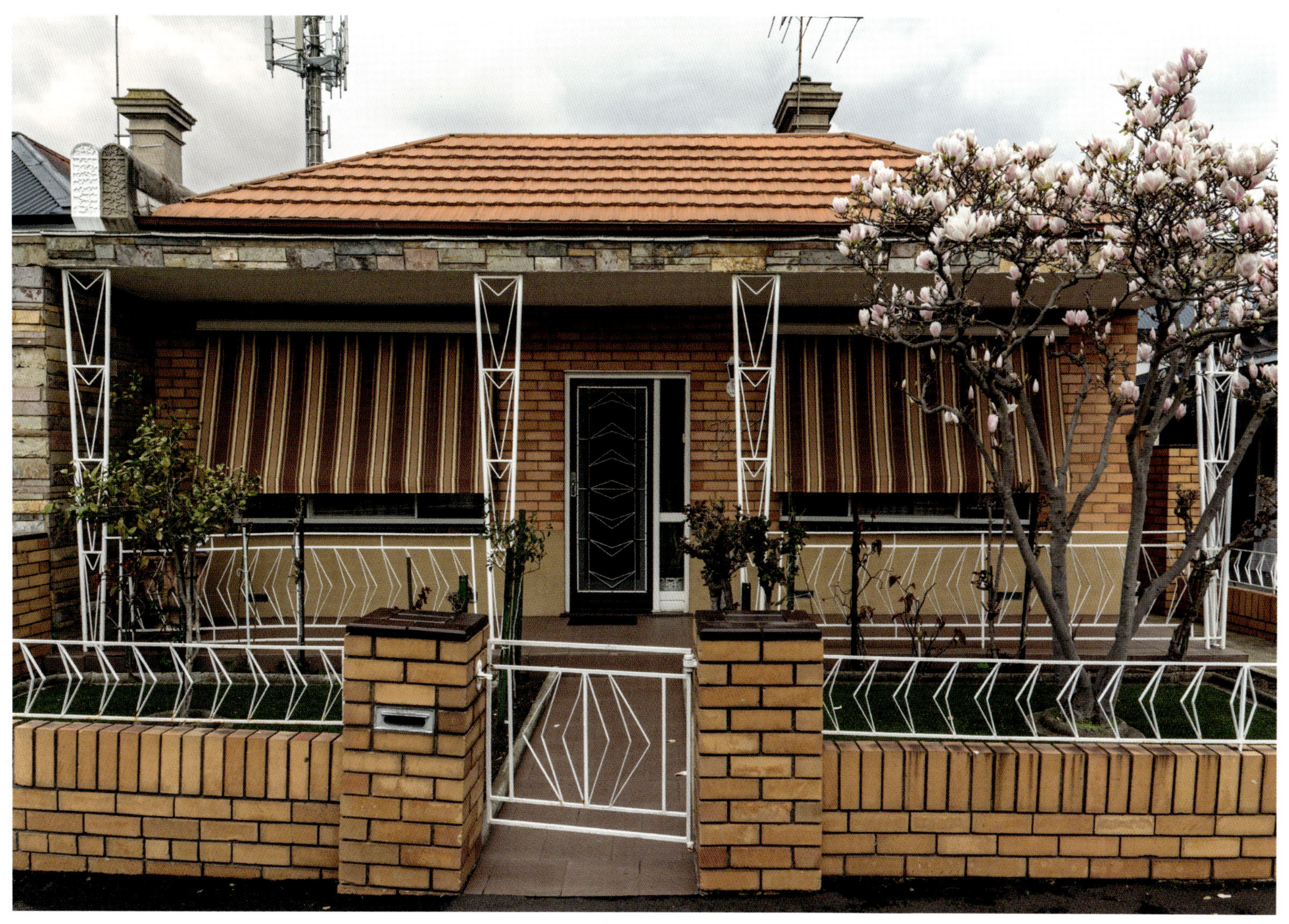

Fitzroy North

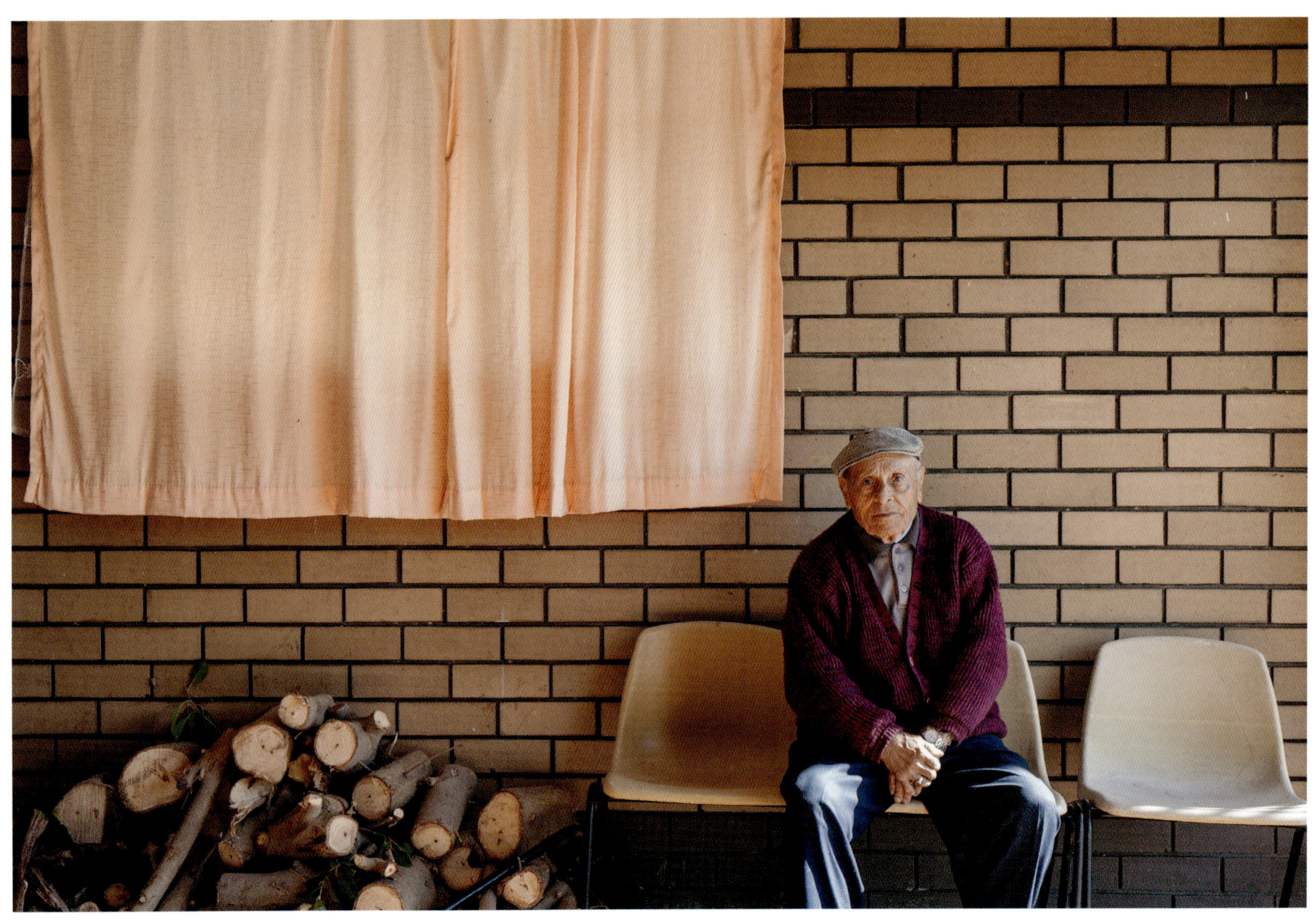

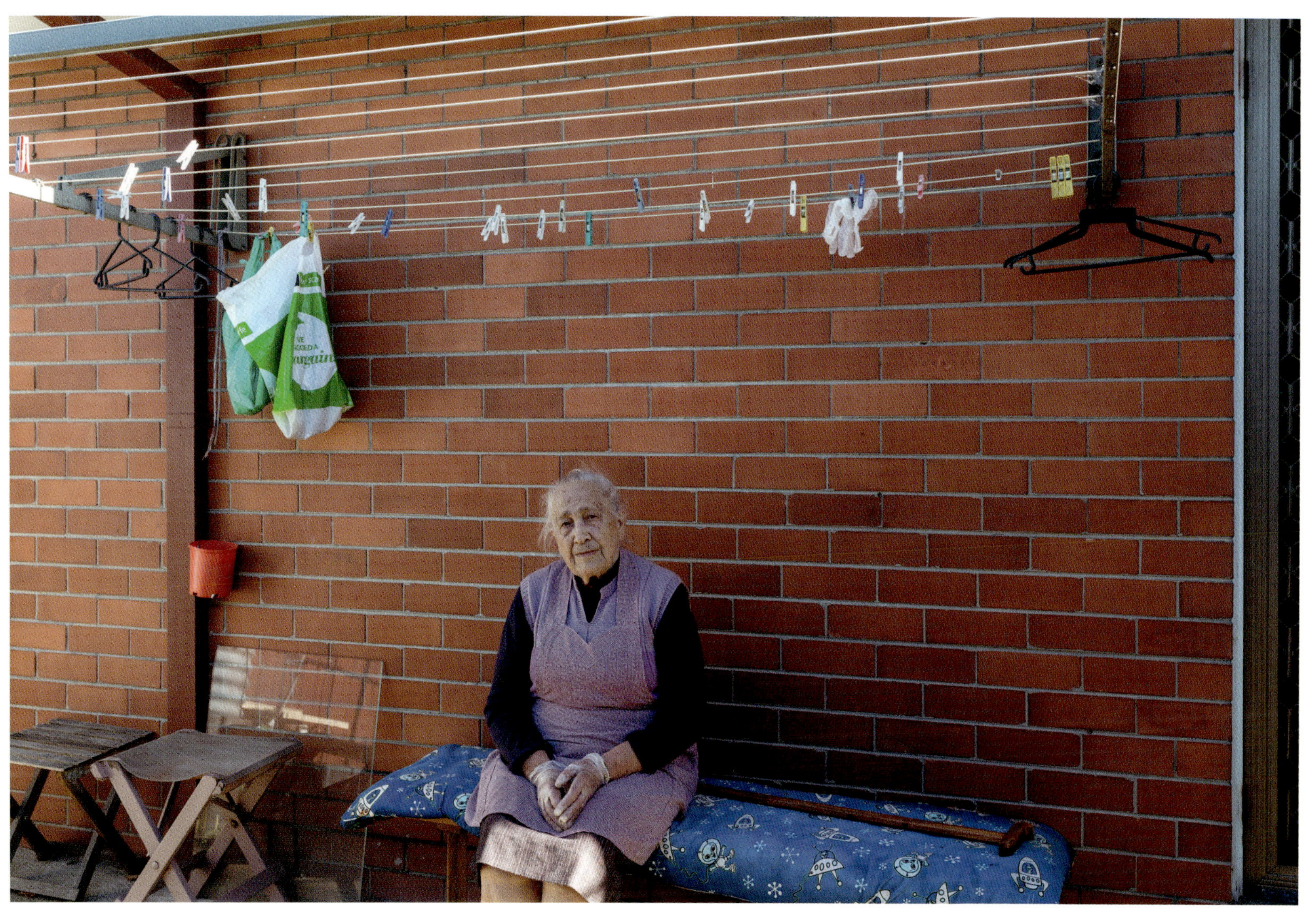

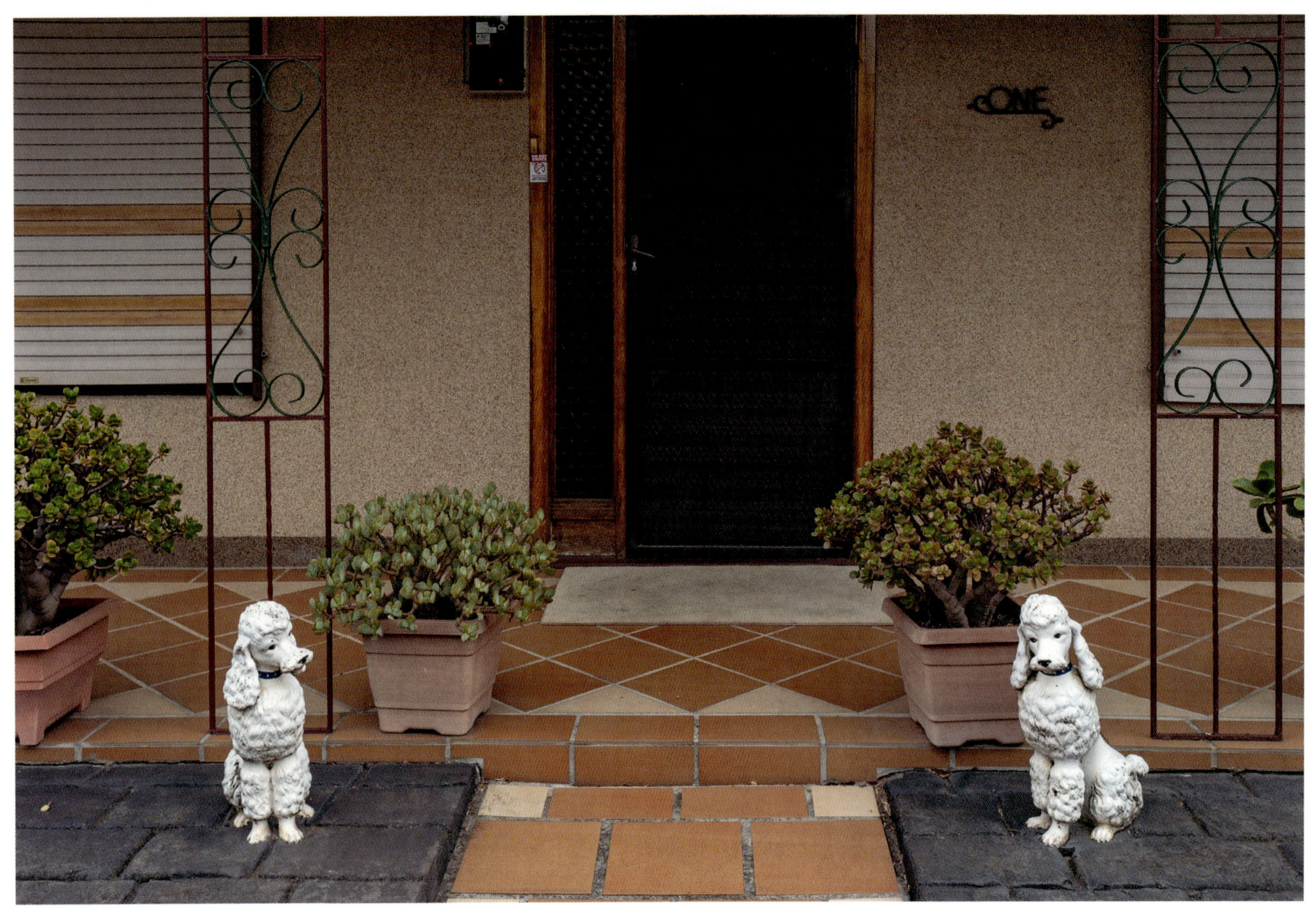

Brunswick

112

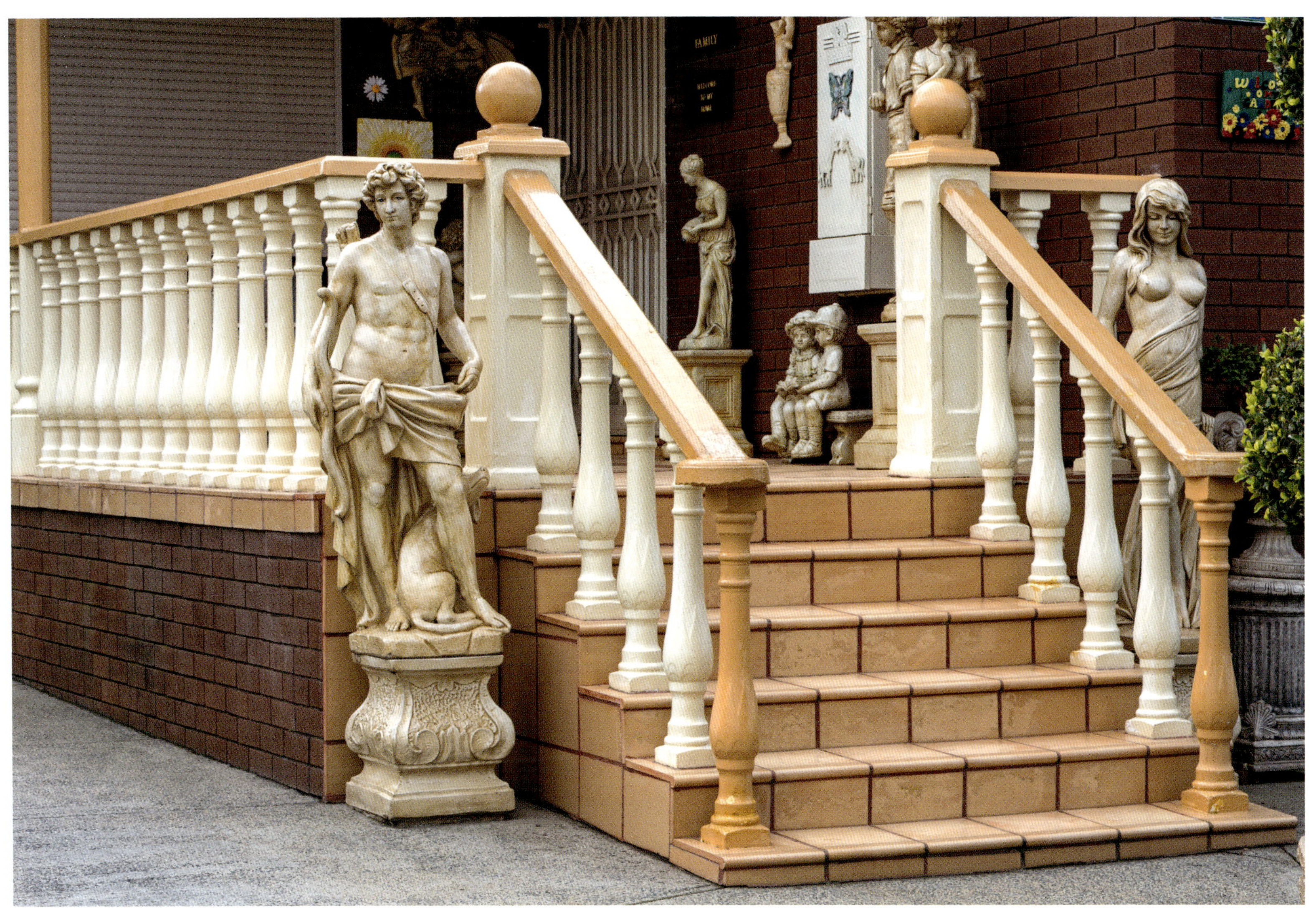

Thomastown

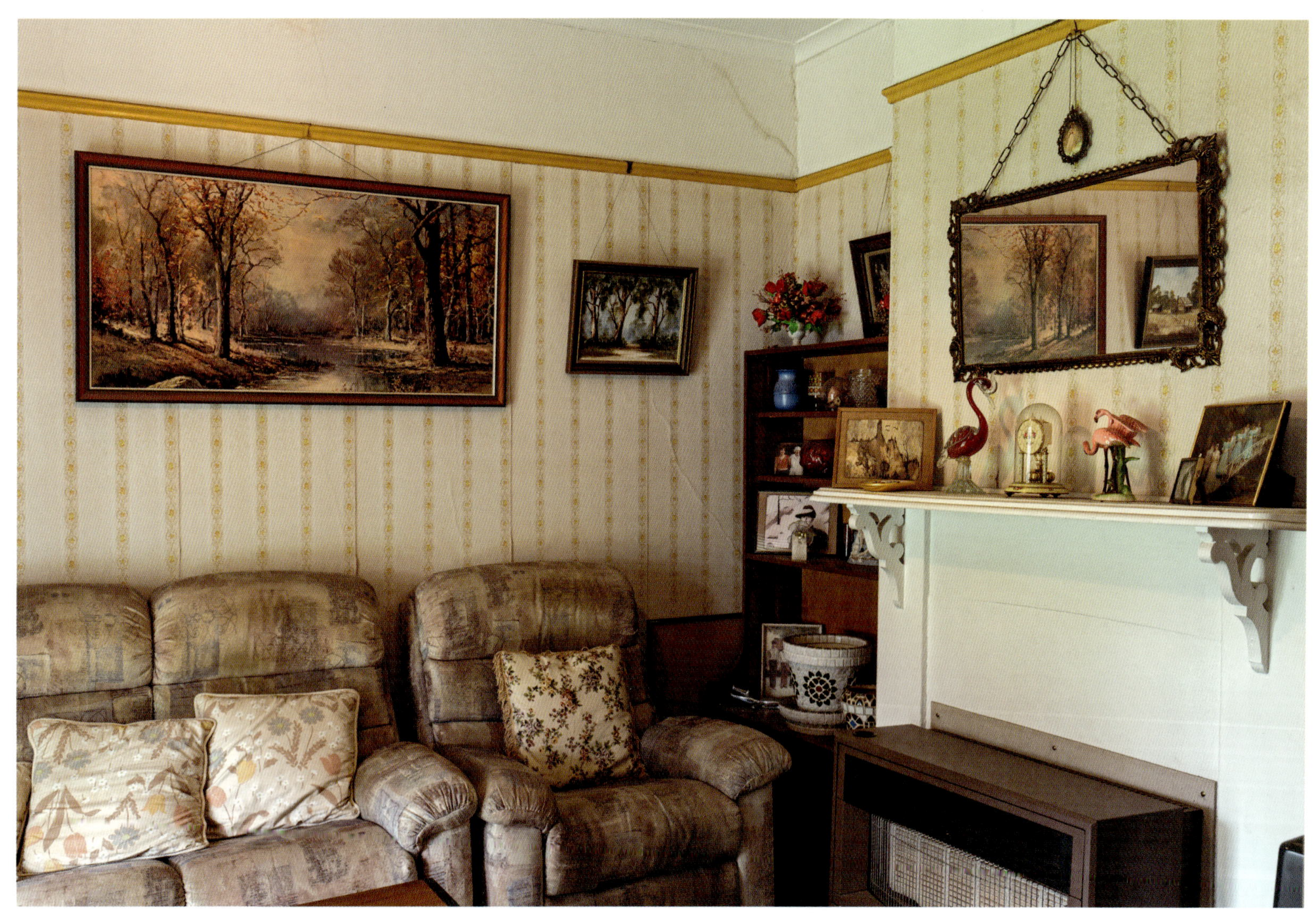

Carlton

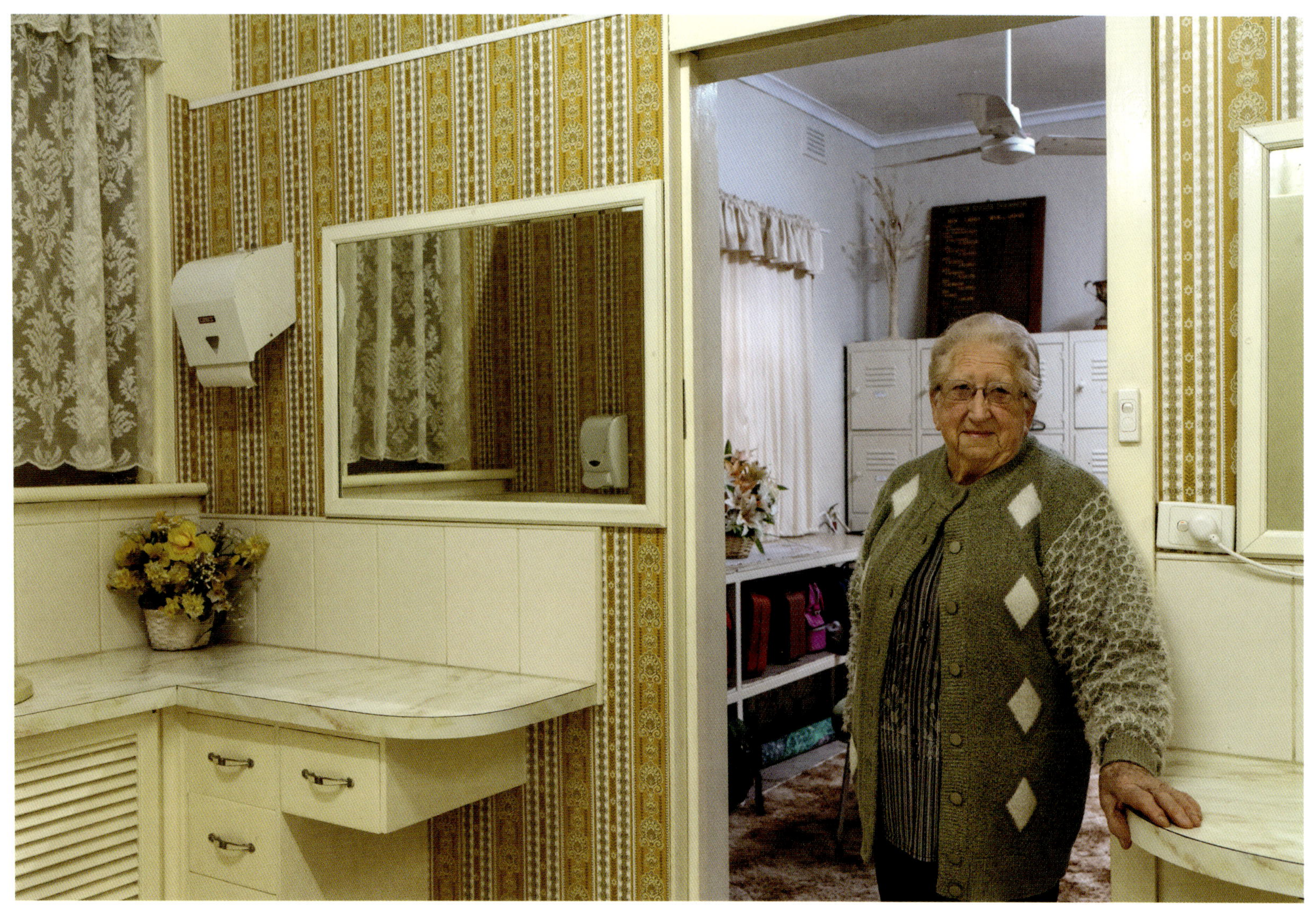

Thornbury

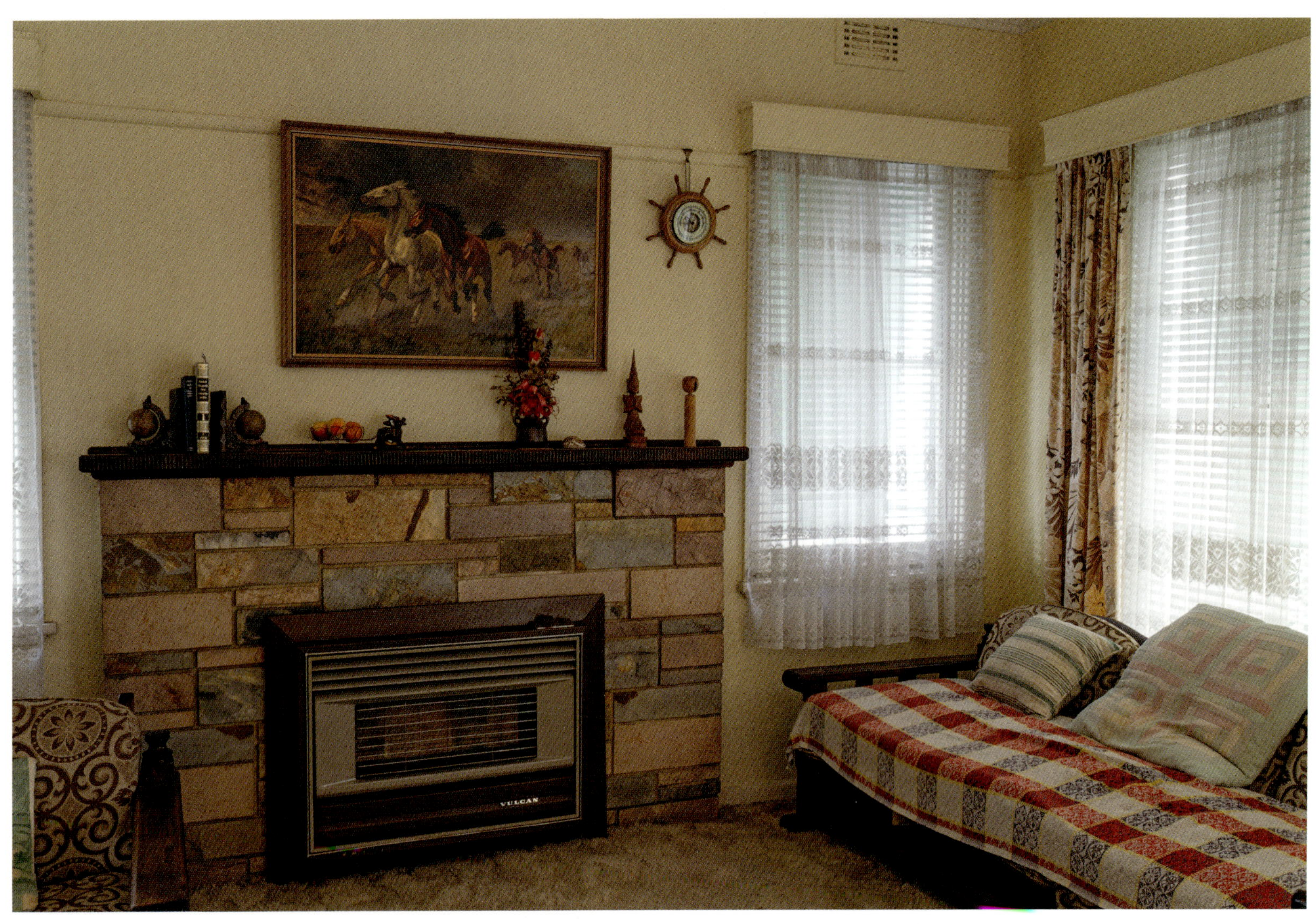

Pascoe Vale South

116

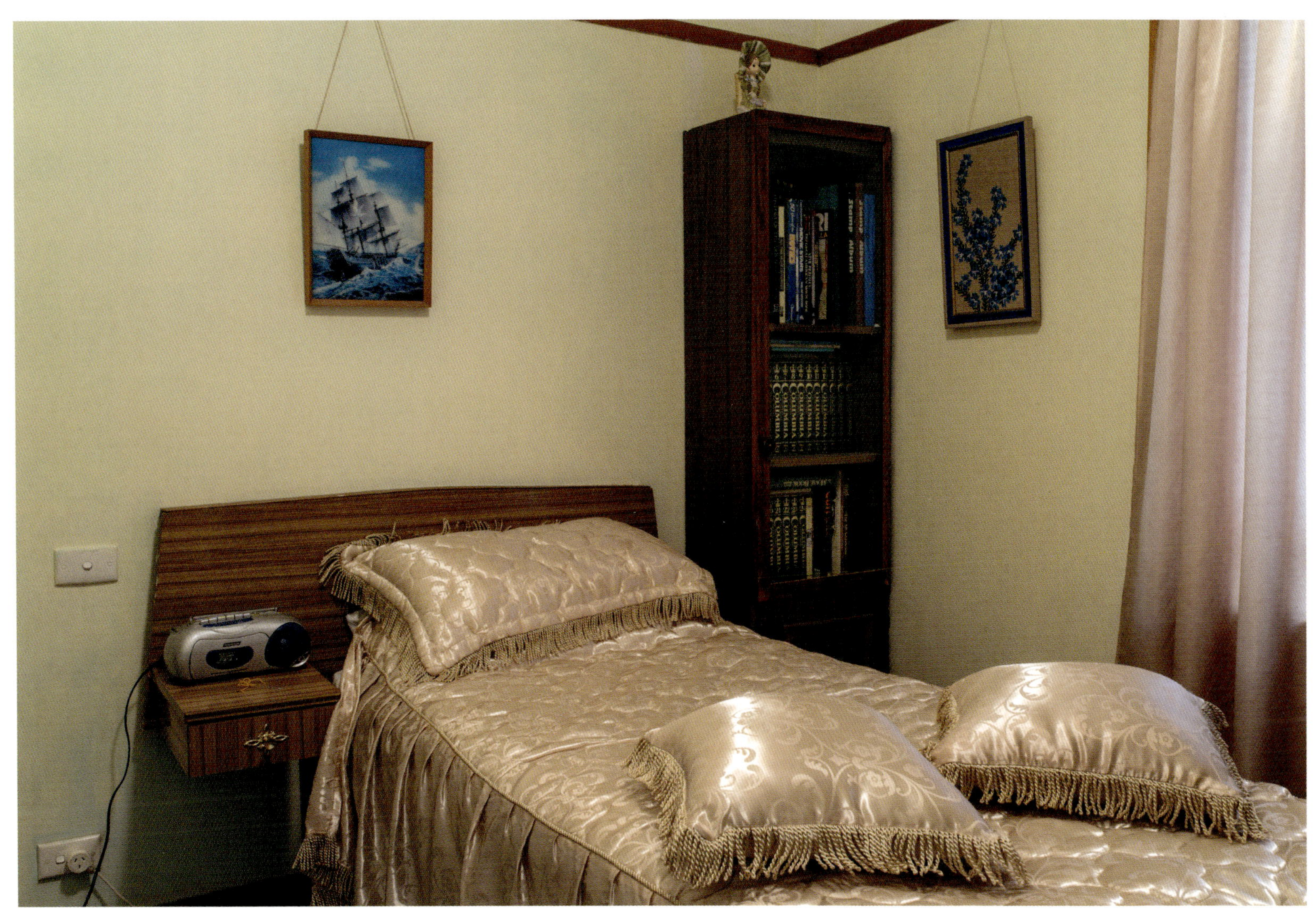

117

Preston

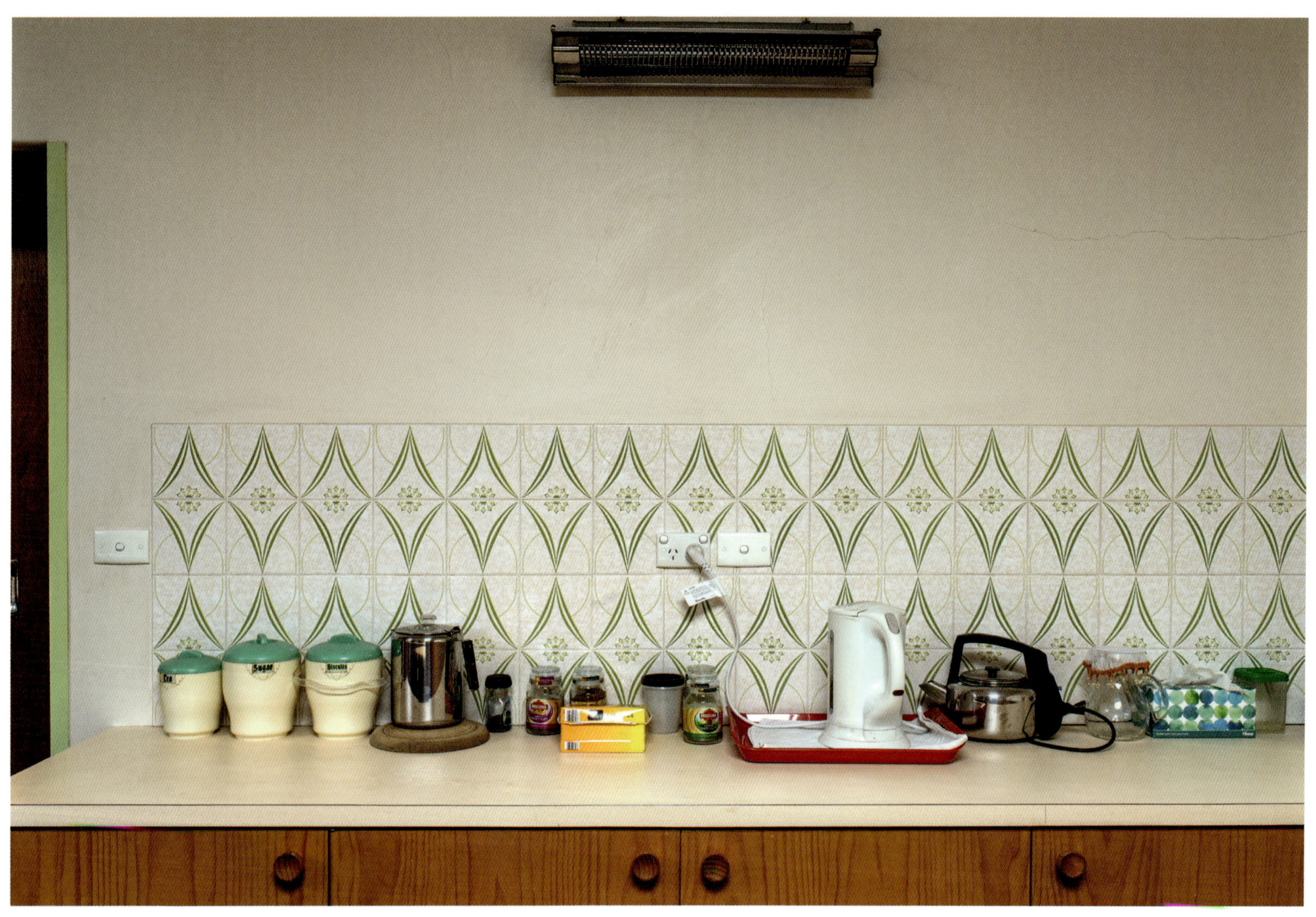

Fitzroy

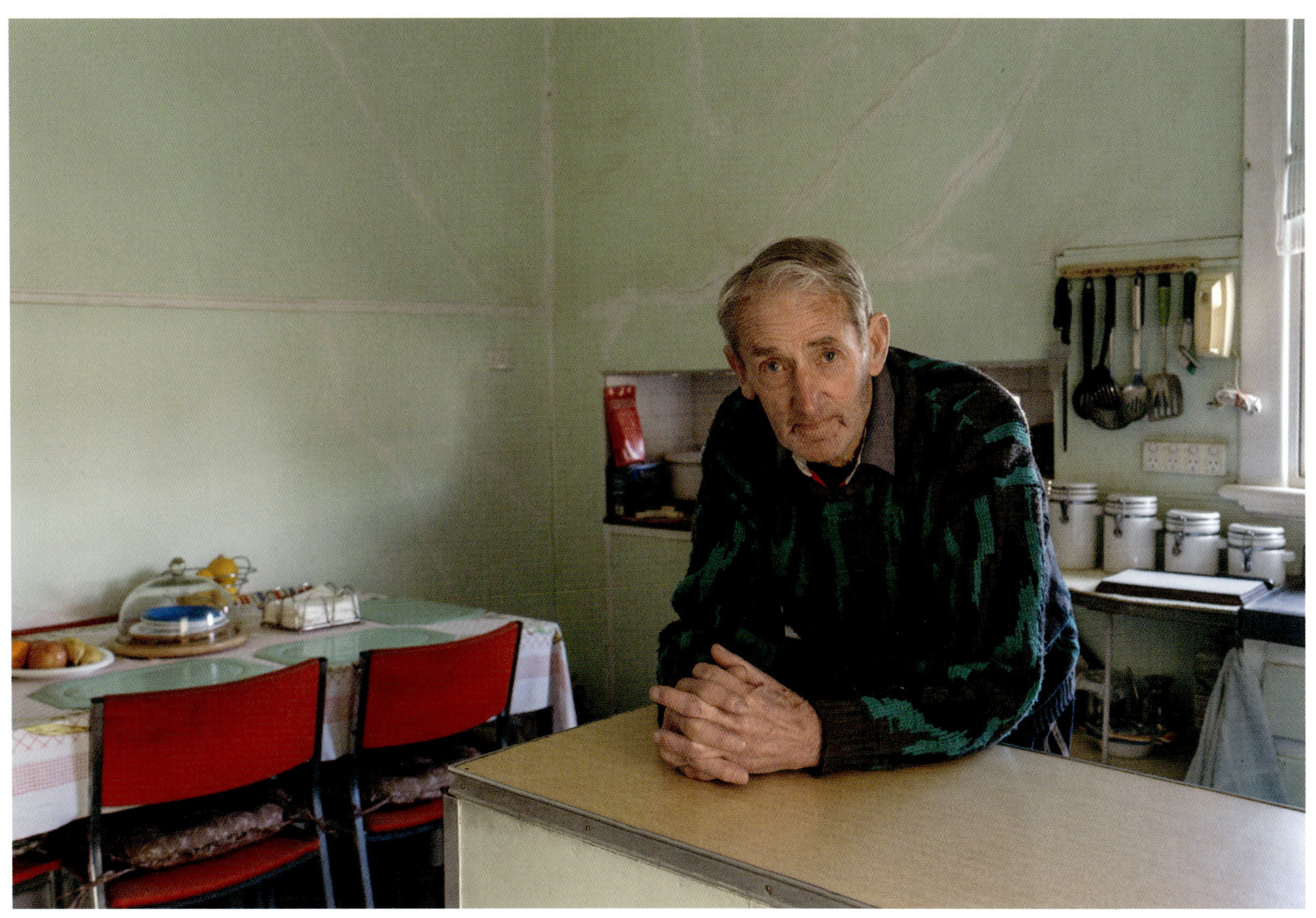

Preston

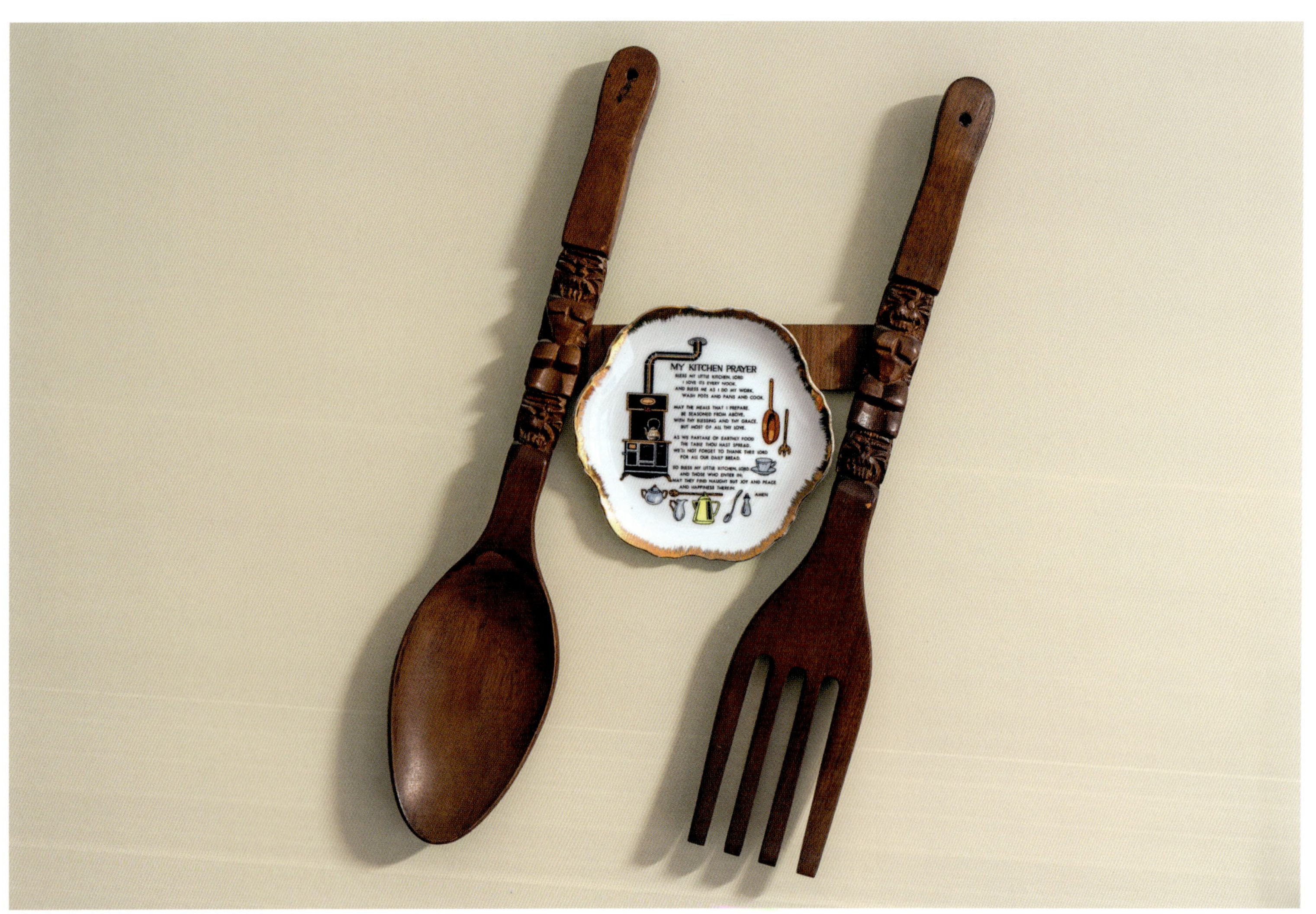

MY KITCHEN PRAYER
BLESS MY LITTLE KITCHEN, LORD
I LOVE ITS EVERY NOOK,
AND BLESS ME AS I DO MY WORK,
WASH POTS AND PANS AND COOK.

MAY THE MEALS THAT I PREPARE,
BE SEASONED FROM ABOVE,
WITH THY BLESSING AND THY GRACE,
BUT MOST OF ALL THY LOVE.

AS WE PARTAKE OF EARTHLY FOOD
THE TABLE THOU HAST SPREAD,
WE'LL NOT FORGET TO THANK THEE, LORD
FOR ALL OUR DAILY BREAD.

SO BLESS MY LITTLE KITCHEN, LORD
AND THOSE WHO ENTER IN;
MAY THEY FIND NAUGHT BUT JOY AND PEACE
AND HAPPINESS THEREIN.
AMEN

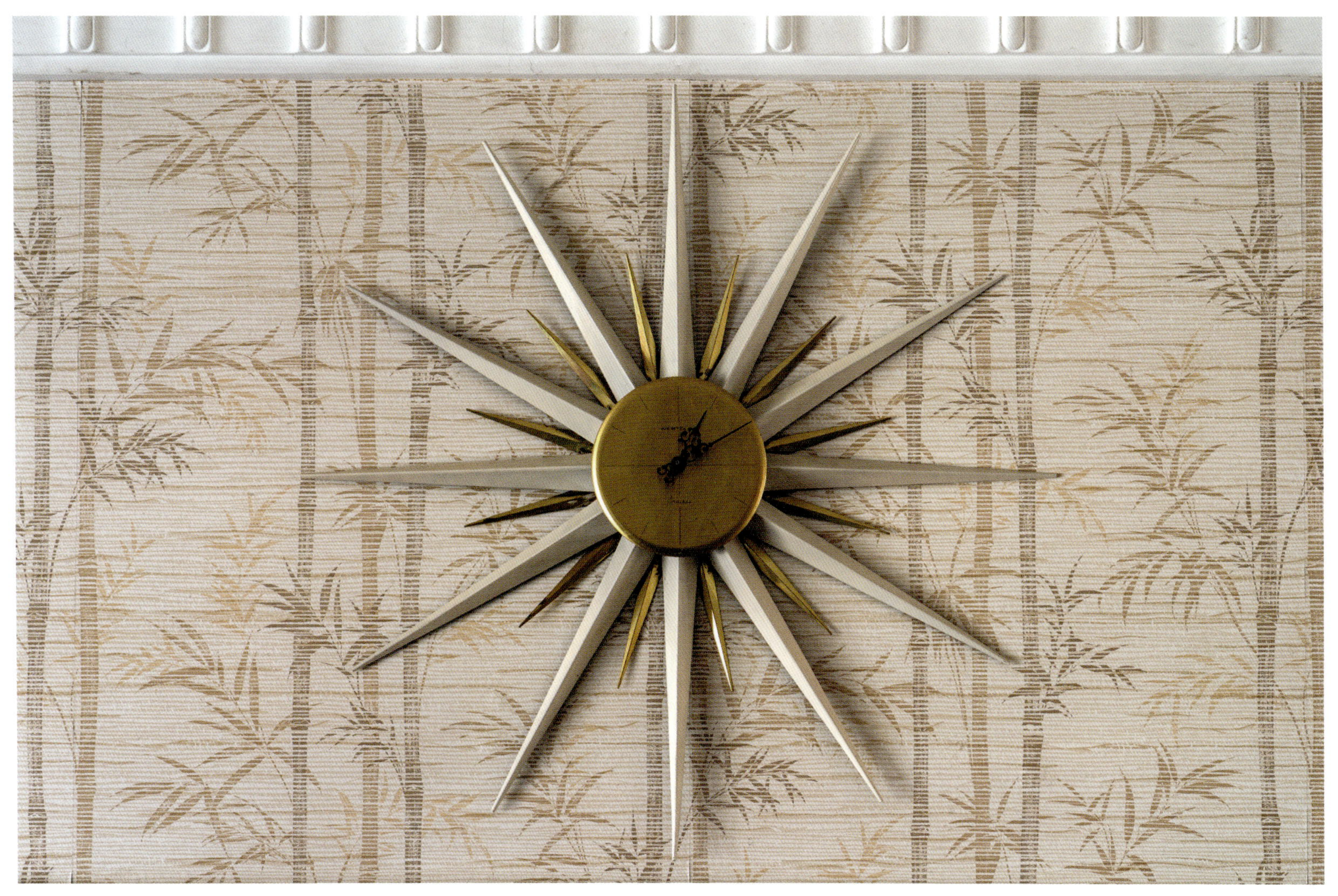

Preston

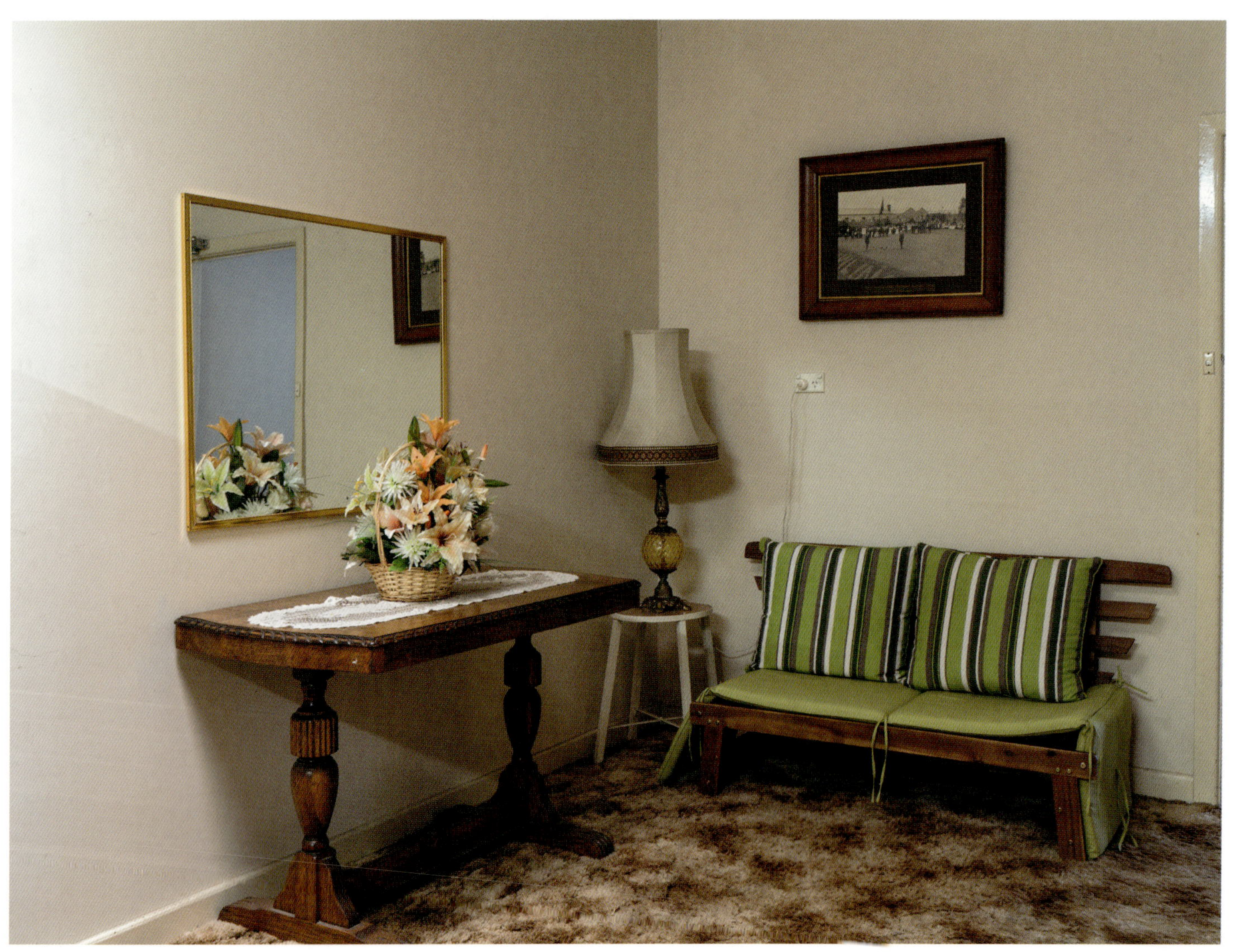

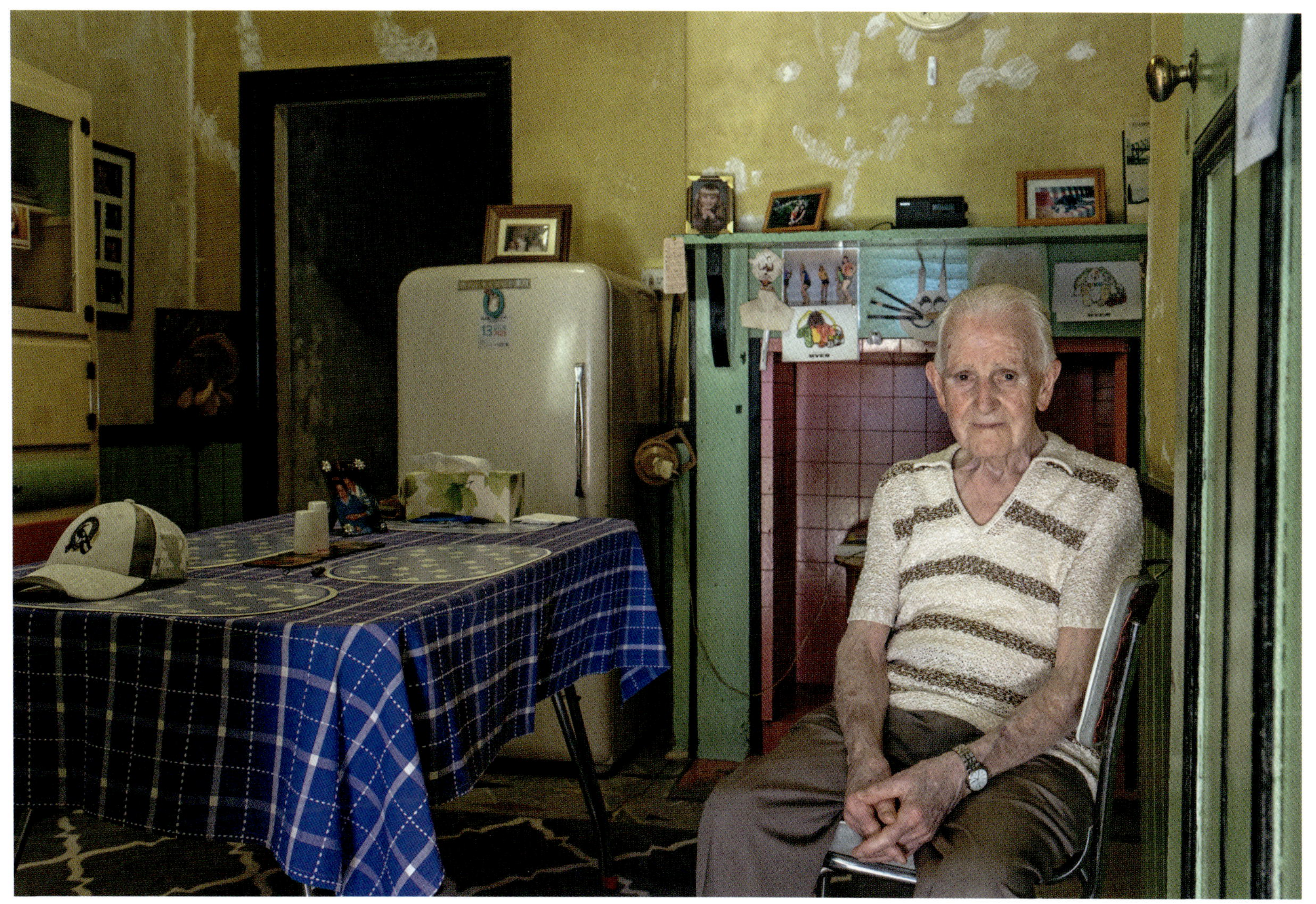

Collingwood

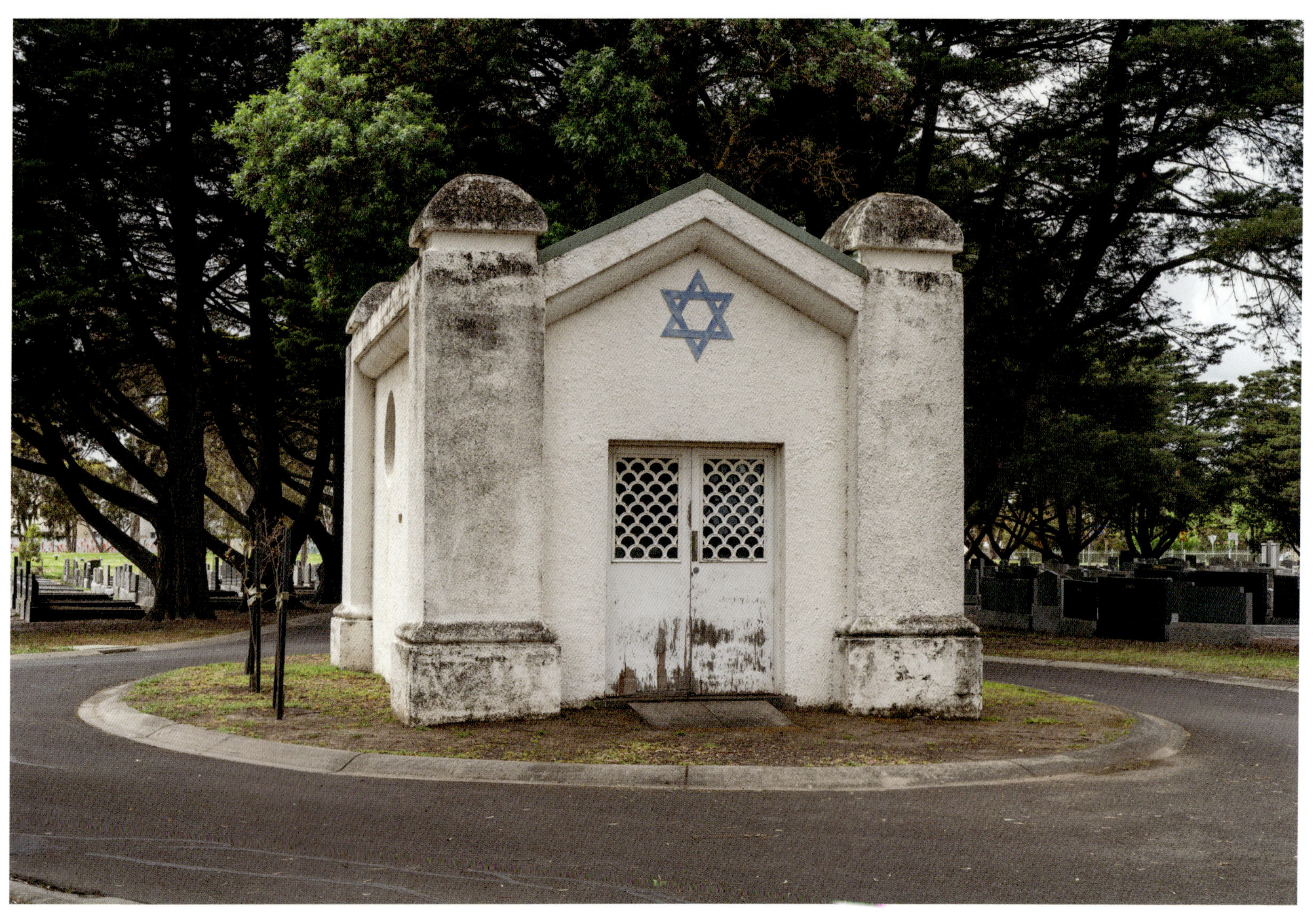

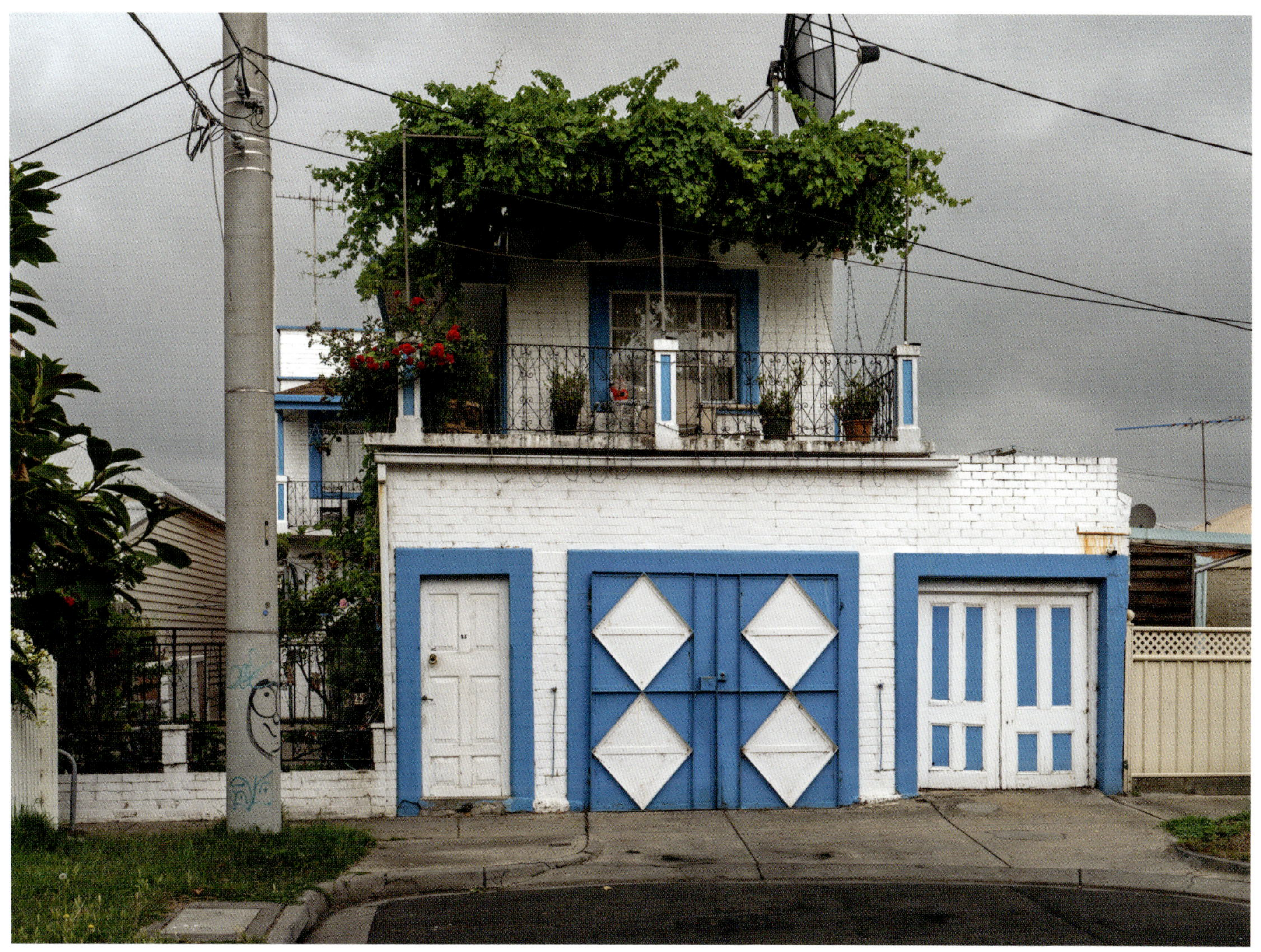

Brunswick

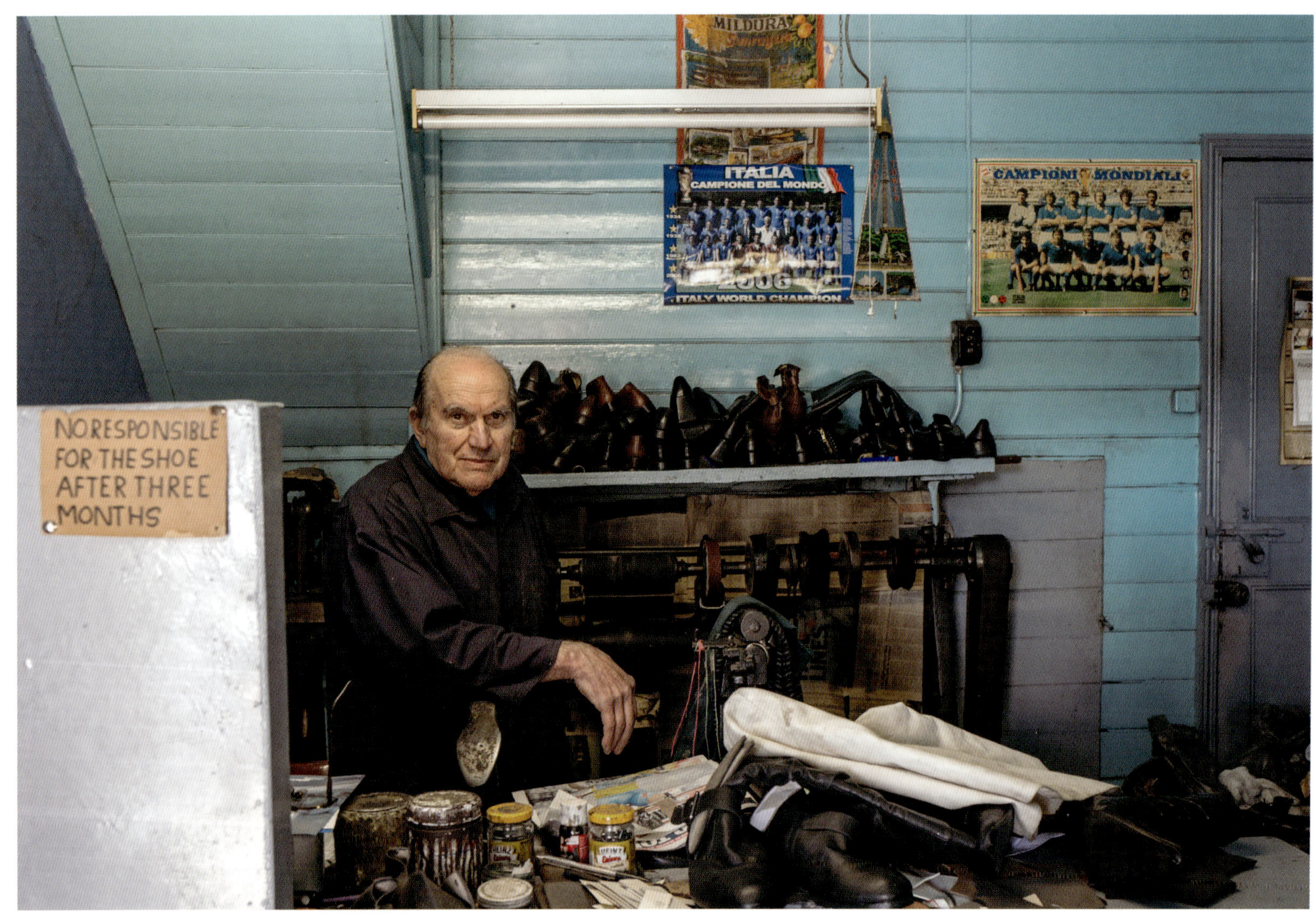

NO RESPONSIBLE
FOR THE SHOE
AFTER THREE
MONTHS
ITALIA
CAMPIONE DEL MONDO
ITALY WORLD CHAMPION
CAMPIONI MONDIALI
MILDURA

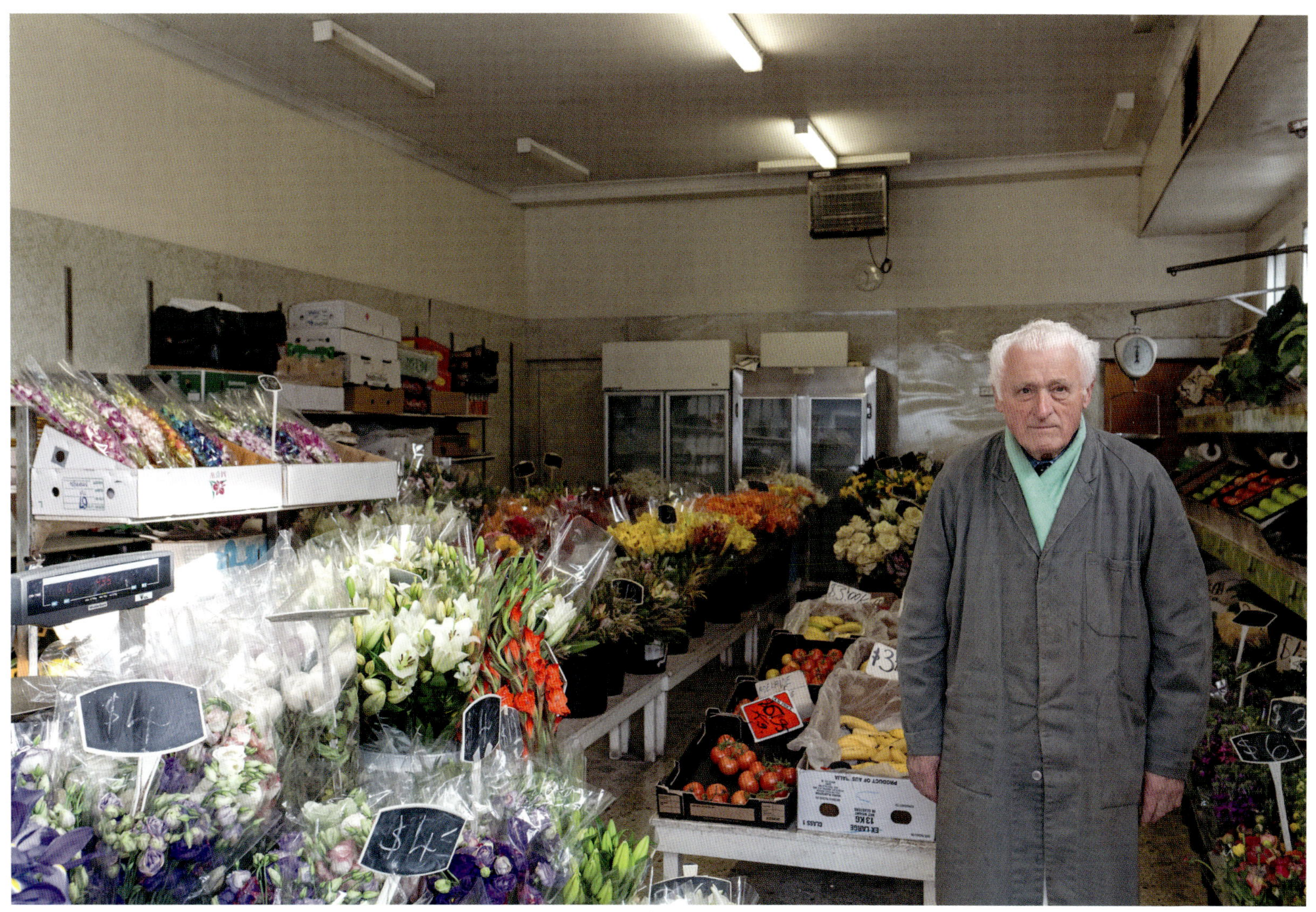

Northcote

249
AUTO ELECTRICIAN
LUCAS
TRADING HOURS
Mon-Fri 8-3.30
249
HELLA
VACC
MOSS
SECURITY
AUTHORISED DEALER

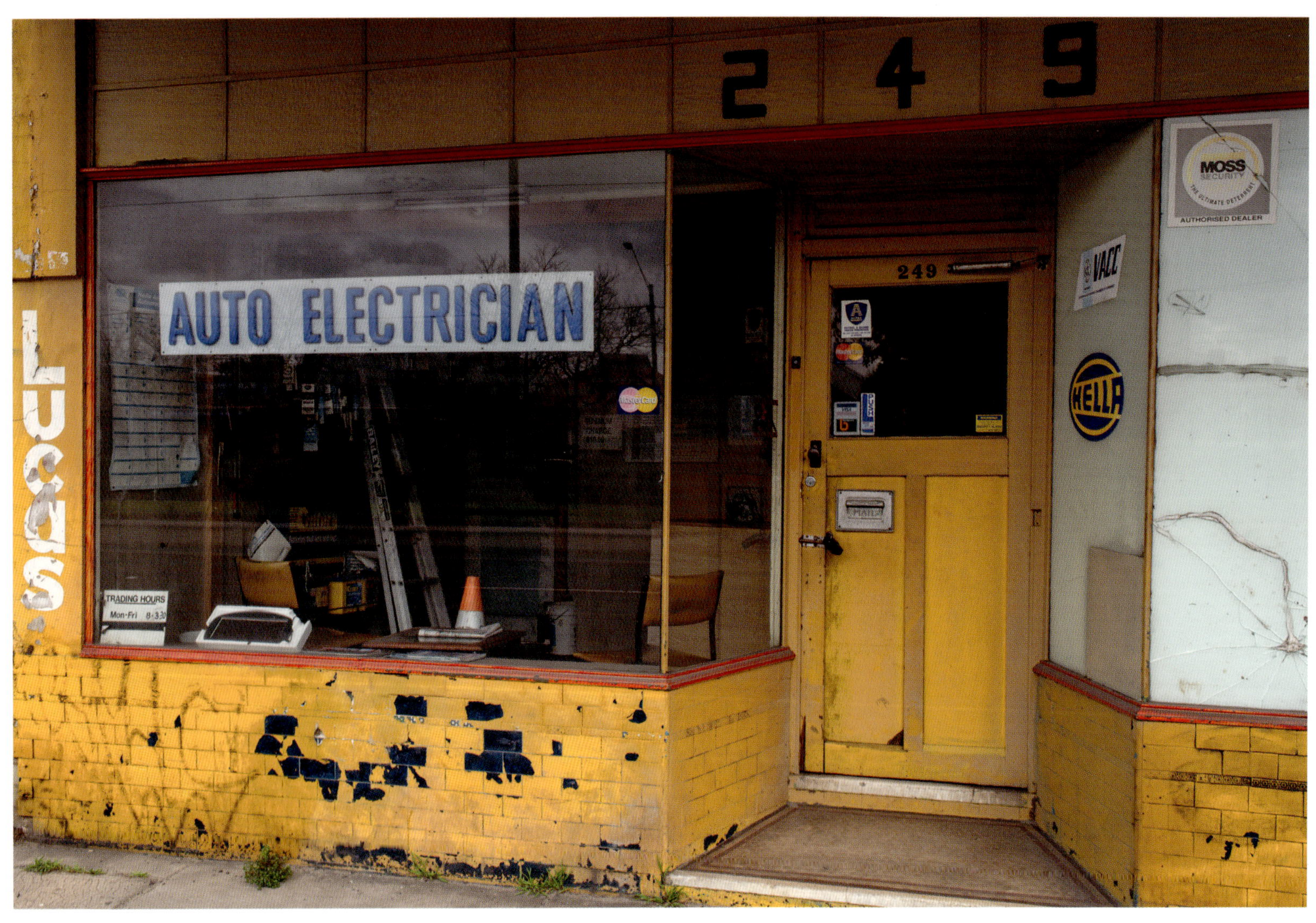

Northcote

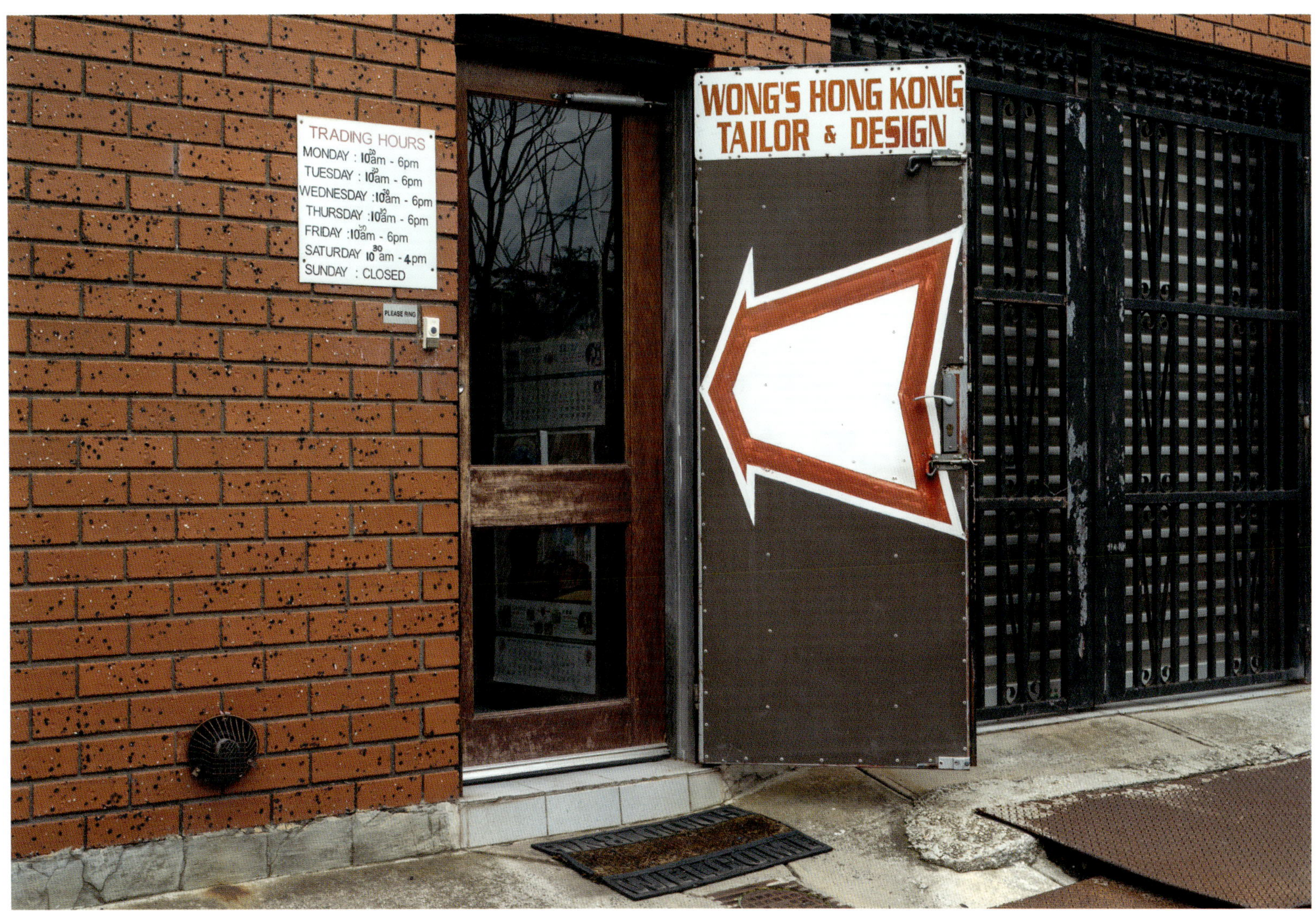
TRADING HOURS
MONDAY : 10am - 6pm
TUESDAY : 10am - 6pm
WEDNESDAY :10am - 6pm
THURSDAY :10am - 6pm
FRIDAY :10am - 6pm
SATURDAY 10 am - 4pm
SUNDAY : CLOSED
PLEASE RING
WONG'S HONG KONG
TAILOR & DESIGN

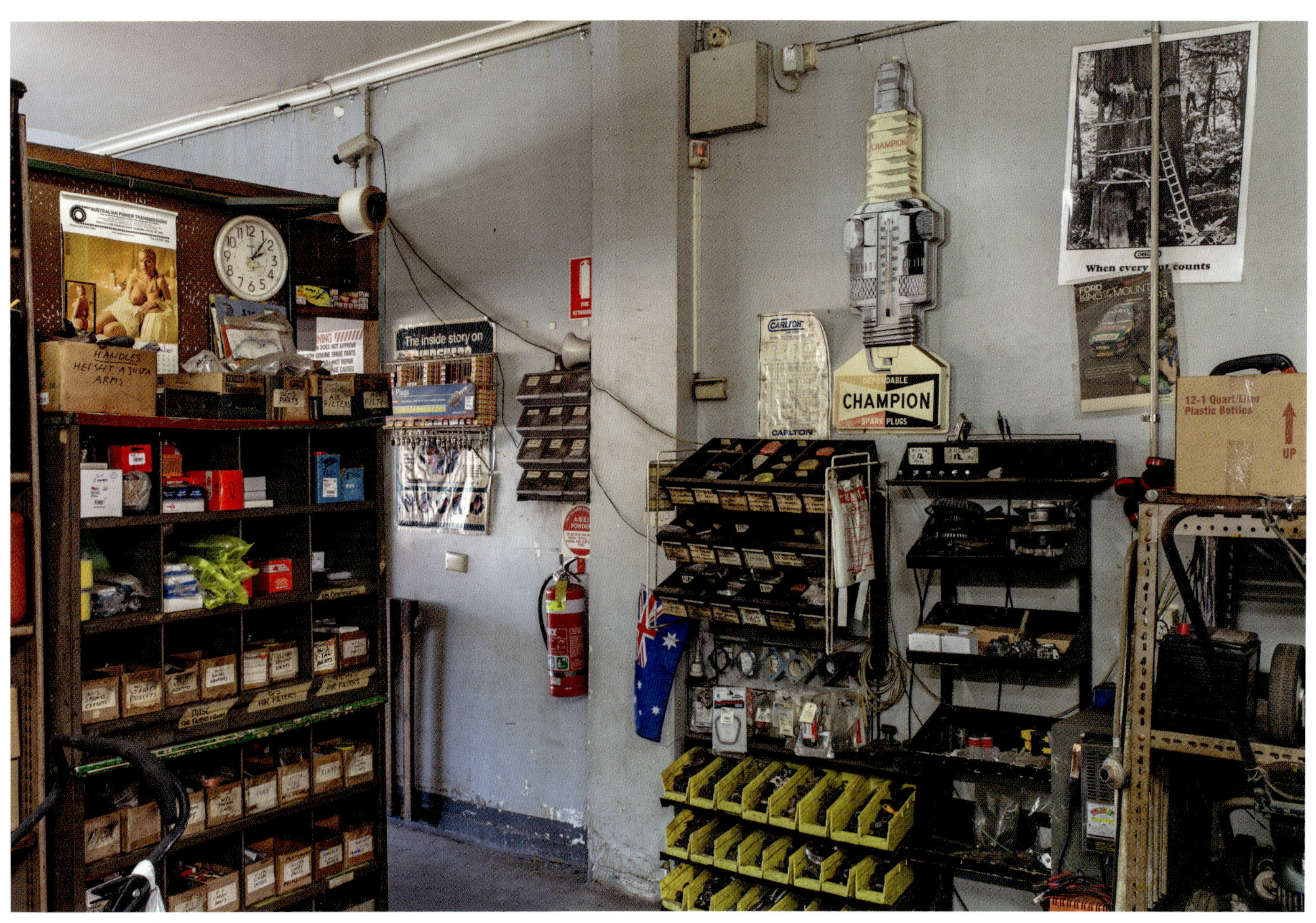

CHAMPION
DEPENDABLE
CHAMPION
SPARK PLUGS
When every our counts
12-1 Quart/Liter
Plastic Bottles
UP
CARLTON
CARLTON

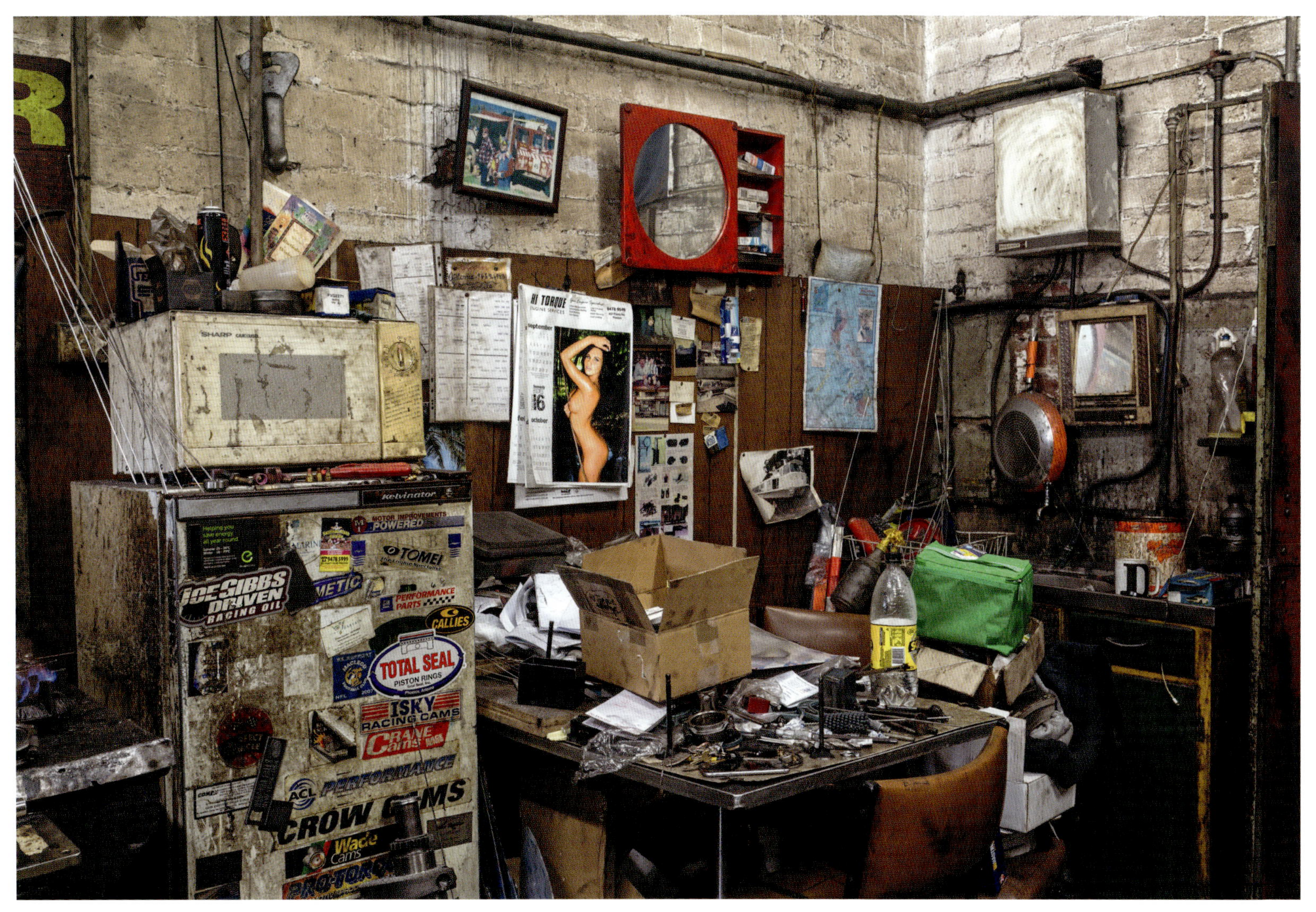

131

Preston

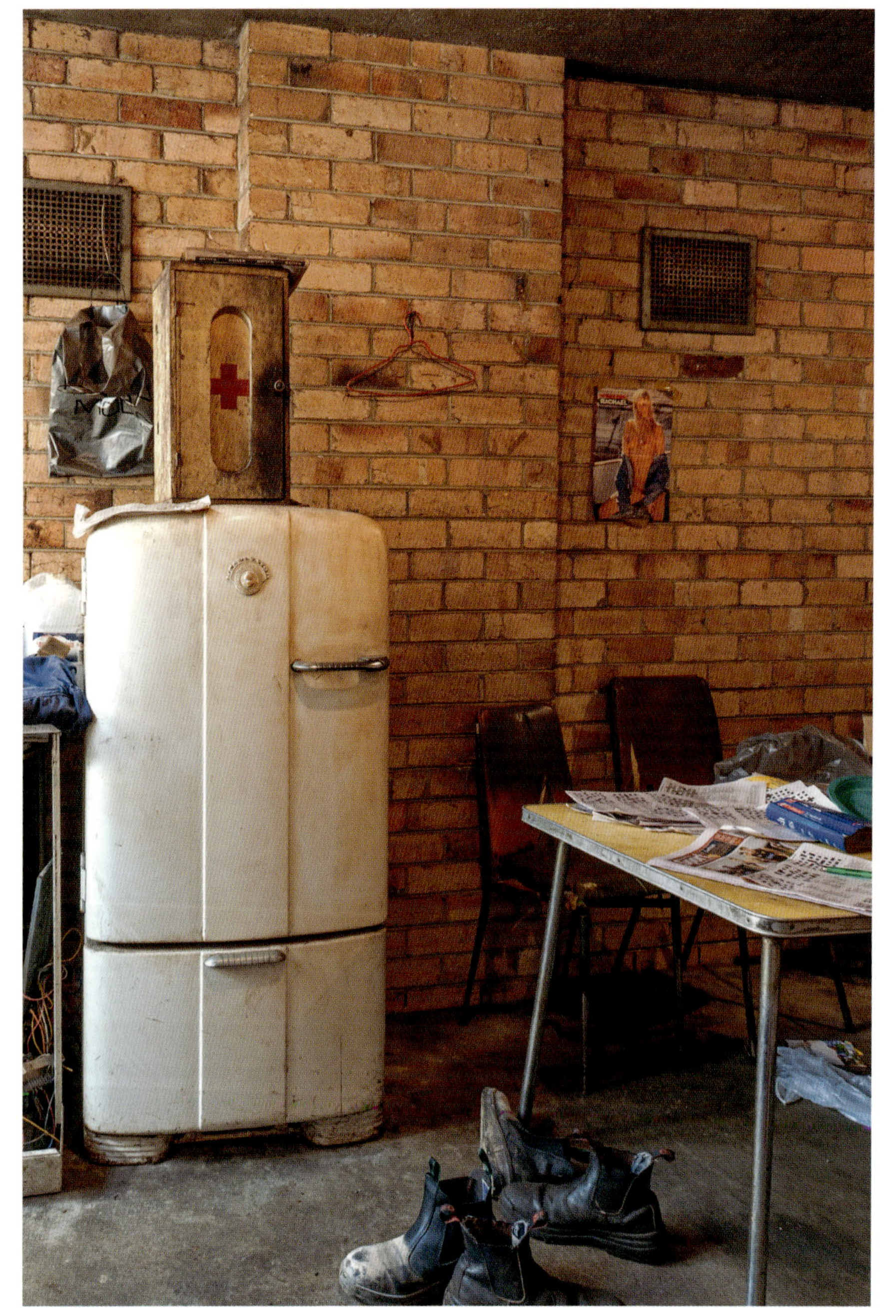

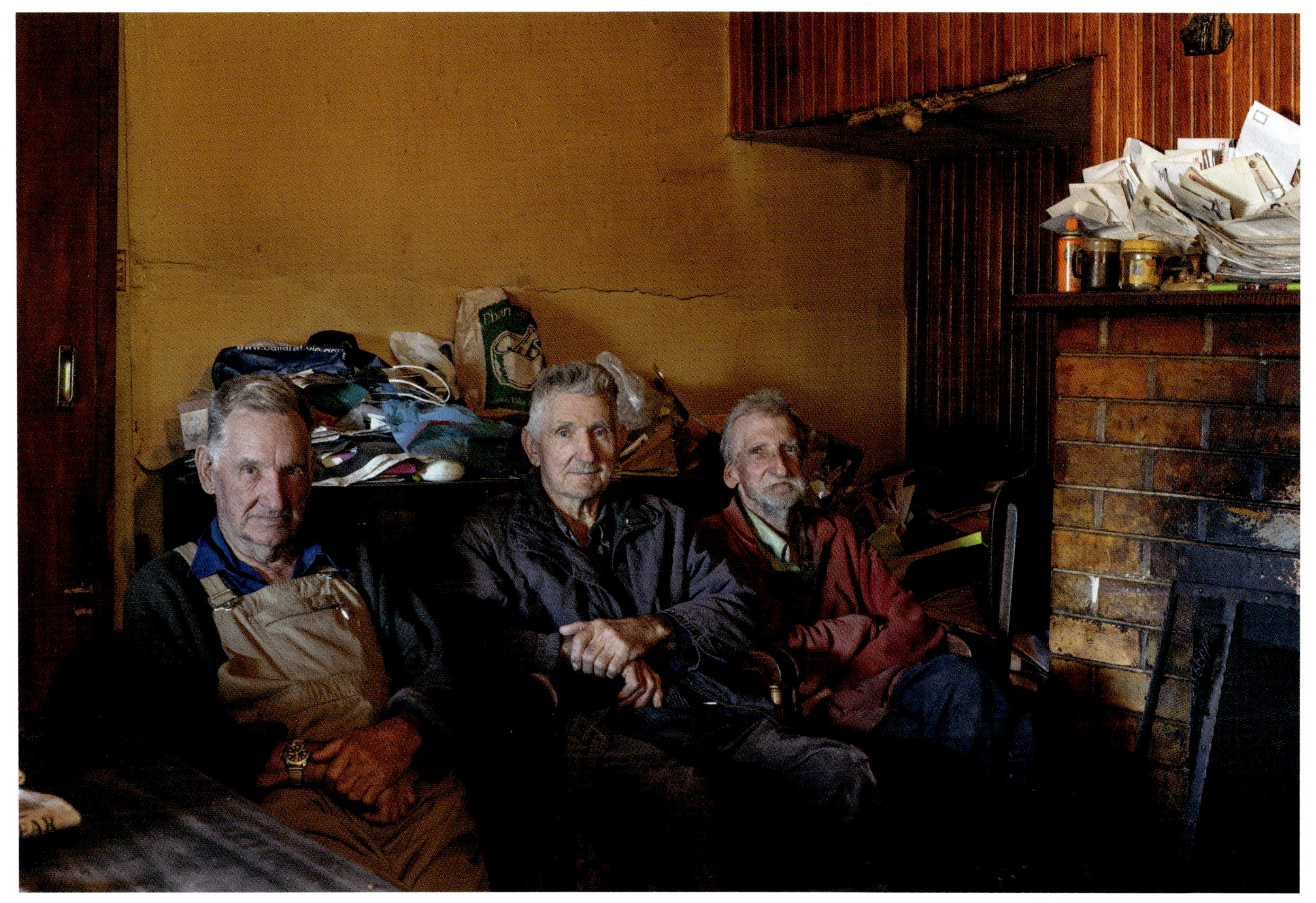

Mickleham

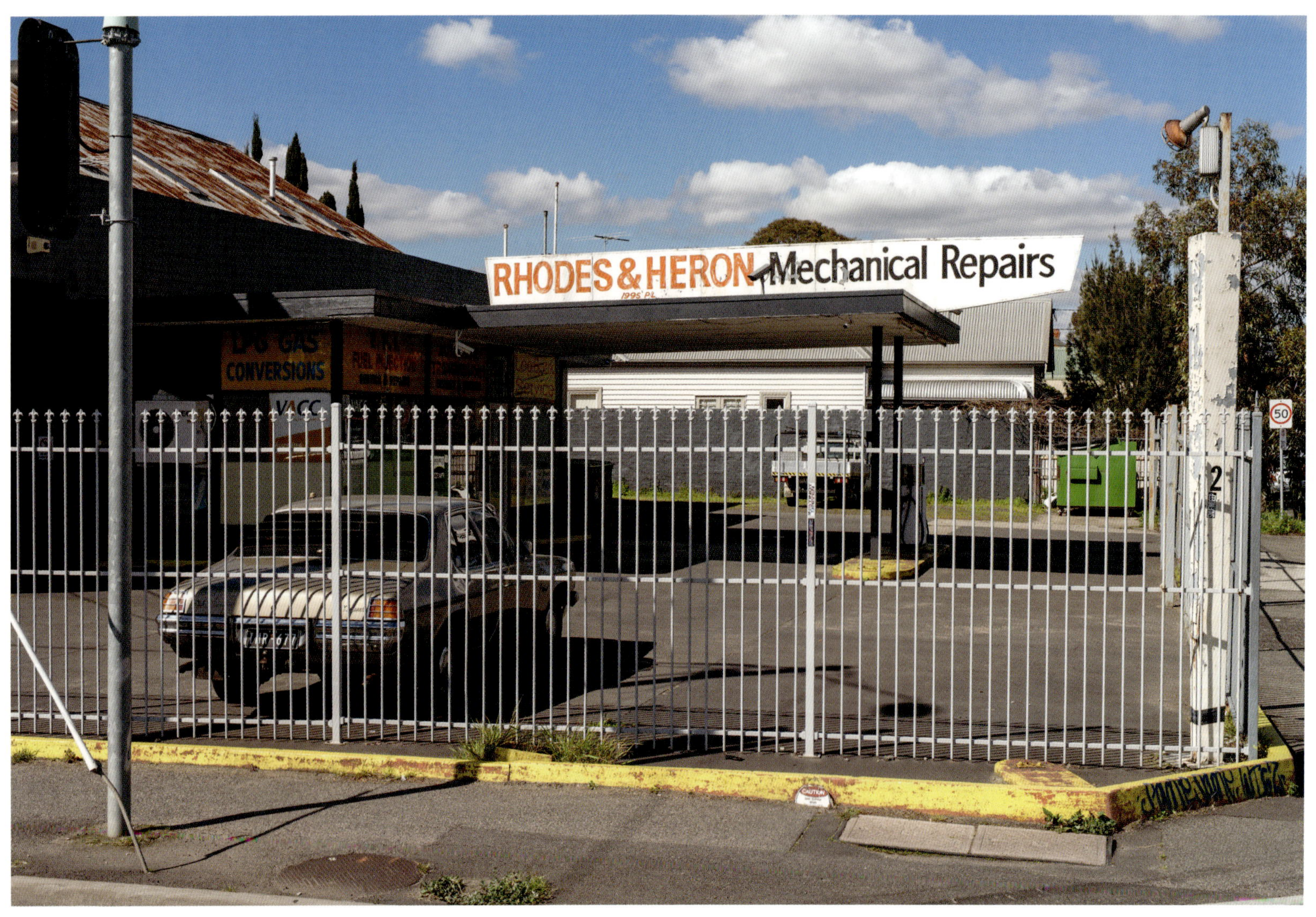

Northcote

134

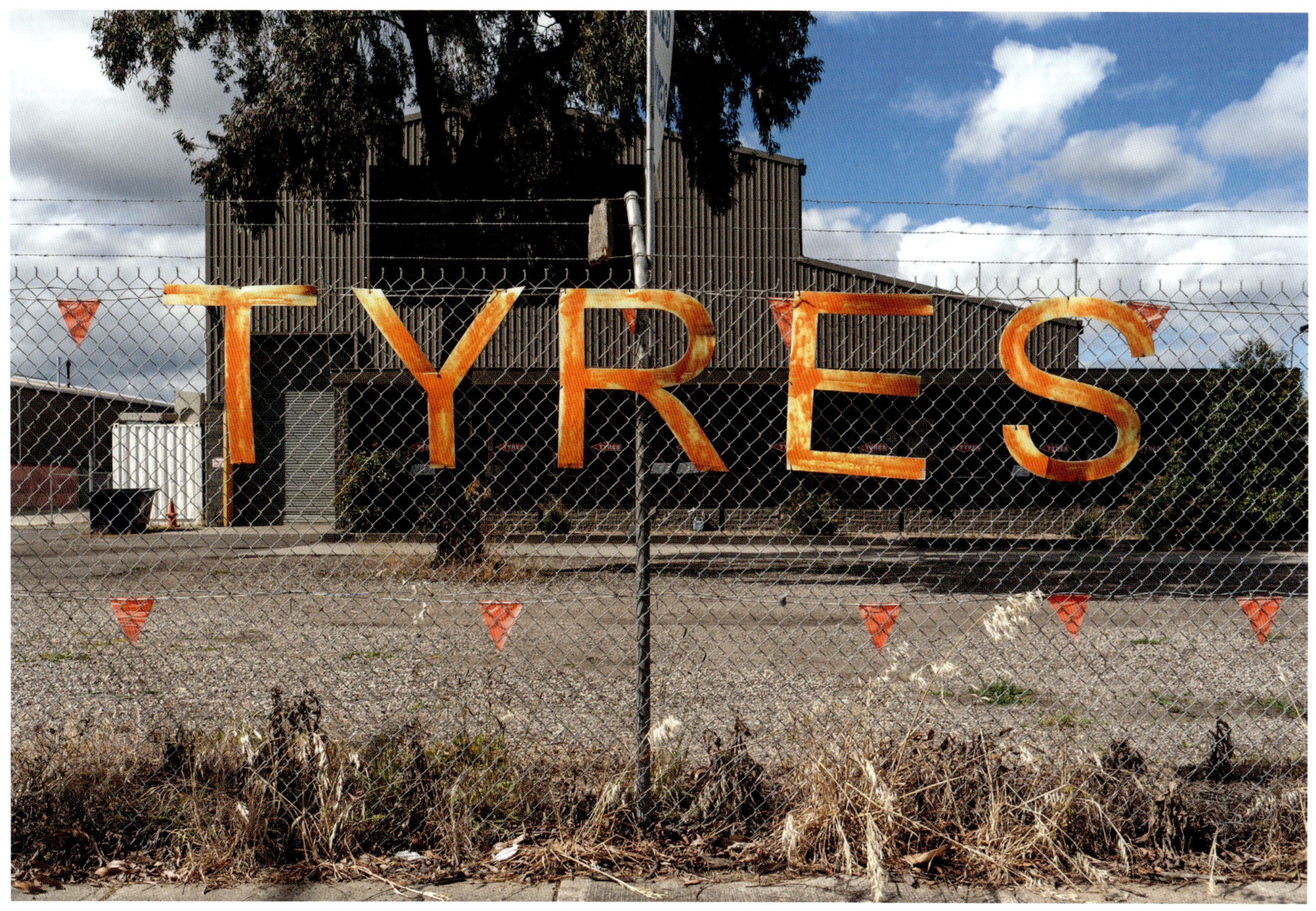

Campbellfield

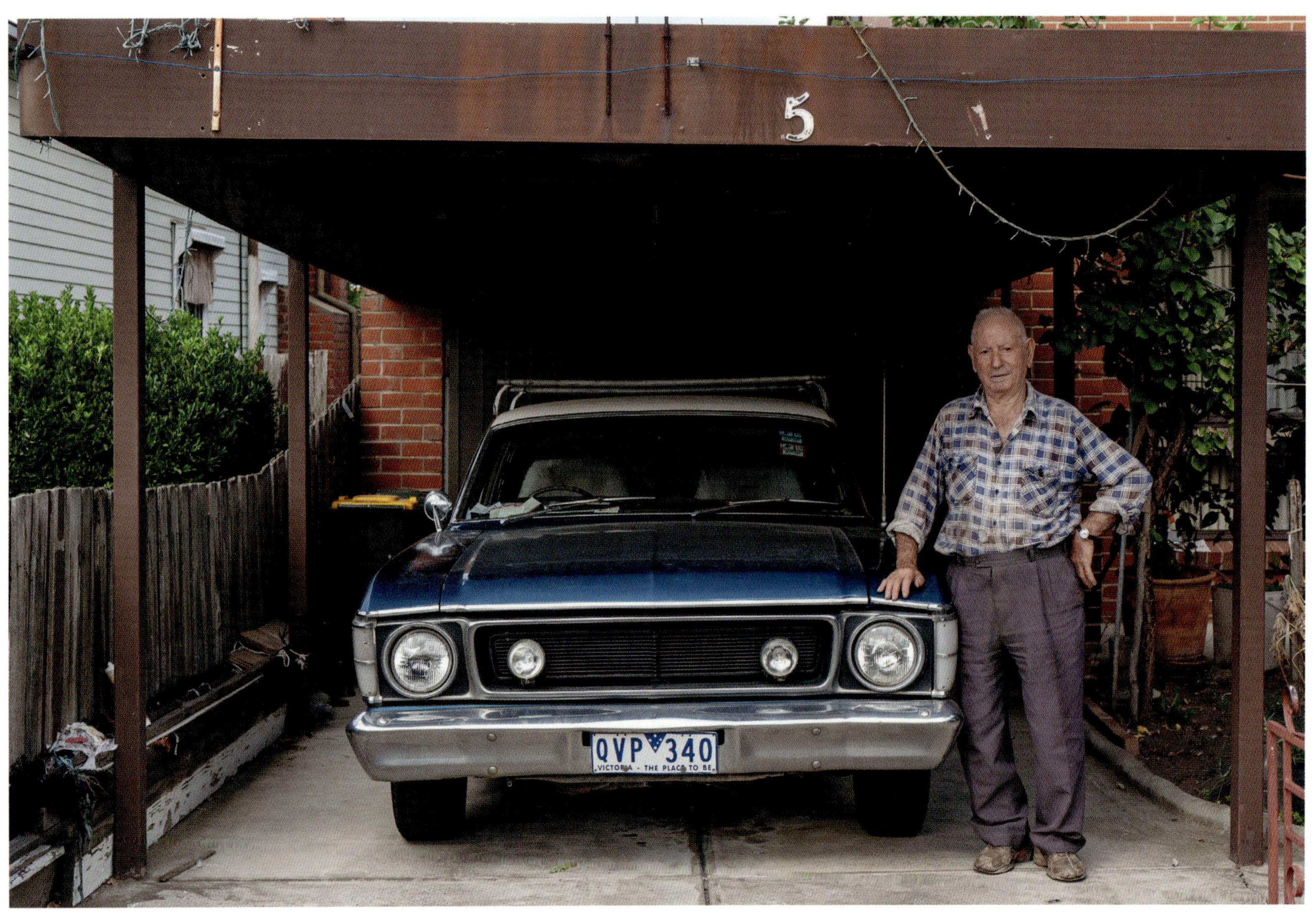
5
QVP 340
VICTORIA - THE PLACE TO BE.

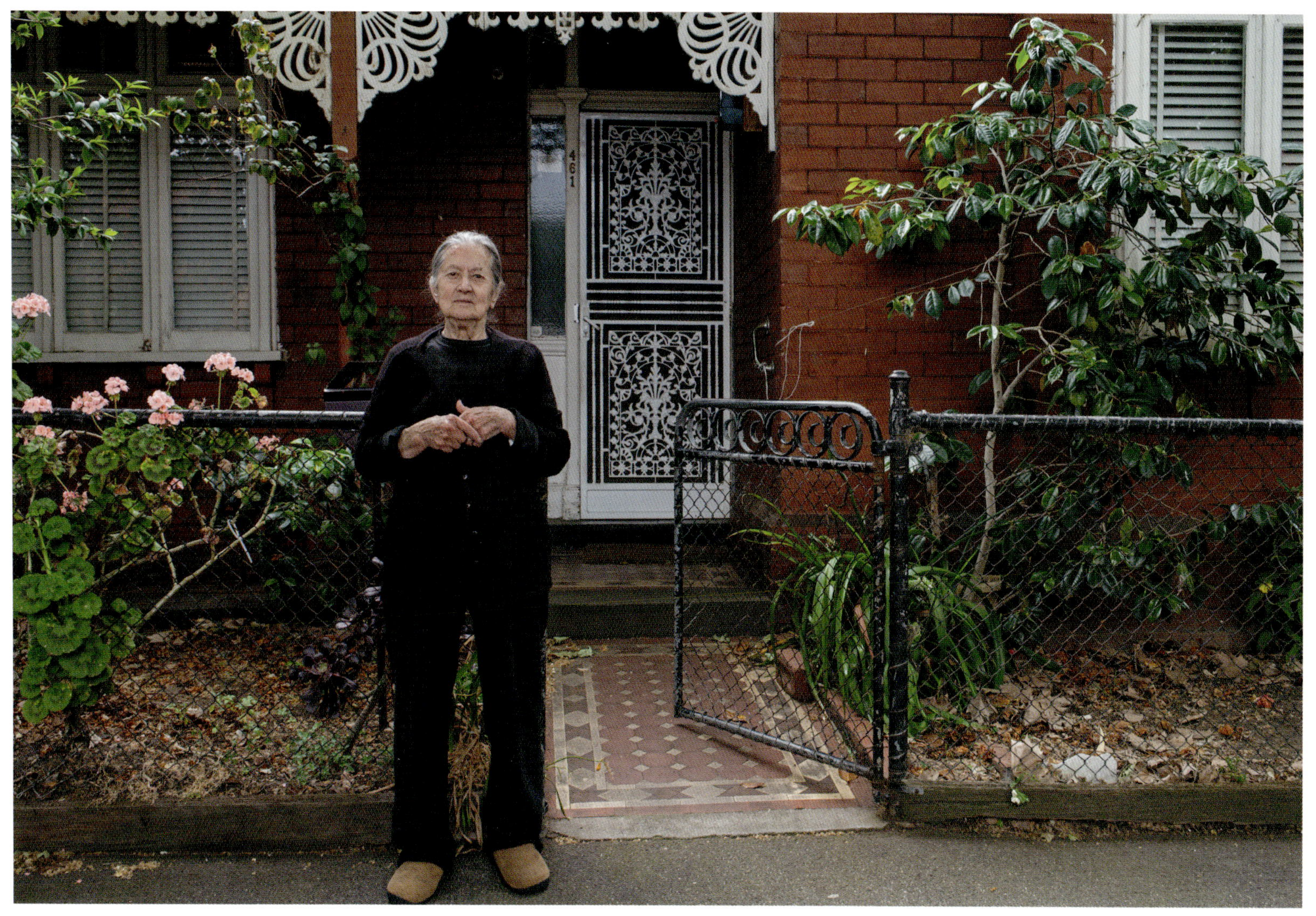

137

Fitzroy

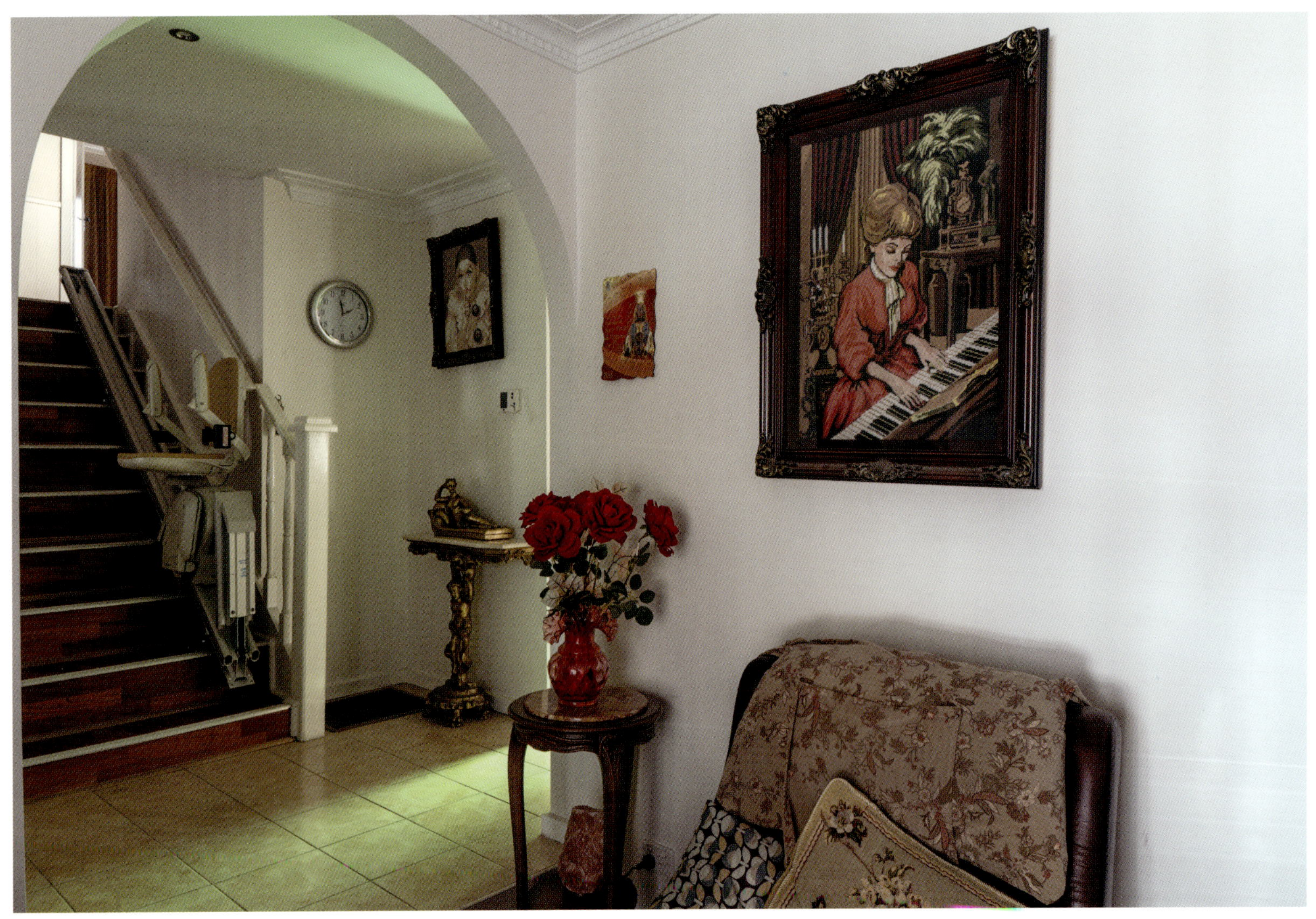

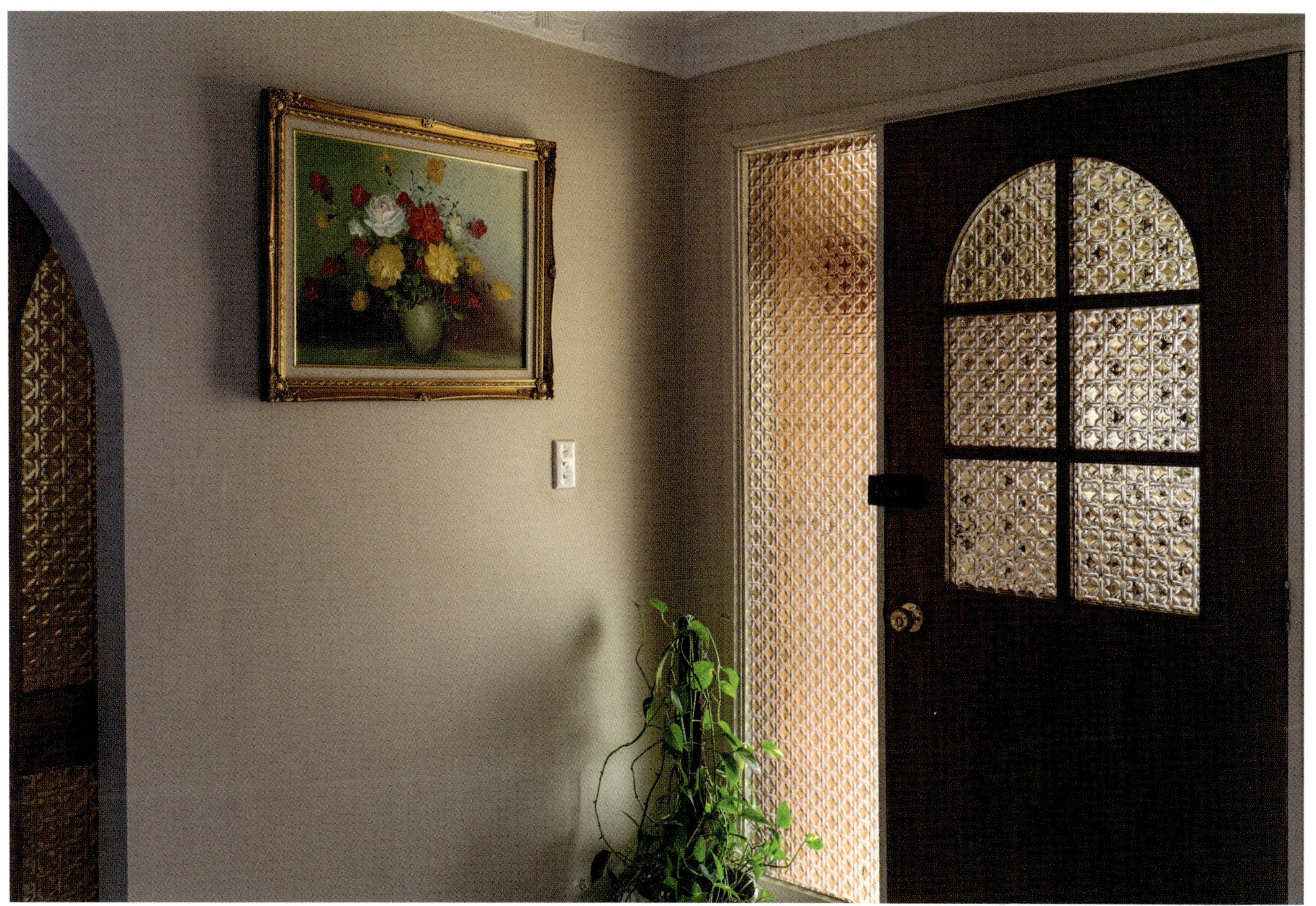

Broadmeadows

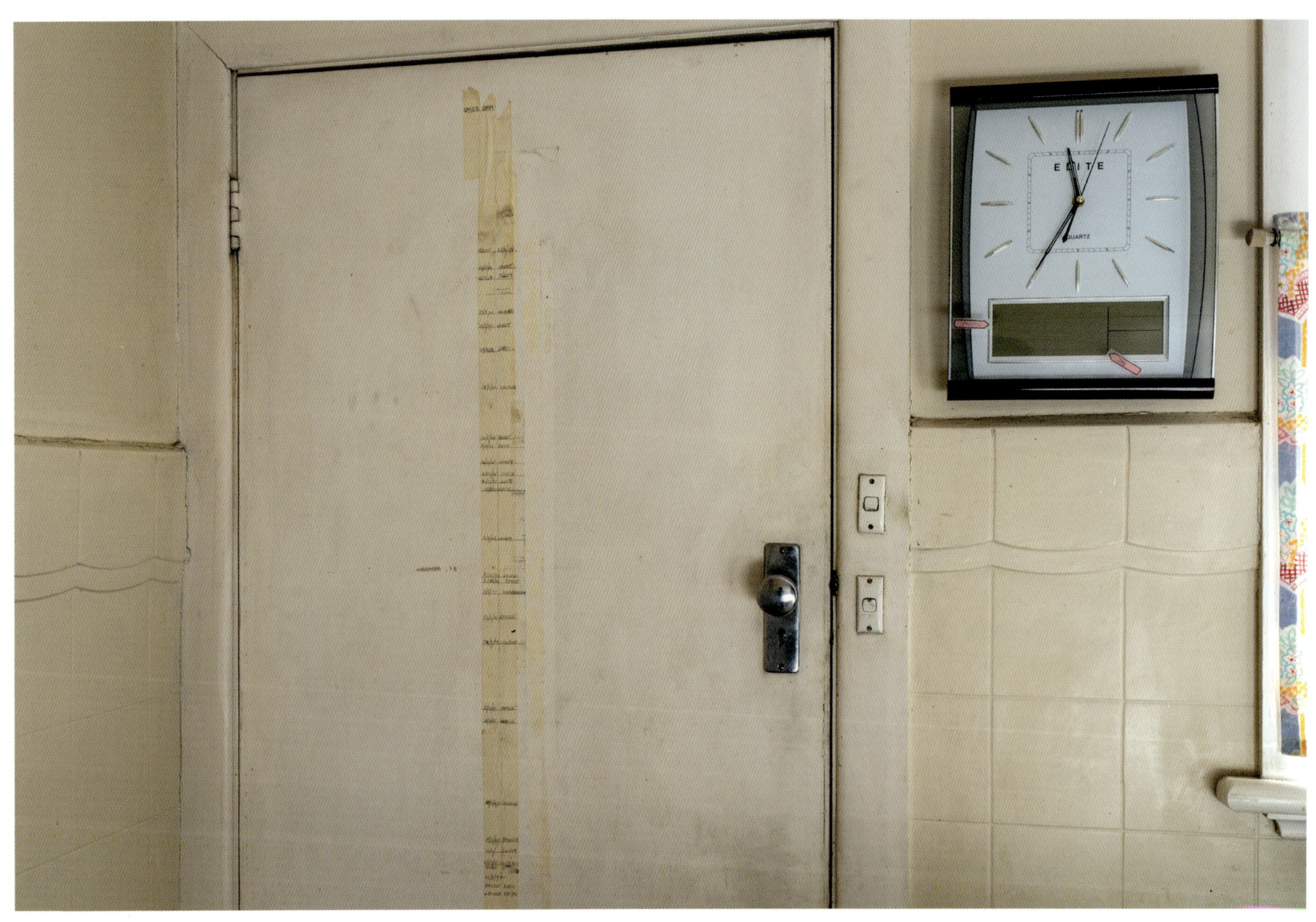

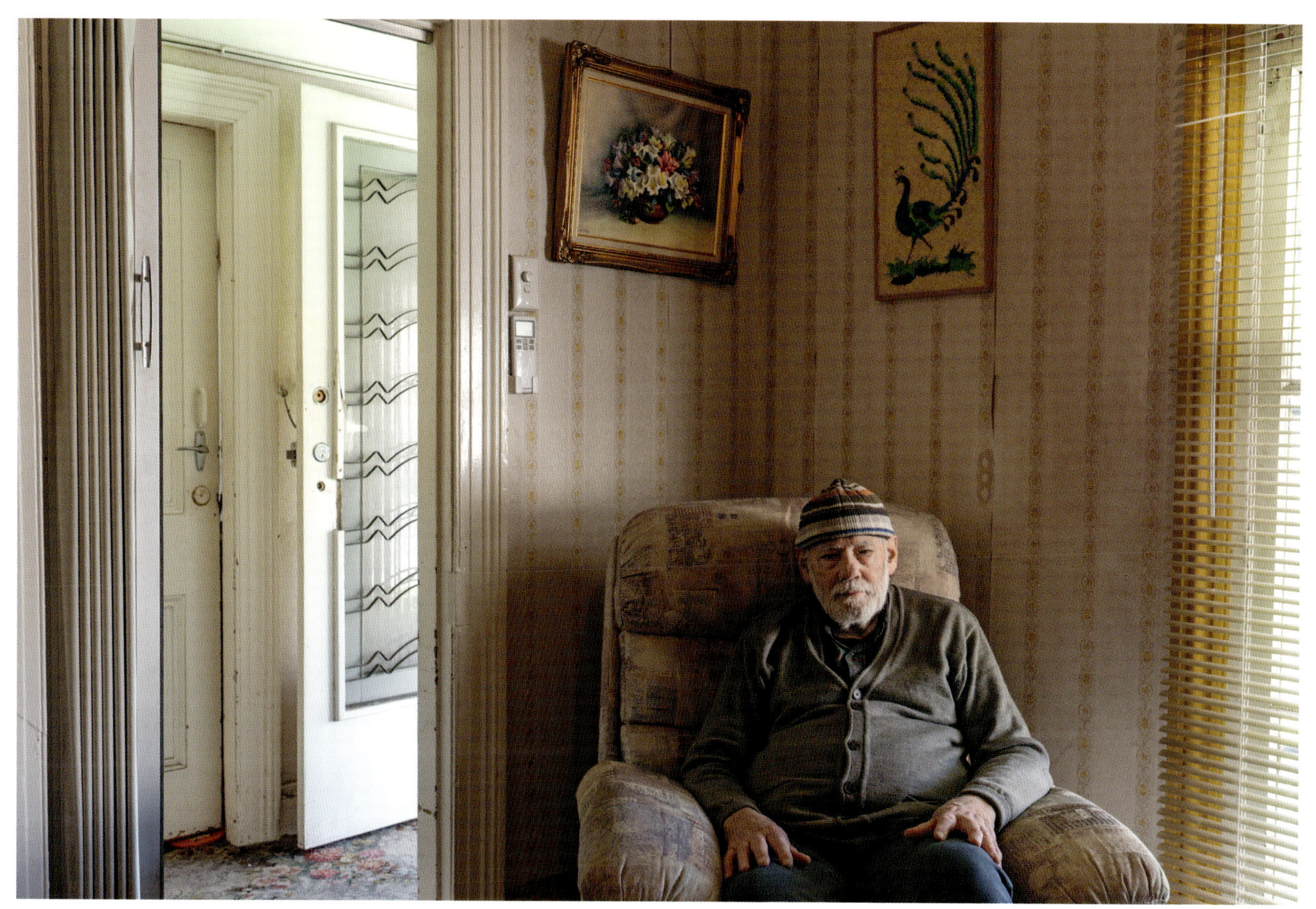

141

Carlton

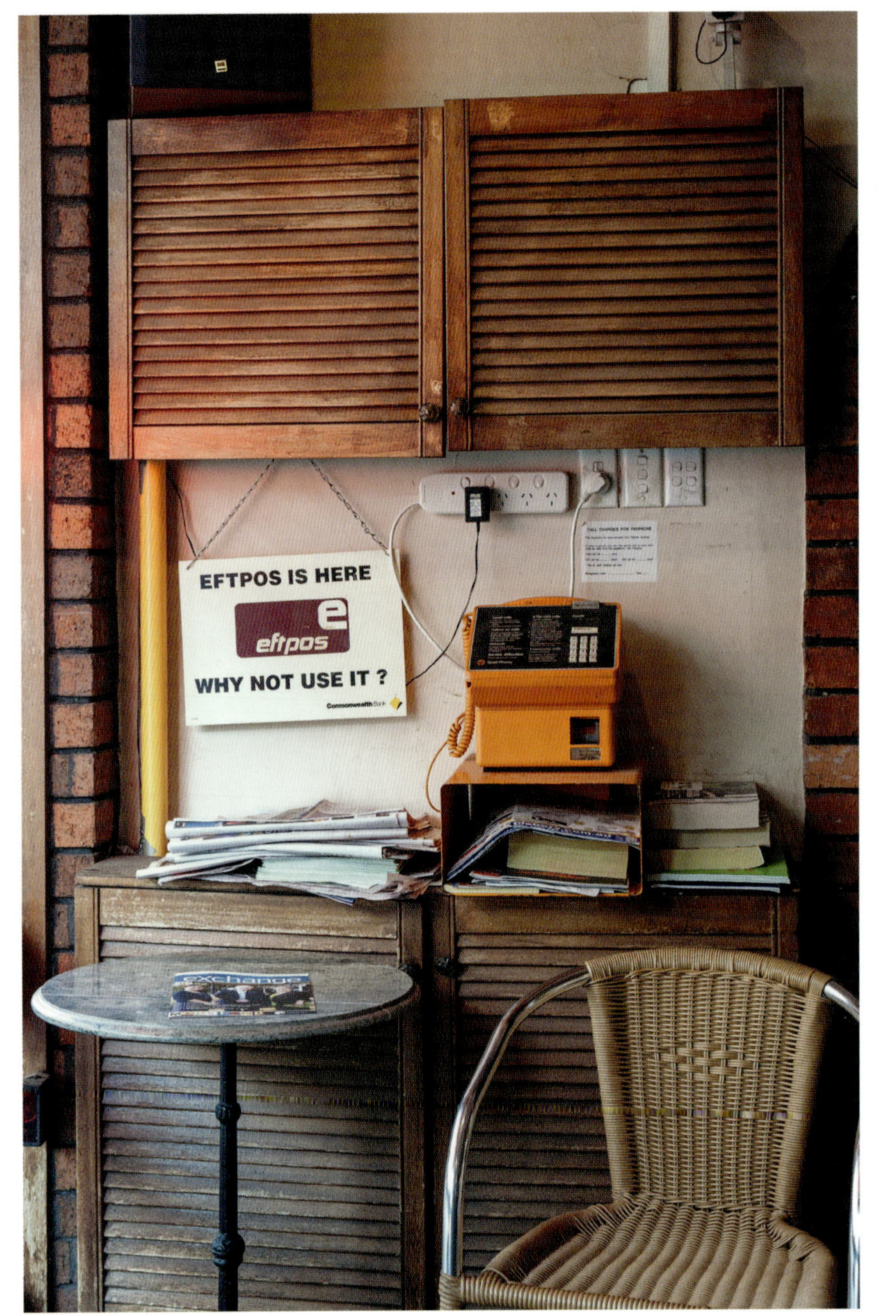

EFTPOS IS HERE
eftpos
e
WHY NOT USE IT ?
exchange